HEROES

HEROES

U.S. ARMY
MEDAL OF HONOR RECIPIENTS

BARRETT TILLMAN

BERKLEY
CALIBER

THE BERKLEY PUBLISHING GROUP
Published by the Penguin Group
Penguin Group (USA) Inc.
375 Hudson Street, New York, New York 10014, USA
Penguin Group (Canada), 90 Eglinton Avenue East, Suite 700, Toronto, Ontario M4P 2Y3, Canada
(a division of Pearson Penguin Canada Inc.)
Penguin Books Ltd., 80 Strand, London WC2R 0RL, England
Penguin Group Ireland, 25 St. Stephen's Green, Dublin 2, Ireland (a division of Penguin Books Ltd.)
Penguin Group (Australia), 250 Camberwell Road, Camberwell, Victoria 3124, Australia
(a division of Pearson Australia Group Pty. Ltd.)
Penguin Books India Pvt. Ltd., 11 Community Centre, Panchsheel Park, New Delhi—110 017, India
Penguin Group (NZ), Cnr. Airborne and Rosedale Roads, Albany, Auckland 1310, New Zealand
(a division of Pearson New Zealand Ltd.)
Penguin Books (South Africa) (Pty.) Ltd., 24 Sturdee Avenue, Rosebank, Johannesburg 2196,
South Africa

Penguin Books Ltd., Registered Offices: 80 Strand, London WC2R 0RL, England

While the author has made every effort to provide accurate telephone numbers and Internet addresses at the time of publication, neither the publisher nor the author assumes any responsibility for errors, or for changes that occur after publication. Further, publisher does not have any control over and does not assume any responsibility for author or third-party websites or their content.

HEROES: U.S. ARMY MEDAL OF HONOR RECIPIENTS

Copyright © 2006 by Tekno Books
Interior photos courtesy of www.HomeOfHeroes.com
Book design by Tiffany Estreicher

This book is an original publication of The Berkley Publishing Group.

First edition: August 2006

ISBN: 0-425-21017-0

An application to register this book for cataloging has been submitted to the Library of Congress.

PRINTED IN THE UNITED STATES OF AMERICA

10   9   8   7   6   5   4   3   2   1

CONTENTS

FOREWORD BY COLONEL
WALTER J. BOYNE

Courage is rightly esteemed the first of human qualities . . .
because it is the quality which guarantees all others.
                                    —Winston Spencer Churchill

Anyone reading this book on the recipients of the highest honor the
United States can bestow, the Medal of Honor, must inevitably be impressed with the towering courage each and every one displayed under
difficult—sometimes impossible—circumstances.

Those who have received the Medal of Honor come from all walks
of life, and all have demonstrated a common trait, an extraordinary
courage in a perilous moment. In too many instances, they have given
their lives so that others might live.

After reading any one of the accounts, most readers will have a very
private moment of reflection to consider how they might have performed in similar circumstances. The question inevitably arises: would
they have had sufficient courage or would they have faltered, succumbing to the familiar fears to which almost everyone is susceptible?

No one knows the answer to this, but the accounts in this book
make it evident that under conditions of war, especially when exposed
to danger while in the company of their comrades, a surprising number
of otherwise average human beings can rise to the occasion, transcend-
ing their fears with a palpable courage that enables them to succeed in
the face of lethal hazards.

The type and duration of the potential hero's exposure to these hazards vary. For some it might be enduring the horrors of a prisoner of war camp; to others it might be suffering an intense bombardment for hours, even days. For others the challenge might come in their first split second in combat, perhaps when their unit is ambushed on the way to the battle.

There are many scenarios that might elicit the overriding heroic behavior that is cited in the award of the Medal of Honor. Such valor is a gift, and no one can know for sure that he will have it at any given time. The spiritual uplift, the exact moment when the need to do the right thing overcomes all hesitation and spurs the nascent hero into action, might stem from many sources. In one instance it might be the patriotism of a warrior who is willing to sacrifice everything for the good of the country. In another, the abrupt, irrevocable decision to risk everything might arise from a deep religious conviction, in which the profound belief in a better life in Heaven enables an individual to risk making the ultimate sacrifice.

But there are many accounts that attribute the selfless act of heroism to a simple desire to protect comrades from harm. There is a bonding within the military service that many never experience, a sense of belonging to a community more tightly associated than even a family can be. This feeling of affection is so profound that it can, in an instant, make a young warrior decide to sacrifice everything to save other members of the unit, at whatever cost.

And of all the prospective motivations, this is somehow the most satisfying, the most realistic. It makes the sacrificial act more plausible, more reasonable, more easily understood. And it makes it easier for the reader to believe that he too might have the courage to perform a similar act of courage.

—Colonel Walter J. Boyne
Former Director, Smithsonian
Air and Space Museum

PREFACE

NORTH Carolina, 1865: in the assault against a Confederate fort, a nineteen-year-old brigade commander picks up the fallen colors and leads his men to the top.

Kansas, 1869: a Pawnee scout races his pony ahead of his troop in pursuit of hostiles and, though accidentally shot from behind, continues the chase.

Cuba, 1898: a thirty-nine-year-old patrician New Yorker leads an egalitarian corps of Ivy Leaguers and bronco busters to the heights occupied by an entrenched enemy.

France, 1918: a fundamentalist deacon brings a bolt-action rifle to a machine-gun fight—and wins.

Philippines, 1944: an automatic rifleman loses both legs in an explosion but refuses evacuation, bleeding to death while covering his platoon's withdrawal.

South Korea, 1951: a thirty-year-old company commander with a fervent belief in cold steel leads an uphill bayonet charge, the last in U.S. history.

South Vietnam, 1967: a twenty-three-year-old medic dashes into open terrain to rescue a wounded GI, then makes repeated trips despite multiple wounds and dies after saving six men.

Somalia, 1993: two commandos insist on attempting the rescue of a downed helicopter pilot amid hundreds of hostiles, dying in the process.

These men and more than 2,300 others received the U.S. Army's Medal of Honor. Some were recognized for initiative; some for self-sacrifice; some for raw courage. All were awarded the five-pointed pendant containing one word: Valor.

The United States Army established the "pyramid of honor" during the First World War. Prior to that time—July 1918—the Medal of Honor (also called the Congressional Medal of Honor) was the nation's only award for military prowess. It had been established some fifty-six years previously, during the War Between the States.

Realizing that combat actions merit various levels of recognition, during the Great War the Army established the Distinguished Service Cross and the Citation Star. The latter was a certificate that evolved into the Silver Star during the 1930s. In World War II, the Bronze Star was authorized, completing the pyramid of awards for combat valor. The Distinguished Flying Cross and the Air Medal were presented to members of the Army Air Forces before establishment of an independent Air Force in 1947.

However, the earliest U.S. military honor was devised at the beginning of the American nation. General George Washington created the Badge of Military Merit, but the award was not widely endorsed (only three were presented), as some Americans believed that military orders and decorations clashed with the democratic concept. Titles of nobility were forbidden, and it was felt that badges and medals smacked of European autocracy.

Despite initial misgivings, there were exceptions. In the Mexican-American War of 1847, the Certificate of Merit was established for noncommissioned officers, and 545 were presented. Brevet commissions also were awarded, usually to officers in recognition of notable service in the field.

A hero of the Mexican conflict, General Winfield Scott, remained opposed to medals even as commander of the Union Army in 1861. He considered decorations "contrary to the spirit of our institutions." Nevertheless, his adjutant general, Colonel Edward Townsend, began lobbying for creation of a military award. Townsend's attitude found favor in Congress, and the Navy established its Medal of Honor several months before the Army.

Throughout its history, the medal has been the focus of respect and admiration; controversy and criticism. Certainly the criteria for presentation have changed or been ignored over the decades. It is subject to political whims, patronage, and favoritism. At least two presidents sought it: Theodore Roosevelt, who lobbied for it (and received it a century later) and Harry Truman, who frankly stated he would rather have the five-pointed pendant than remain in office. Yet the medal's prestige remains undiminished in the public eye.

This volume describes the actions of many of the 2,300-plus soldiers awarded the Medal of Honor. Some familiar tales are omitted in order to recognize lesser-known recipients. Therefore, the exploits of notables such as Joshua Lawrence Chamberlain, Mary Walker, Alvin York, the "lost battalion," and Audie Murphy are only touched upon.

Finally, no Army aviation Medals of Honor are included here. They were addressed in my previous volume, *Above and Beyond: The Aviation Medals of Honor*.

Thanks to Carol Cepregi of the Congressional Medal of Honor Society; Gregg Clemmer, Sons of Confederate Veterans; J.C. Cooper, Mike Force Association; Randy Everette; Mark Feldbin, 27th Division website; Noel Garland; Marty Greenberg, Tekno Books; Robert R. Haas, 40th Division Association; Les Jensen, West Point Museum;

Philippe Jourdan; Luther Kantner, 2/28th Recon; Arlette King, Army Personnel Command; Donald R. Kocks; Dave Mocabee; Carolyn Pfaus; Eulis Presley; Ray Smith, 1/69th Armor; Doug Sterner, Home of Heroes; Vickie Wendel, Second Minnesota Artillery; and Scott K. Williams.

HEROES

CHAPTER ONE

A HOUSE DIVIDED:
THE CIVIL WAR

■

I N a curious way, the history of the Medal of Honor began before it existed. The first action occurred in an unexpected time and place.

In February 1861, Bernard J. Irwin was an assistant surgeon in the U.S. Army, a twenty-nine-year-old Irish immigrant serving on the Southwest frontier. The Chiricahua Apache band led by Cochise had seized captives and fled the area of Fort Breckenridge in southern Arizona.

The Apaches had taken young Mickey Free in October 1861; the Army, perennially under strength, was unable or unwilling to pursue for three months. In late January, Lieutenant George Bascom set out with fifty-six men of the Seventh Infantry and encountered Cochise en route. Cochise denied having taken hostages, a claim Bascom doubted. Negotiations produced nothing but violence. Both sides seized captives, and Cochise's band killed or tortured to death several American and Mexican citizens.

Word got back to the fort, one hundred miles away, and though the situation was confused, it was clear that Bascom could not hold out in-

Asst. Surgeon Bernard J. Irwin

definitely; he had been under siege since February 5. The garrison commander could afford only fourteen men for a relief expedition, but Irwin volunteered. Without available horses, his soldiers mounted themselves on mules and set off across the Sonoran desert in a winter snowstorm.

It was an epic effort. Irwin's men covered sixty-five miles in one day, arriving at Bascom's position on February 10. En route they had overtaken Apaches herding stolen livestock and recovered the animals while taking prisoners. The Irishman deployed his troops to deceive the Indians as to his true strength. The ruse worked. In concert with two companies of dragoons, Irwin broke Cochise's siege and rescued Bascom's command. The soldiers then pursued the renegades into the mountains near Apache Pass, east of Tucson. Bringing Cochise's band to bay, the officers entered negotiations resulting in release of a white boy.

Having found Cochise's mutilated victims, Irwin demanded revenge. He hanged several of his captives, an act endorsed by the senior dragoon. But three of the condemned were relatives of Cochise; the Apache wars had barely started, but they lasted another twelve years.

Though some officers decried the hangings, Irwin's leadership and initiative certainly merited recognition, but at that time the U.S. Army had no decorations for valor. Irwin returned to his medical duties and probably thought little more of the events.

Nor did the Army. Beyond chasing hostile Indians in the western territories, far greater concerns were afoot in the thirty-four not so United States. Two months after Irwin's valiant effort, the Union was split when eleven Southern states exercised their right of secession. They organized themselves as the Confederate States of America, declaring their independence from the federal government in Washington, D.C.

NATIONAL FRATRICIDE

Knowing that federal troops were en route, on April 12, Confederate forces fired on Union-held Fort Sumter in Charleston Harbor, and the War Between the States violently rent the nation. Over the next four years, some 650,000 Americans would perish before the South was forced back into the Union at bayonet point. Eventually, more than 1,500 Union men received the Medal of Honor for their role in the Civil War. Eighty percent of them—some 1,200—were members of the U.S. Army.

The American Civil War established many and varied precedents. It was the first war in which railroads played a significant role, and it introduced the rifle to widespread military use. It was also one of the first major conflicts with a high degree of literacy, hence the treasure trove of memoirs and primary sources. In 1860, nearly 97 percent of Northern adult males were literate, compared to 56 percent of white Southerners.

In that pivotal year, Senator James W. Grimes of Iowa proposed legislation that led to establishment of the Medal of Honor. As chairman of the Senate Naval Committee, Grimes advocated a medal to recognize significant actions by enlisted members of the U.S. Navy and Marine Corps. The bill passed both Congress and the Senate, and was signed by President Lincoln on December 12.

In fairness to the Army, a comparable decoration was proposed by Senator Henry Wilson of Massachusetts. The new medal was intended for enlisted men who "shall most distinguish themselves by their gal-

■ *Right to Secede?*

When the eleven Southern states voted to leave the Union in 1861, they claimed the inherent right to secede. Portions of two border states (Kentucky and Maryland) joined them. The Constitution, ratified in 1788, was ambiguous on the matter. It neither permitted nor denied individual states the right to exit the federal entity. Most Northerners insisted that because there was no explicit provision for secession, it was illegal. States rights advocates argued that the Tenth Amendment enabled such action, since it ceded to the states all powers not specifically granted to the federal government. Southerners also insisted that "once in, never out" deprived individuals as well as states the option of nonviolent response to perceived injustice from Washington.

In his first inaugural speech that same year, President Abraham Lincoln seemed to have it both ways. He was an astute politician, seeking to maintain the Union while appeasing zealots on both sides of the Mason-Dixon line. He said that whenever American citizens grow tired of their government, "they can exercise their constitutional right of amending it, or their revolutionary right to dismember or overthrow it." The South chose dismemberment, but Lincoln (whatever his pronouncements) was never going to permit it.

However, the Confederate States of America erred fatally in firing on Sumter, giving the federals the moral position of responding to offensive action. And morality featured hugely in the Civil War. The smoldering issue of slavery combined with states rights to spark the dry tinder of conflict. Later, Lincoln said that if he could preserve the Union by freeing some, all, or no slaves, he would do so. His objective was a return to the *status quo ante*—a goal he achieved at expense of his own life.

lantry in action and other soldier-like qualities." Wilson's proposal took the form of a resolution rather than legislation, but the results were comparable. Lincoln granted approval on July 12, 1862. For the first time in its history, the U.S. Army had a decoration for its troops.

In March 1863, the Medal of Honor legislation was amended, authorizing presentation to officers and permitting retroactive awards to the start of the war. Therefore, technically, Surgeon Irwin's action was not eligible for the medal because his action occurred nearly a year before it was created and two months before hostilities began.

Even more noteworthy was the fact that Irwin did not receive the decoration for thirty-three years. It was presented retroactively in 1894, when the old campaigner was sixty-four years old. His award represented a long line of exceptions to the regulations that continues into the twenty-first century.

It is noteworthy that the original criteria for the medal included not only combat action but also "other soldier-like qualities." The concept of "above and beyond the call of duty" lay decades in the future.

Pvt. Francis Brownell, 11th New York

The first Medal of Honor action after the decoration was established went to twenty-year-old Private Francis E. Brownell of the Eleventh New York Infantry. On May 24, 1861, the day after Virginia seceded, his unit advanced into Alexandria, Virginia, across the Potomac from Washington. At the Marshall House hotel the proprietor, James T. Jackson, had hung a Confederate flag, outraging the Eleventh's commanding officer, Colonel Elmer Ellsworth, a former law student in Abraham Lincoln's Illinois office. With some of his soldiers, Ellsworth rushed to the roof to remove the banner of insurrection. On the way down, he encountered Jackson, equally passionate about the flag, who raised his shotgun to kill Ellsworth. In the close quarters, Brownell responded, trying to deflect the shotgun, but Jackson's blast killed the colonel. Brownell then shot Jackson and finished him with the bayonet. Brownell later was commissioned and left the Army as a lieutenant in 1863.

Frank Brownell's award came well after the war, in 1877. At that time, veterans could propose themselves for the medal, and Brownell succeeded the third time, with support of his congressman.

The first significant battle of the war occurred near Washington, D.C., on July 21, 1861. It lasted most of the day, to the entertainment of the Washington elite who arrived by carriage to spread picnic blankets and enjoy the spectacle while beneath their parasols. It ended in an absolute rout.

Though a solid Confederate victory, the First Battle of Manassas (aka Bull Run) yielded Medals of Honor to seven officers, four enlisted men, and a civilian. Perhaps the most deserving went to Colonel John F. Hartranft and Captain Walter H. Cooke of the Fourth Pennsylvania Militia. Though their terms of service had expired, they remained as aides to the regimental commander. Hartranft, a twenty-nine-year-old colonel, was credited with rallying Union regiments that had withdrawn in the confusion of combat.

The First Michigan Infantry received two of the twelve decorations that day. Colonel Orlando B. Willcox led charges until wounded and captured, while Captain William H. Withington remained on the field to tend his commander. Both their medals were presented in 1895.

One award was presented for an exceptional record that began at Bull Run. First Lieutenant Samuel N. Benjamin of the Second U.S. Artillery distinguished himself over the next three years, culminating with the Battle of Spotsylvania in May 1864. A product of the West Point class of '61, he became one of the noted artillerists of the war. At Knoxville in 1863, he was credited with a 2,500-yard, one-round shot on a house containing rebel sharpshooters.

In 1878, one of Benjamin's former foes wrote a member of his battery, saying in part, "Nothing that I admire more on the battlefield than bravery, and if the old Yanks who had the makings of Benjamin's battery was not brave men, I never saw any during the war. And all brave men who was at Sharpsburg certainly had great respect for the members of your battery, and if we ever meet you can count on a hearty shake."

Benjamin died in 1886, only age forty-seven.

MILITARY MEDICS

Lieutenant Charles J. Murphy, Thirty-eighth New York, was a quartermaster, but he took a rifle and fought in the ranks. When his regiment was forced back, he remained to care for wounded and was captured. In camp, he became known as "Doctor Murphy" for his treatment of the sick and injured. Subsequently, he escaped, rose to colonel, and received his medal in 1880.

A genuine doctor was Mary Walker, a contract surgeon from New York, who tended the wounded at Manassas as well as Washington, D.C.; Chattanooga in 1863; and Atlanta in 1864. She was captured and held as a POW from April to August of that year. However, because she was not a member of the armed forces, her award was withdrawn in the 1917 review but was reinstated by the Carter administration sixty years later.

Additional medical personnel receiving the medal included a half dozen surgeons:

Richard Curran, Thirty-third New York, tended the wounded amid enemy fire at Antietam in 1862.

Gabriel Grant, U.S. Volunteers, rescued wounded men under fire at Fair Oaks, Virginia, in 1862.

Andrew Davidson, Forty-seventh Ohio, tried to run the rebel batteries at Vicksburg in 1863.

George E. Ranney, Second Michigan Cavalry, saved a wounded private lying between the lines in Georgia in 1864.

William R. D. Blackwood, Forty-eighth Pennsylvania, retrieved wounded under fire at Petersburg in 1865.

At Hatchers Run, Virginia, in 1865, Jacob F. Raub of the 210th Pennsylvania noticed Confederate forces flanking his position, informed the commanding general, and joined in repelling the attack.

MARTIAL MUSICIANS

One of the many anomalies of the Civil War was the time warp: technological progress overlapping earlier conventions. The importance accorded flag bearers and field musicians are but two examples, but both figured in Medal of Honor citations.

There was still a battlefield role for military musicians in the nineteenth century. One of the youngest in the Union Army was William "Willie" Johnston, a drummer boy not yet twelve. Though born in New York, he enlisted from St. Johnsburg, Vermont, and was allowed to follow his father into Company D, Third Vermont Infantry, at age eleven. He was enlisted in December 1861. Willie survived the appalling Peninsula Campaign, including the retreat from the Seven Days battle. At the end of that time he was reportedly the only drummer in his division still in possession of his instrument, and was permitted to parade the division during assembly at Harrison's Landing. The boy's fidelity was noted by Brigadier General William F. Smith, commanding the Second Division, VI Corps, and evidently President Lincoln heard of it. Consequently, Willie's award was issued by Secretary of War Stanton in September 1863, the first presentation after Andrews' Raiders.

Probably the next-youngest recipient was a friend of Willie's in the Third Vermont. Julian Scott of E Company was fifteen when he joined the regiment in 1861, and received the medal for helping wounded soldiers to safety across a creek at Lees Mills, Virginia, in April 1862. Like Johnston, Scott was nominated by General Smith. Scott later became a noted artist, painting Civil War murals and scenes of the frontier.

At Antietam, Maryland, that September, Battery B of the Fourth Artillery sustained a terrific bombardment from Confederate guns. The battery bugler, fifteen-year-old John Cook, offered to help man one of the guns and did a man's work.

At least one other musician received the medal. William J. Carson of the First Battalion, U.S. Infantry, literally played a major role in the Battle of Chickamauga in September 1863. When the XIV Corps was wavering, on his own initiative Carson raised his bugle and blew "To the Colors" amid the Eighteenth Infantry, which formed on him. Minutes later, he repeated the process with the Second Ohio. His citation said "This bugling deceived the enemy who believed reinforcements had arrived. Thus they delayed their attack."

■ *Civil War Rifles*

The fact that the U.S. Army did not adopt a cap lock rifle until the verge of the Civil War is testament to the power of bureaucratic inertia. By the time the federal establishment converted to percussion ignition, the flintlock had been in use for three centuries. Even with development of the Forsyth cap lock in 1807, five decades passed before the Army caught up with technology.

Ironically, in view of later events, in 1855, the Ordnance Board recommended to Secretary of War Jefferson Davis that the Army adopt a new weapon. It was a .58 caliber rifle, as opposed to a smoothbore musket, capable of firing the French-devised minié ball, a conical projectile, rather than the traditional round ball. With sixty grains of black powder, the bullet left the 40-inch barrel at some 950 feet per second, yielding a practical range of three hundred yards or more. It was a tremendous advancement: muskets were rarely useful beyond one hundred yards, and then only in volley fire.

Originally, the Model 1855 was produced with the Maynard tape ignition system: reliable enough under good conditions but prone to failure otherwise. The conversion to percussion caps made firearms almost 100 percent reliable.

However, rate of fire was slower for rifles than muskets. The soldier had to stand up to reload, pouring powder and ball into the barrel from his paper cartridge. The combination then had to be seated by a ramrod, without which the rifle was useless except as a bayonet mount.

Repeating rifles appeared from nongovernmental armories such as Henry and Spencer. With such weapons "you could load on Sunday and shoot all week." However, they saw relatively limited service (primarily in the cavalry) owing to logistical concerns over new weapons and ammunition.

THE GREAT LOCOMOTIVE CHASE

Discounting retroactive awards, almost a year passed before the first Medal of Honor action occurred after the award was created. In April 1862, twenty-two men from Brigadier General Ormsby Mitchell's Ohio brigade volunteered to disrupt the Confederate railroad between Atlanta, Georgia, and Chattanooga, Tennessee. They were led by James J. Andrews, an agent of the federal government, with William Campbell.

Necessarily wearing civilian clothes (and therefore subject to execution as spies), the raiders stole a locomotive called *The General* at Big Shanty, Georgia, some two hundred miles into enemy territory. Two soldiers declined to continue the mission, leaving twenty-two raiders.

Both sides recognized the importance of rail traffic, and the Union men were determined to cripple part of the Confederacy's transport.

"Andrews' Raiders" stoked *The General*'s boiler and fled northward. It went into history as "The Great Locomotive Chase," an eighty-seven-mile pursuit with Andrews' men still attempting to burn bridges and destroy tracks while cutting telegraph lines along the way. The raiders would have escaped were they pursued by less determined men. *The General's* engineer, Jeff Fuller, grabbed two friends and set out in pursuit.

The Southerners' determination was exceptional. They started the seemingly fruitless chase with a handcart, then alternately ran from two to three miles around torn-up tracks before commandeering other locomotives. Andrews was delayed by traffic, allowing Fuller's men to close the gap. Eventually, Fuller overtook Andrews in a locomotive called *The Texas*. The raiders jumped off and ran for cover, still doggedly pursued.

In a matter of days, the raiders were caught and sent to prison; eight were tried and executed, including Andrews and Campbell. As civilians, they were not eligible for the Medal of Honor, though their role in the episode was pivotal.

The fourteen Ohioans remaining in captivity realized their chances of survival were slim. Presumably with nothing to lose, they staged an escape; eight succeeded. The other six were recaptured but permitted to live.

On March 25, 1863 (the same month that officers became eligible for the medal), the escapers arrived in Washington. That day, Secretary of War Stanton presented medals to six, then introduced them to Lincoln. Eventually, nineteen of Andrews' twenty-two raiders received the medal. (That ceremony became the basis of Medal of Honor Day, begun in Washington State.) Nine more were awarded in September; the others between 1864 and 1883.

The six, in order of presentation, were Privates Jacob Parrott (33rd Ohio); William Bensinger (21st); and Robert Buffum (21st); Sergeants Elihu Mason (21st) and William Pittinger (2nd); and Corporal William H. Reddick (33rd).

As civilians, Andrews and William Campbell were not eligible for

Pvt. William Bensinger, Andrews' Raiders

Pvt. Jacob Parrott, Andrews' Raiders

*Pvt. Robert Buffum
Andrews' Raiders*

the medal. In June, with six others, they were hanged as spies. Four of the latter were posthumously recognized after the war.

THE SECOND YEAR: 1862

Counting retroactive awards, about twenty medals eventually were presented for 1861. However, 171 were awarded for 1862 actions. One of the most deserved medals of the war went to First Lieutenant William R. Shafter of the Seventh Michigan. On May 31, 1862, "Pecos Bill" Shafter led a detail of twenty-two men assisting with bridge construction near Fair Oaks, Virginia. Learning of an impending Confederate attack, he returned to Company I's position

---

■ *Medal of Honor Trivia*

The children of two raiders, Privates Jacob Parrott and Wilson Brown, married. John M. Parrott was the only son of Jacob; Edith was one of Wilson Brown's eight children. *The General* was restored in 1961, and the centenarian locomotive was placed on exhibit in Kennesaw, Georgia.

---

and played a significant role in defending the position, though eighteen of his men were killed or wounded. As the black powder smoke cleared, Shafter was afoot, his horse having been killed beneath him. He had also sustained "a severe flesh wound" that he kept concealed from his superiors. He remained on duty for the next three days until the other wounded had been cared for or removed. Thirty-six years later, he commanded all American troops in Cuba.

Some Civil War awards were made for repeated valor over a period of months and years. One such case was Private Thomas T. Fallon, an Irishman who enlisted upon arrival in New Jersey. His citation mentions two engagements in May 1862—Williamsburg and Fair Oaks, Virginia, where he engaged Confederate skirmishers and reported for duty though still ill. Two years later, he led his fellow New Yorkers into the rebel defenses at Big Shanty, Georgia.

One of the most unusual Army awards went to Sergeant James H. Burbank of the Fourth Rhode Island. A native Hollander, he was detached to the gunboat *Barney* during action near Franklin, Virginia, in October 1862. No other awards were made for similar service, so it appears that Burbank's naval service was extremely rare, if not unique, for an Army man.

The nineteen medals awarded the raiders did not remain a record. At the Battle of Antietam (Sharpsburg to the Confederacy), twenty soldiers were recognized for actions on September 7, 1862. Three months later, twenty-one were honored for the gallant, doomed Union effort at Fredericksburg, Virginia.

FREDERICKSBURG

The story of Marye's Heights is oft told on both sides of the Mason-Dixon line, partly because Scots-Irish regiments fought so well and so hard for both North and South. Throughout the final day, December 13, Major General Ambrose Burnside refused to learn the obvious lesson. With 100,000 troops to Robert E. Lee's 72,000, Burnside squandered his strength and repeatedly threw new regiments at the stone wall atop the heights. Federal losses were appalling: more than 13,000 blue-coated men were killed or

1st Lt. William R. Shafter, 7th Michigan

wounded; they fell by companies and battalions. Today, it may seem incredible, but men in the nineteenth century placed more value on honor than survival. For that matter, so did men of the early twentieth century, witness Paaschendale and the Somme.

The Fredericksburg medals went to men from seventeen regiments representing eight states. Pennsylvanians predominated, with one-third of the awards for the battle, followed by three each from Massachusetts and New York.

Elsewhere, the Union attack dislodged the Nineteenth Alabama, on the left flank of A. P. Hill's Division. Lieutenant Colonel A. J. Hutchins' command was surrounded by two Pennsylvania units: the Seventh assaulting from the front and the Second on the left and rear. Most of the proud Southerners broke after sustaining nearly ninety killed, leaving the color guard a small gray island in a sea of blue. Twenty-five-year-old

Evan M. Woodward of the Second Pennsylvania Reserves advanced between the lines to demand the colors of the Nineteenth Georgia. The Pennsylvanians counted 107 prisoners, including most of the Irish company. It was nearly the only Union bright spot in an otherwise dismal day. Woodward received his medal thirty-two years and one day later.

Private Martin Schubert of the Twenty-sixth New York ignored a furlough to recover from wounds and returned to his unit. Finding Company E on the field, he picked up the flag after the designated color bearers had been shot and carried the banner until he was wounded again. Likewise, Private Joseph Keene raised the colors in Company B and led the regiment's charge.

Officers occasionally gained fame as color bearers as well. In the Nineteenth Massachusetts, Second Lieutenant John Adams grasped the national and regimental colors from the dying hands of the bearers and carried both flags across the lethal field, standing firm to provide a rallying point.

Other regiments also were stopped or repelled by the Confederate's massed riflery. Colonel Zenas R. Bliss led his Seventh Rhode Island into the Fredericksburg cauldron, the regiment's first battle, where the soldiers were told to lie down to avoid the worst of the rebel fire. Bliss, a Maine man, exhorted his Rhode Islanders by example. He rose to his feet, strode ahead of the line, and fired his revolver at the stone wall before walking back. Somehow he avoided being killed, and lived to receive his medal shortly after the Spanish-American War.

Corporal John G. Palmer and Private Wallace A. Beckwith of the Twenty-first Connecticut were among the first six men volunteering to assist an artillery battery in danger of being destroyed. The infantrymen remained with the gunners until the fight was ended; upon their return, the F Company commander said he never expected to see the men alive again. It is unknown why the other four volunteers were not decorated.

THE THIRD YEAR: 1863

Increasing numbers of medals were awarded throughout 1863, in all theaters of war. An indicator of the extent of the war was the number of medals awarded in a five-day period in May: nine at Vicksburg, Mississippi; twenty-four at Chancellorsville; and fourteen at Fredericksburg, Virginia, including nearby Salem Heights and Brooks Ford. "Second Fredericksburg" drove the Confederates from Marye's Heights where Union dead had carpeted the ground the previous December. The Vicksburg campaign would last into July.

Meanwhile, in May, the Battle of Chancellorsville, Virginia, went into history as Lee's greatest victory. Outnumbered nearly two to one, he split his army not once but twice and drove the federals from the field. Still, Union men displayed unquestioned valor amid defeat.

Captain Hubert Dilger of the Ohio Light Artillery fought his battery until enemy pressure forced a withdrawal. Moving one gun by hand, Dilger's men rolled the piece to a final protective position. The crew executed rapid-fire drill until finally forced to retreat; Dilger was the last of his command to depart.

Four men of the Sixty-sixth Ohio were recognized for battlefield heroism of perhaps the rarest kind: saving an enemy. Sergeants Henry Heller and Thomas Thompson led privates William Cranston and Elisha Seaman and retrieved a wounded Confederate officer within the rebel lines. The citation credited their efforts with producing "valuable information."

Chancellorsville represented the pinnacle of Lee's stunning career. Sixty days later, he plummeted from that lofty height.

The record for Civil War awards was ninety-six at Vicksburg, Mississippi, on May 27. Most of the recipients were members of the "volunteer storming party." In all, 120 medals were presented for the siege.

VICKSBURG

On the afternoon of May 19, 1863, Grant ordered an attack against the weakened Confederate defenses at Vicksburg, Mississippi. The assault failed, resulting in redoubled efforts three days later. A massive attack—most of three corps—was thrown against the Southern line. Taking the brunt of the defenses were 150 men of the volunteer storming party.

The storming party was equipped with hastily constructed bridging material to span the gap in the defensive ditch around the enemy lines. Speed was essential in order to overwhelm the defenders at the crucial point, and as the first rank, the volunteers in the storming party knew that they would absorb horrendous casualties.

The storming party was not as suicidal as it may be perceived 150 years later. In the nineteenth century, the British concept of "the forlorn hope" was well established, especially in siege warfare. For reasons both apparent and obscure, some soldiers were drawn to the prospect of an all-or-nothing assault against a seemingly impregnable position. Some followed their more determined comrades; others enjoyed the acclaim accorded survivors; a few were just curious as to whether their number was up.

The party was drawn from the Second Division, XV Corps. It comprised fourteen regiments from Illinois, Indiana, Missouri, Ohio, and West Virginia.

Brigadier General Hugh Ewing, commanding the Third Brigade, reported, "At 10:04 A.M. of the twenty-second, a storming party, composed of fifty volunteers from each brigade of the division, bearing the colors of my headquarters, and followed by my troops in column, charged down a narrow, deep-cut road upon a bastion of the enemy's works. They were instructed to bear to the left and cross the curtain if the ditch at the salient could not be bridged. They made a footpath at the salient, by which Captain (John H.) Groce, commanding, Lieutenant O'Neal, Private Trogden, the color bearer, and others, crossing, climbed halfway up the exterior slope, and planted the flag upon it unfurled. The Thirtieth Ohio, next in order, moved close upon the storming party, until their progress was arrested by a front and double flank fire, and the dead and wounded which blocked the defile. The second company forced its way over the remains of the first, and a third over those of the preceding, but their perseverance served only further to encumber the impassable way. The Thirty-seventh Ohio came next, its left breaking the column where the road first debouched, upon a deadly fire. After the check, a few passed on, but were mostly shot. They fell back, and, with the remainder of the brigade and division, came over a better route.

"I formed my troops as they came up on the brow of the hill running from the road to the left, parallel to and seventy yards from the intrenchments. Here we protected our advanced men and wounded until they were gradually withdrawn, and, with a heavy and well-directed and sustained fire, covered the after attempt to charge over the intrenchments made down the same road by the brigade of General Mower.

"At night, the wounded, dead, and colors were brought seventy yards back to the hill, where the brigade remains, intrenching and skirmishing with the enemy."

The color bearer whom Ewing cited was Private Howell G. Trogden of the Eighth Missouri. His citation, like all those from Vicksburg, was brief but carried the additional note, "He carried his regiment's flag and tried to borrow a gun to defend it."

Following a seven-week siege, Vicksburg capitulated on July 4, 1863. The Union had lost 925 dead or missing, plus 3,700 wounded. Some 31,000 Confederates surrendered. Most of the storming-party medals were awarded in 1894, but meanwhile events were accelerating in the eastern theater as well. They climaxed at a Pennsylvania crossroads called Gettysburg.

GETTYSBURG

Fifty-eight medals were awarded for the crucial Battle of Gettysburg in July 1863. The steely determination of Colonel Joshua Lawrence Chamberlain has passed into legend for the Twentieth Maine's defense of Little Round Top on the second day of battle, including Chamberlain's color sergeant, Andrew Tozier.

The Gettysburg awards were reasonably well distributed among thirteen privates, twenty-eight NCOs, and eighteen officers, including two generals. The fifty-eight medals represented forty units from eleven states. Not surprisingly, Pennsylvania topped the list with eleven awards, followed by New York (ten) and Massachusetts (seven). Ten were awarded for the first day, July 1, with twenty-two and twenty-six on the next two days.

Reinforcements arrived on both sides during the first night, and by dawn on July 2, some 65,000 Confederates opposed 85,000 Northerners. Nevertheless, new Union commander George Meade felt desperate enough to authorize "the instant death of any soldier who fails to do his duty in this hour."

Commanding the Union III Corps was flamboyant Major General Daniel Sickles, a New York politician securing the Union left. He was concerned about the low ground south of Cemetery Ridge, so, against orders, he moved his two divisions (with regiments from seven states) forward to command the ground near the peach orchard. With the new disposition, his left rested near the base of Little Round Top in a rocky area called Devil's Den. Though he now commanded the ground to his front, both flanks were unhinged from the main Union line. His opposite number, Lieutenant General James Longstreet, took the opportunity. He attacked.

Whatever his judgment, Sickles "displayed the most conspicuous gallantry . . . vigorously contesting the advance of the enemy and continuing to encourage his troops after being severely wounded." Nobody ever questioned Dan Sickles' courage, though his wisdom is still debated today. His bobtailed corps was torn apart in vicious fighting throughout the afternoon; his left leg was shattered as well. Unperturbedly puffing a cigar, he watched the amputation and arranged for the bones to be sent to an army hospital in Washington, which he regularly visited the rest of his life. Charged with dereliction of duty and threatened with court-martial, instead he received the Medal of Honor. It was not the last time a goat was declared a hero.

Other heroes abounded that day, and the Sixth Pennsylvania Reserves accounted for six medals on July 2. Belonging to the Third Division of Major General George Sykes' V Corps, Colonel W. H. Ent's men made a forced march to arrive on the field before that afternoon. Upon moving off Little Round Top, the unit was taken under accurate fire from a log house near Devil's Den, and the call went out for volunteers to storm the position. Six men replied, all noncoms from companies A, D, and G. They were sergeants John Hart, Wallace Johnson, and George Mears, with corporals Chester Furman, Levi Roush, and Thaddeus Smith. The volunteers flanked a squad of rebel sharpshooters, forced their surrender, and brought them into the Union lines. The medals were awarded between 1897 and 1900.

The First Minnesota had fought every battle of the Army of the Potomac since Bull Run, and paid the price for its credentials. Winfield Scott Hancock, II Corps commander, saw the imminent danger of his center along Cemetery Ridge and threw in his reserve. Outnumbered six to one, the 262 Minnesotans charged a Confederate brigade. In military terms, it was a local spoiling attack, buying time until significant reinforcements could repulse the Alabamans. It worked. But that evening, only forty-seven of the First Minnesota remained alive and unwounded, a record 82 percent casualty rate. They were at it again the next day, when two Medals of Honor represented the sacrifice of the many.

On July 3, the remnants of the First Minnesota protected artillery batteries opposing Pickett's Charge against the federal center. Corporal Henry O'Brien picked up the unit colors, ran ahead of the line, and was badly wounded. But he held the flag aloft until struck again.

Meanwhile, Private Marshall Sherman managed to seize the colors of the Twenty-eighth Virginia, earning wide acclaim. He was wounded the next year, losing a foot, but retained his trophy long after the war. Upon receiving the Medal of Honor in December 1864, he delivered the Virginia flag to the War Department yet somehow regained possession thereafter. Sherman presented the flag to the Minnesota Historical Society and died in 1896.

The story did not end there. In 1905, most Confederate flags were returned to the state of origin, but Minnesota kept the Twenty-eighth Virginia's. In 2002, the Army and Commonwealth of Virginia both requested return of the banner, but Minnesota declined, having had possession most of the previous 139 years. Governor Jesse Ventura stated, not unreasonably, "We won it."

A twenty-eight-year-old brigadier, Alexander S. Webb, exhibited "distinguished personal gallantry in leading his men forward at a critical period in the contest" for Cemetery Ridge. Webb commanded a brigade of four regiments in the Second Division of Hancock's II Corps. Called the "Philadelphia Brigade," Webb's command had largely been raised in that city. Now it prepared to defend Pennsylvania soil against George Pickett's men.

Webb had deployed his regiments near the low stone wall that formed "the angle." On command, his two largest regiments stood and fired into the approaching gray ranks of Brigadier Lewis Armistead. The Sixty-ninth and Seventy-first delivered close-range volleys and received Confederate fire in turn. Webb had placed the Seventy-second and part of the 106th on the reverse slope, out of artillery fire, but now called them forward. The enemy pressure was enormous: men of the Seventy-first were pushed back into the ranks of the Seventy-second. Soldiers milled about, screaming, loading, and firing. Blue and gray alike fell dead or crippled from enemy and "friendly" fire.

Webb dashed ahead of the Seventy-second, trying to restore order. It was fruitless in that awesome noise and confusion. He saw Armistead cross the wall with about a hundred Virginians and, sensing the battle hung in the balance, he ordered the Seventy-second to the crest within forty yards of the Southerners. Most of the Sixty-ninth and Seventy-first held tight, even with enemy passing to their rear. The Union cannon were overrun and more rebels

Brig. Gen. Alexander S. Webb, Philadelphia Brigade

surged into the woods. It was a riot of gunfire, black powder smoke, bayonet thrusts, and clubbed rifles. Then more Union troops arrived; the fight was decided.

The hilltop fell silent. Alexander Webb had fallen, wounded, but received the Medal of Honor twenty-eight years later. He had held the line at the high tide of the Confederacy.

Artillerymen constituted a small minority at Gettysburg but four "redlegs" received recognition; three on July 2. Lieutenant Edward M. Knox, Fifteenth New York Battery, held his ground after other batteries had pulled back. While helping withdraw a field piece by hand, he was severely wounded but received the medal in 1892.

Private Casper R. Carlisle, Pennsylvania Light Battery, saved a gun from possible capture while under heavy rifle fire, with most of the horses killed and drivers wounded.

Meanwhile, Bugler Charles Reed of the Ninth Independent Massachusetts Light Battery rescued his commanding officer who had fallen wounded between the lines.

German-born Frederick Fuger faced Pickett's Charge on July 3. A sergeant in the Fourth Artillery, he found himself the senior noncom in Battery A after all officers had fallen. Five guns had been disabled under the remorseless pounding of Confederate artillery, but Fuger supervised the remaining gun, keeping up a fire into the gray lines advancing toward him, until ordered to withdraw.

The Nineteenth Massachusetts was heavily engaged on the third. Major Edmund Rice was in the forefront of the counterattack against Pickett's division, falling badly wounded amid the Confederates. Sergeant Benjamin Jellison of Company C and Private John Robinson of Company I captured the colors of the Fifty-seventh Virginia and assisted in taking prisoners. Meanwhile, Corporal Joseph DeCastro, also of Company I, was credited with taking the flag of the Nineteenth Virginia.

The color sergeant of Company A was Benjamin Falls, killed while capturing an enemy flag, one of a handful of posthumous recipients.

POSTHUMOUS AWARDS

In marked contrast to the high mortality rates among later Medal of Honor recipients, very few Civil War medals were posthumous. Other than Falls, they included:

Corporal John P. McVeane, a Canadian law student in the Forty-ninth New York, captured colors at Fredericksburg Heights in May 1863 and compelled the surrender of rebels in a barn. He was killed a year later in the Wilderness, and his medal was approved in 1870.

Private Henry M. Hardenbergh, Thirty-ninth Illinois, captured a flag at Deep Run, Virginia, in August 1864, but he died at Petersburg two weeks later.

At Winchester, Virginia, on September 19, 1864, Sergeant Charles H. Seston, Eleventh Indiana, was cited for "gallant and meritorious service in carrying the regimental colors."

Ten days later at Chapin's Farm, Virginia, privates George A. Buchanan and Henry Wells of the 148th New York advanced ahead of the skirmishers and drove rebel artillerymen from their guns until shot down. In the same battle, Sergeant Richard Gasson, Forty-seventh New York, fell dead while planting the regimental colors on the enemy's works at Chapin's Farm, Virginia.

In April 1865, Captain Edwin F. Savacool, First New York Cavalry, received mortal wounds seizing an enemy flag at Sayler's Creek, Virginia.

BLACK RECIPIENTS

Far to the south of Gettysburg, two weeks later, the Fifty-fourth Massachusetts played a leading role in the attack on Battery Wagner in South Carolina, the action depicted in the 1989 film *Glory*. Though Sergeant William Carney did not appear in the movie, clearly his actions inspired part of the climax of that fruitless assault. When the regimental color sergeant fell, Carney took the flag and led the way to the top of the parapet, where he planted the colors. Under close-range, high-volume fire, the Fifty-fourth fell back, and Carney brought the flag with him despite being wounded twice. He received his medal in 1900.

Some 180,000 blacks served in the Union Army during the war (and an unknown number joined the Confederacy). Sixteen black soldiers received the medal for Civil War action; fourteen were decorated for Chapin's Farm, Virginia, September 29–30, 1864. They belonged to five regiments of the U.S. Colored Troops, and most were senior NCOs who assumed responsibility beyond their rank.

The Fifth Regiment sustained potentially crippling losses among its

Sgt. William Carney, 54th Massachusetts

officers, but the noncoms stepped into the breach. First Sergeant James H. Bronson took command of Company D when the officers were killed or wounded, as did First Sergeant Powhatan Beaty of Company G. So did Sergeant Major Milton Holland, a twenty-year-old Texan in Company C. Corporal Miles James of the Thirty-sixth ignored a critical wound to one arm, continuing to load and fire one-handed, directing his squad within thirty yards of the Confederate defenses. He lost his arm but gained the Medal of Honor.

DOWN SOUTH IN '63

One of the highest proportion of medals for any action went to the Second Minnesota. Near Nolensville, Tennessee, on February 15, 1863, Company H garnered eight medals. First Sergeant Lovilon Holmes; corporals William A. Clark, Milton Hanna, and Samuel Wright; privates Joseph Burger, James Flannigan, Byron Pay, and John Vale were among sixteen men who defended a supply train against a hundred or more Confederate cavalry. It is unknown why the other half of the detachment was not decorated.

Nine awards were presented for Chickamauga, Georgia, September 19–20. The Union debacle occurred in the second-bloodiest battle of the war: General William S. Rosecrans sustained 16,000 federal casualties;

and Braxton Bragg, 18,400 Confederate. General James Longstreet's corps broke the Union right, putting the defenders to rout. But though the rebels garnered a treasure trove of supplies, they were too badly hurt to pursue the Yankees.

Colonel Ferdinand Vanderveer commanded the Third Brigade, Third Division. His topographical engineer was Captain Clinton A. Cilley of the Second Minnesota. But when another brigade broke and fled through the lines, Cilley grasped the colors of a retreating regiment and reversed its course, leading it back into action. A gunner of the brigade was so disgusted that he used his rammer to flatten a fleeing captain and damn him for a coward.

Another notable from the Second was Sergeant Axel H. Reed, who was under arrest when his unit was committed. Nevertheless, he "excused himself" from detention, pushed to the front, and secured a rifle and ammunition. After fighting through both days, he was formally released. At Missionary Ridge two months later, he led Company K to the Confederate earthworks, where he was severely wounded in one arm. The limb was amputated, but Reed declined discharge and served throughout the rest of the war. His medal, presented in 1898, truly represented "devotion to duty above and beyond."

Mostly the Chickamauga citations reflected steadiness in the face of disaster. An ordnance captain, Horace Porter, rallied "enough fugitives" to hold the ground long enough to effect escape of the baggage train.

Some federal regiments stood long enough to run short of ammunition; two medals were awarded for obtaining extra cartridges. Second Lieutenant Orville T. Chamberlain, Seventy-fourth Indiana, was sent in search of an adjacent regiment and found it—no small feat in the confusion of a disintegrating army amid massed formations firing black powder. He secured extra ammunition and returned to his company.

William G. Whitney was a twenty-two-year-old sergeant with the Eleventh Michigan, which was hard-pressed during the day. Seeing Confederate forces grouping for an attack, he left his lines to scavenge ammunition from the dead and wounded. He distributed cartridges to the men of Company B, who withstood the next charge.

Still, there were moments of success—even glory. Corporal William A. Richey, Fifteenth Ohio, found himself between the lines and captured a Confederate major on horseback.

Repeated hard-fought battles occurred in Tennessee during November 1863. Among the notable performances at the Battle of Lookout Mountain was the 149th New York on November 23–24. The regiment was led by Colonel Henry A. Barnum, who remained at the head of his troops despite repeated wounds. First Sergeant Norman F. Potter (Company E) and Private Peter Kappesser (Company B) captured the flag of Confederate General Braxton Bragg's army. The unit's own flag featured in the action of Company D's Sergeant John Kiggins, who waved the colors to identify the New Yorkers as friendlies to Union batteries firing on the 149th. In the process, he drew "concentrated fire from the enemy."

Elsewhere in Tennessee that same month, the Seventeenth Michigan received five medals. Another color bearer was Private Joseph Brandle of Company C. At Lenoire on November 16, Brandle was already wounded when he was blinded in one eye. Nevertheless, he retained his grip on the flag until the regimental commander ordered him back.

That same day, Lieutenant Colonel Frederick W. Swift ignored the enemy fire directed at the color bearers, three of whom were killed or wounded. He grasped the standard and helped rally the Seventeenth, which was in danger of being routed.

At Knoxville on November 20, corporals John A. Falconer and Irwin Shepard volunteered with a few other men to burn buildings that had shielded rebel sharpshooters. While so engaged, the Confederates counterattacked and the half dozen Michiganders were ordered back, but Shepard remained to complete the task.

Other Tennessee battles in the second half of November accounted for thirty medals. They included Lenoire, Campbell Station, Knoxville, and Missionary Ridge. The latter, November 25, resulted in seventeen medals, nine to Ohioans, mainly for capturing colors.

Prominent among the latter was Private James C. Walker. After the Thirty-first Ohio lost two color bearers, he took up the flag and carried it into an enemy artillery position. Not content with that feat, he then captured the standard and bearer of the Forty-first Alabama. Meanwhile, the Fifteenth's Private Robert Brown, barely nineteen, compelled the surrender of the Ninth Missippi's flag.

British-born Corporal George Green of the Eleventh scaled the Confederate defenses and, in a hand-to-hand tussle, helped Private Hiram Howard seize the Eighteenth Alabama's colors.

1st Lt. Arthur MacArthur Jr.
24th Wisconsin

Another Buckeye, Sergeant Freeman Davis, saved the Eightieth's national and regimental flags from capture.

At Missionary Ridge, First Lieutenant Arthur MacArthur Jr. of the Twenty-fourth Wisconsin displayed valor beyond that expected of a regimental adjutant.

During the assault, the color bearer was bayoneted by a Confederate soldier; the next man to raise the flag was decapitated by cannon. The eighteen-year-old officer took up the regiment's colors, shouted "On Wisconsin!" and advanced to the enemy defenses at the crest of Missionary Ridge. By the end of the war, MacArthur was nineteen: the youngest colonel in the U.S. Army.

MacArthur's medal was awarded in 1890, when his third son was ten years old, the same Douglas MacArthur who would receive the award upon evacuating the Philippines in 1942.

THE FOURTH YEAR: 1864

In the third full year of the war, significant battles were fought in Virginia. The meat-grinder Wilderness campaign produced twenty-two medals, while Spotsylvania, also fought that May, garnered thirty-six.

At the Wilderness, the Sixty-second New York received two medals, both related to flags. Sergeant Charles E. Morse and Private James Evans dashed into the Confederate lines to seize the regimental banner from the color sergeant who lay mortally wounded. Though himself wounded, Morse bore the flag through the remainder of the engagement.

In the Spotsylvania fight, Private William Noyes of the Second Vermont demonstrated exceptional coolness. Standing atop the breastworks, he ignored the extreme danger by loading and firing at least fifteen rounds at the rebel line a few yards away. Incredibly, he got away with it. Meanwhile, a fellow Vermonter, Second Lieutenant Augustus Robbins, showed more initiative than usually expected of a staff officer. He successfully withdrew a regiment from a dangerously exposed position and, though wounded, led it to the safety of the Union lines.

That fall, the battles of Winchester and Cedar Creek, also in Virginia, added their own tales of heroism to the mounting toll.

A few medals were presented for killing or capturing Confederate officers. At Crosby's Creek, Tennessee, in January 1864, the Fifteenth Pennsylvania Cavalry pursued Brigadier Robert B. Vance's Carolina brigade to retrieve captured supply wagons. Sergeant Everett W. Anderson single-handedly captured Vance, who spent the war in prison. Seven months later, Private George Lucas of the Third Missouri Cavalry rode to fame in Arkansas when he chased down and killed Brigadier General George Holt of the Arkansas Militia, returning with his horse and weapons.

In Virginia that October, a New Jersey trooper, Sergeant James T. Clancy, killed Brigadier General John Dunovant (a brigade commander under Wade Hampton) in a cavalry charge, "thus confusing the enemy and greatly aiding in his repulse."

Near Resaca, Georgia, in May 1864, Sergeant Thomas D. Collins of the 143rd New York captured an enemy flag. It was just one of several notable exploits of the young soldier, who became a favorite of General William T. Sherman. Though an infantryman, he spent much time in the saddle as a scout and lost four horses in combat "and one from eating hardtack." Later that year, Collins was recommended for a commission but could not be promoted owing to his age. He was still sixteen. However, Collins' treatment contrasts with the treatment accorded another youngster.

THE LAST YEAR: 1865

The last four months of the war produced a deluge of Medals of Honor. The hard-fought battle at Fort Fisher, North Carolina, on January 15, featured one of the most remarkable characters of the war. Born at Valley Forge, sixteen-year-old Galusha Pennypacker recruited one of the original companies of the Ninety-seventh Pennsylvania Volunteers in 1861 and was elected captain. For the next three years, he rose in rank and prominence to become regimental commander at nineteen. At Fort Fisher, Colonel Pennypacker led his New York/Pennsylvania brigade over a traverse and picked up the Ninety-seventh's flag when the color bearer fell wounded. Pennypacker planted the colors on the parapet before being badly hit himself. However, he remained in service and, in April, he was promoted to brigadier general at age twenty. He remained in the Army, rising to major general before retiring to run a newspaper.

In March, a relatively small cavalry engagement occurred at Waynesboro, Virginia, resulting in one of the highest medal-to-combatant ratios of the war. Some 2,500 of Sheridan's horsemen clashed with

Col. Galusha Pennypacker, 97th Pa. Volunteers

1,600 Confederates under Jubal Early, resulting in a clear-cut federal victory. Fifteen medals were awarded to members of three New York regiments: the First, Eighth, and Twenty-second Cavalry.

Some two hundred Army awards eventually were presented for April 1865, the last month of hostilities. More than half occurred on two days: fifty-two at Petersburg on April 2, and fifty-six near Deatonsville on the sixth.

Corporal Harris S. Hawthorne of the 121st New York was credited with capturing Brigadier General G. W. Custis Lee, son of the Confederate commander, at Sayler's (aka Sailor's) Creek on April 6, 1865. Other sources credit a Connecticut artilleryman, Private Dennis Moore, but Hawthorne received the medal.

The battle that became known as Sayler's Creek yielded fifty-two Medals of Honor, though it was a wholly lopsided contest. On April 6, elements of three Union corps surrounded one-fourth of Robert E. Lee's army, capturing 6,000 men (including his son Custis). Medals were presented to members of twenty-six regiments, including twenty-three awards to New Yorkers. More than thirty of the total went to cavalrymen from seven states, led by seven recipients of the Second New York and six of the First West Virginia. One of the horsemen already was known for flamboyant courage bordering on foolhardiness.

Lieutenant Thomas W. Custer, Sixth Michigan Cavalry, received two medals in two years. The younger brother of Brevet Major General

George Custer, Tom was called "the bravest of the brave." The teenage lieutenant also had the famous Custer luck. At Namozine Church, Virginia, in May 1863, he led a charge against a Confederate cavalry regiment fighting a rearguard action. Jumping his horse over a barricade, he seized a flag and supervised capture of some fourteen prisoners. Reportedly his trophy belonged to the Second North Carolina.

Almost two years later, on the staff of his brother's division, young Custer saw another chance at glory's golden ring near Sayler's Creek. Eager for another flag, he jumped his horse over rebel defenses, probably expecting a repeat of his previous success. He was badly astonished to find a second defensive line behind the first.

1st Lt. Thomas W. Custer, 6th Michigan Cavalry

Lieutenant Colonel E. W. Whitaker, George Custer's chief of staff, described the action. "Tom led the assault upon the enemy breastworks, was first to leap his horse over the works on top of the enemy while they were pouring a volley of musketry into our ranks. Tom seized the rebel colors and demanded their surrender. The color bearer shot him through the face and neck, so close to the muzzle Tom's face was spotted with burnt powder. He retained the colors with one hand, while with the other he drew his revolver and shot the rebel dead." Custer then spurred his mount back to the lines, where his brother had to have him restrained for treatment of a severe wound.

In the same action, Second Lieutenant Elliott Norton of Company H raced ahead of his column to seize the flag of the Forty-fourth Tennessee.

Tom Custer received both medals the month after the war ended, still barely twenty years old. He died with his brother on a barren Montana hillside eleven years later. He was the only soldier with two awards in the Civil War, though Captain Frank Baldwin of the Nineteenth Michigan earned his first in 1864 and the second ten years later. Two other men each received two medals during the Indian wars.

The last event resulting in a Civil War medal occurred on April 19 at Greensboro, North Carolina. Lieutenant Colonel Charles M. Betts was scouting with seventy-five troopers of the Fifteenth Pennsylvania Cavalry when they sighted a battalion of Confederate horsemen. Betts quickly deployed his men, who surrounded the approaching enemy and compelled their surrender.

Before month's end, the Confederate States of America had ceased to exist.

LOST COLORS

Several Confederate regiments repeatedly lost flags to the enemy. The Eighteenth North Carolina's colors were seized twice during 1864 and 1865, and nearly a third time. During a hand-to-hand struggle at Gravelly Run, Virginia, on April 1, 1865, Sergeant Albert O'Connor of the Seventh Wisconsin killed a Southern officer and grasped the colors. However, O'Connor was quickly surrounded and forced to return the flag.

Between 1862 and 1864, the Thirteenth Alabama lost its colors at Antietam, Gettysburg, and Nashville. Each Union man received the Medal of Honor.

The record, however, was undoubtedly held by the Ninth Virginia, which lost four flags: one at Gettysburg and three more during April and May 1865.

AFTERMATH

After the war, 864 men of the Twenty-seventh Maine received the medal for extending their term of enlistment by four days to include the Battle of Gettysburg. Some 309 accepted the extension, but bureaucracy permitted an award to the entire regiment. Ironically, the Twenty-seventh did not participate in the battle. In 1917, the regiment's awards were among a total 911 revoked, including those to twenty-nine members of Lincoln's funeral guard, plus six civilians (scouts such as Bill Cody, plus Mary Walker).

From 1890 to 1897, some seven hundred veterans applied for the medal. President William McKinley had had enough: He directed the Army to develop objective criteria that included recommendation by someone other than the honoree and a limit of one year between the action and recommendation. There was at least one exception, as in 1907, Congress approved award of the medal to Corporal Monroe Reisinger of the 150th Pennsylvania for action at Gettysburg.

In 1917, Corporal Henry Lewis and Private Henry Peters received Civil War decorations for Vicksburg, the "last-last" such awards. The fact that both served in the Forty-seventh Ohio indicates political influence behind the awards. There were, of course, more downstream. In 1915, similar legislation provided for an award to Major John Skinner for the January 1873 Indian battle at the Lava Beds in Oregon.

In the face of continuing exceptions, the time requirement subsequently was altered, and more than a century can pass between the event and the award. In fact, since the 1990s, time constraints have effectively been eliminated, regardless of statutory limitations.

If not the last, the most recent medal for the Civil War was awarded in 2001. Corporal Andrew Jackson Smith of the Fifty-fifth Massachusetts was recognized for his role at Honey Hill, South Carolina, in 1864. When the color sergeant was killed, Smith took up the banner and, though the regiment sustained 30 percent losses, he carried the flag through artillery fire and prevented its capture. Smith thus became the eighteenth black soldier to receive the nation's highest honor. (Six black sailors also received the Medal for Civil War action.)

CONFEDERATE MEDALS

During the War of Southern Independence, there was no Confederate equivalent of the Medal of Honor. Southern fighting men received no awards or decorations, as a British-style "mention in dispatches" was about all that could be expected. In 1896, former Lieutenant General Stephen D. Lee addressed the precursor of the Sons of Confederate Veterans (SCV), urging them to preserve the memory and valor of their parents. In 1977, the SCV began publishing an equivalent of the "Confederate Medal of Honor" to recognize notable warriors of the Lost Cause. As of 2006, the organization had cited fifty-five men and women. They include names familiar and obscure: Forrest, Garnett, Hampton, and Mosby, plus seventeen privates or seamen and four noncoms. The largest contingent is the seven-man crew of the submarine *Hunley*, lost after destroying the USS *Housatonic* off Charleston in 1864.

CHAPTER TWO

ON THE FRONTIER

■

O FFICIALLY, the Indian wars lasted nearly forty years, producing 423 Medals of Honor from 1861 to 1898. In that period, 1,031 Regular Army troops were killed fighting Indians, and one-third perished in just three battles: the Fetterman fight in Wyoming in 1866 (80); Little Big Horn, Montana, in 1876 (250); and White Bird Canyon, Idaho, in 1876 (33). By one reckoning, of the 15,000 people killed during the frontier wars, 9,800 were Indians.

The Indian campaigns were fought in fifteen states or territories as well as the Republic of Mexico. By far the most activity occurred in Arizona, with more than 150 Medal of Honor citations, mainly in 1868–69. For much of the frontier era, conflict was nonstop, and the most medals were awarded for actions over eleven consecutive years, 1867–77.

The Indian wars were largely a cavalry affair. More than three-quarters of the Western medals went to horse soldiers, though the infantry received sixty-seven, with artillery receiving five and the medical service six. Indian scouts, usually attached to cavalry, were awarded at least fifteen Medals of Honor.

To readers of Eastern newspapers and dime novels, service in the West often seemed adventuresome, even glamorous. The troopers knew better. They sang, "Forty miles a day on beans and hay in the Regular Army-oh!" They were poorly paid and undertrained; few were proficient with their weapons. Often they were poorly fed—remains examined from the Custer battlefield in the 1980s showed signs of malnutrition. Others suffered serious spinal problems from years of jarring horseback maneuvers on the McClellan Saddle.

The Indian-fighting army was composed in large part of immigrants; over one-third of the bluecoats were foreign born. Among the 423 Medal of Honor recipients on the frontier, 148 came from abroad, as far afield as Germany and Australia. Ninety-one were from the British Isles, including seventy-four from Ireland. In fact, the sons of Erin accounted for fully half the immigrants among Medal of Honor men. Germans comprised the next largest contingent, though all were born before Bismarck unified the nation. Others were Canadians, Swiss, and French, with one each born in Mexico, the West Indies, Australia, Denmark, and Sweden.

During the Indian wars, eighteen black soldiers received the medal, including eleven "buffalo soldiers" from the Ninth Cavalry, one from the Tenth, and two from the Twenty-fourth Infantry. Four Seminole-Negro Indian Scouts also were decorated.

Unquestionably the most famous frontier regiment was the Seventh Cavalry, which garnered forty-three Medals of Honor. Yet other regiments received more. The Eighth, fighting in Arizona and New Mexico, received ninety-one (21 percent of the total) while the Sixth received four more than the "Garry Owens."

Details of most of the Medal of Honor actions are lost to history. The citations are maddeningly brief, frequently as short as "Bravery" or "Gallantry in action." It is clear that many were awarded simply for doing one's duty. A cavalry sergeant at Wounded Knee, South Dakota, "assisted the men on the skirmish line, directed their fire, encouraged them by example, and used every effort to dislodge the enemy." Even by nineteenth-century standards, he was doing no more than required of a noncom. In an Arizona incident, an Irish trooper was recognized for defeating four Apaches separating him from his troop. In other words, he fought to survive. During another episode, a farrier of the Fourth Cavalry was decorated for "the gallant manner in which he faced a desperate Indian." However, the "above and beyond" concept did not arise until later, and any action that brought comment was likely to be recommended for the medal.

Frederick W. Gerber, a sergeant of engineers, received his medal for "gallantry in many actions and in recognition of long, faithful, and meritorious service" between 1839 and 1871—a period of thirty-two years.

Actually, the second Medal of Honor for the Indian wars was presented while the Civil War was well underway. In July 1862, just before the Second Battle of Bull Run, First Sergeant Charles Taylor of the Third Cavalry gained note for an action in Arizona. The next two frontier awards were granted for events in 1865.

Captain F. R. Bernard, an experienced soldier, led eight expeditions against Apaches in 1869. By far the most notable was the punitive effort following the slaying of stagecoach passengers and their escort in October of that year. Bernard took his force from Fort Bowie to Chiracahua Pass and, in three engagements, claimed killing thirty hostiles. It set up one of the most remarkable actions in Medal of Honor history.

On October 20, four troopers named Smith, from the same unit, received the medal for the same action. Company G of the First Cavalry was hotly engaged with Apaches, as privates Theodore, Thomas, Thomas J., and William H. Smith were cited for gallantry in action. Nor was that all. In the same area that day, Sergeant Andrew J. Smith and Private William Smith of the Eighth also received the medal. Finally, Private Otto Smith of the Eighth was rewarded for bravery in 1868–69, making a total of seven Smiths decorated for essentially the same event, including two Williams and two Thomases.

■ Guns Out West

A variety of military and civilian arms are credited with "winning the West." From the Army perspective, the most important was the series of rifles generically called Trapdoor Springfields, developed in 1865 at the end of the Civil War. The trapdoor concept permitted breech loading with metallic cartridges versus the conventional paper-wrapped fodder. Because loading was so much faster, rate of fire dramatically increased, even with single-shot rifles.

Trapdoors were so named because a portion of the barrel was machined with a hinged segment that was elevated to insert the cartridge into the breech. The "trap door" then was closed, the hammer cocked, and the rifle was fired. The Model 1865 was chambered in .58 caliber rim fire from a weapon nearly six feet long with a three-foot barrel. Over the next twenty-four years, no fewer than thirteen additional models were tested or produced. The definitive versions fired the .45-70 cartridge, denoting a .45 caliber bullet propelled by seventy grains of black powder. The standard cavalry arm was the Model 1873 carbine, a lighter, handier version of the infantry weapon firing the same cartridge.

But the horseman's traditional weapon, apart from the largely useless saber, became the six-shot revolver, variously chambered in .44 or .45 caliber. Colt's Model 1873 Single-Action Army became famous as the "Peacemaker," a rugged, reliable handgun that defined the Westerner. Other popular side arms were Remington and Smith & Wesson designs circa 1871–72. A top-break revolver advocated by Major George Schofield was based on the Smith & Wesson with an improved latch for the hinged barrel. It was issued in 1875, thanks in part to the major's brother John, a general and Civil War Medal of Honor man.

In contrast to the large number of Indian-fighting awards, only two were posthumous. Private George Hooker of the Fifth Cavalry was killed in Arizona in January 1873, aged twenty-six. He was buried at Fort Bliss, and his award was issued two and a half years later.

In September 1874, Private George W. Smith and several Sixth Cavalry troopers were carrying dispatches when attacked by as many as 125 hostiles on the Wichita River in Texas. In a daylong fight, Smith was mortally wounded and succumbed the next morning. His medal was authorized in 1876.

CIVILIANS AND SCOUTS

The frontier army relied heavily upon civilians: experienced plainsmen who knew the terrain and were familiar with hostile Indians. Certainly

Scout William F. Cody, 3rd Cavalry

Scout William "Billy" Dixon, 6th Cavalry

the most famous was William F. Cody, who scouted for the Third Cavalry in Nebraska during April 1872. He received the medal, which was rescinded in 1916 because he had been a civilian. The same applied to William "Billy" Dixon and Amos Chapman who served with the Sixth Cavalry along the Wichita River in September 1874. James B. Doshier also scouted for the Army, receiving his award for an 1870 action on the Wichita River. All four awards were restored in 1989.

Dixon is best known in frontier lore for "the impossible shot" at Adobe Walls, Texas, in June 1874. One of fewer than thirty whites besieged by perhaps 700 Comanches, Cheyenne, and Kiowas, he unlimbered a .50 caliber buffalo rifle and sighted a mounted Indian on the skyline almost a mile away. Applying the right elevation and incantation, Dixon touched off the Sharps, and several seconds later the hostile toppled from his horse. The likely distance was about 1,200 yards. It remains probably the greatest documented shot in history, though Dixon was astute enough to disclaim any factor other than fabulous luck.

The controversy as to whether civilians are eligible for military decorations seemingly was resolved in World War II and Vietnam. At least one aircraft company technical representative received the Silver Star for assisting firefighters aboard USS *Bunker Hill* in 1945, as did a war correspondent covering the Seventh Cavalry's battle in the Ia Drang Valley twenty years later. Long after the war, reporter Joe Galloway was honored for exchanging his camera for an M16 during the prolonged firefight at Landing Zone X-ray.

Indian scouts also were widely recognized. As members of the Army they were immediately eligible for the medal, and they provided intimate knowledge of the enemy that no white man could match, however experienced. Alchesay, Blanquet, Chiquito, Elsatsoosu, Jim, Kelsay, Kosoha, Machol, Nannasaddie, and Nantaje all received their awards for action against hostile Apaches in the Arizona Territory between 1871 and 1873. Jim and Rowdy were sergeants; the latter decorated for "gallant conduct" during March 1890.

Co-Rux-Te-Chod-Ish (also called Mad Bear) earned his award the hard way. As a sergeant of Pawnee Scouts during July 1869, he was engaged in a fight along the Republican River in Kansas when he ran ahead of his men, chasing a dismounted hostile. However, some of his scouts continued firing and he was shot from behind. Though badly wounded, he survived.

Four members of the Seminole-Negro Indian Scouts also received the medal. Established in 1870, the Scouts were formed from descendants of escaped slaves who returned to the United States from Mexico. During operations near the Red River in Texas, four demonstrated valor in the field. Colonel R. S. Mackenzie cited Private Adam Paine for "invaluable service" to the Fourth Cavalry in September 1974.

Three other Scouts were honored for saving their officer. On the Pecos in April 1875, Lieutenant John L. Bullis of the Twenty-fourth Infantry was

Blanquet

Jim

Rowdy

Sgt. John Ward, Indian Scouts

1st Lt. Frank D. Baldwin, 5th Infantry

patrolling with three scouts when they encountered Comanches. At first, the soldiers had the advantage and surprised the hostiles in tall grass, but the odds quickly turned against them. In the ensuing firefight, Bullis' mount went down and the scouts turned back for him. Trumpeter Isaac Payne and Private Pompey Factor provided covering fire while Sergeant John Ward pulled Bullis onto his horse. Under close-range fire—his rifle sling and stock were hit—Ward grasped Bullis and galloped to safety. By one account, the Scouts participated in a dozen engagements without losing a man; they were disbanded in 1914.

DOUBLE AWARDS

Only a handful of soldiers received two Medals of Honor before legislation limited presentation "one to a customer." Tom Custer earned both of his in the Civil War, but two other men were recognized twice each as frontier fighters. First was Sergeant William Wilson, who received two medals within six months of 1872. Riding with the Fourth Cavalry in Texas, he pursued a band of cattle thieves in April and fought Indians at the Red River that September.

An Irishman, Henry Hogan, got two awards fighting Indians in Montana. As first sergeant of Company G, Fifth Infantry, he distinguished himself on Colonel Nelson Miles' expedition of 1876–77. That summer, he carried his severely wounded lieutenant to safety at Bear Paw Mountain.

A fourth two-time recipient was Captain Frank D. Baldwin, who got his set a decade apart. Fighting with the Nineteenth Michigan in 1864, he captured two Confederate officers and a guidon. In Texas ten years later, his Fifth Infantry company rescued two white girls from a superior force of renegades.

AMERICA'S CENTENNIAL

On July 4, 1876, the United States gave itself a joyous centennial, observing one hundred years of independence. However, events "out west" less than two weeks before cast a dreary shadow over the festivities.

The campaign to return thousands of Indians to their Montana land produced a succession of medals, beginning with the Third Cavalry's fight on the Rosebud on June 17. A week later came the disaster on the Little Big Horn.

Lieutenant Colonel (Brevet Major General) George Custer had always relied on audacity and luck. On June 25, he retained the former and completely expended the latter. With barely six hundred men, he piled into the largest encampment of Indians ever recorded: a village three miles long with perhaps 5,000 Sioux and Cheyenne warriors. Neither knowing nor caring about the odds, he split his force into three battalions. Then he attacked.

While Custer's five companies were destroyed to the last man (and nearly the last horse), the rest of the regiment consolidated positions. Major Marcus Reno and Captain Frederick Benteen had each taken three companies while Company B kept the packs, eventually joining Reno and Benteen's commands. Among their 250 troopers, medals went to thirteen privates, two artificers, and eight NCOs. They included eleven of Benteen's men, four of Reno's, and six from the Company B reserves. Sergeant Richard P. Hanley and Private Peter Thompson belonged to Tom Custer's troop but survived Little Big Horn, apparently because six men were detached from Company C.

Probably the most notable individual was Thompson, a Scot, who volunteered to fetch water and suffered a gunshot wound to the head. Nevertheless, he made two more trips, "notwithstanding remonstrances of his sergeant."

Half of the medals awarded for Little Big Horn involved risky efforts to bring water, which ran short on the first day. Consequently, Company H's Sergeant George Geiger, Private Henry Windolph, saddler Otto Voit, and blacksmith Henry Mechlin held an exposed position on the brow of the hill facing the Little Big Horn River. Standing erect, they fired constantly for more than twenty minutes, diverting fire and attention from another group filling canteens that were desperately needed. Windolph and Voit were German, while several other recipients that day were English, Scottish, Irish, and French.

Ammunition was almost as critical as water. Realizing that need, Sergeant Richard Hanley caught a pack mule that had panicked and dashed through the perimeter. The Massachusetts NCO survived an incredible twenty minutes under fire, returning with boxes of .45–70 cartridges.

Sergeant Benjamin C. Criswell rescued the body of an officer from within Indian lines, then retrieved ammo and fought in an exposed position. Another Company B sergeant, Thomas Murray, brought up the pack train and on the second day delivered rations while under fire.

The Seventh Infantry was engaged along the Big Horn in mid-July, and pursuit of the Indians continued unabated. The winter campaign made use of harsh weather to compel Indian compliance with the government's demands.

From October 1876 to January 1877, thirty-seven medals were presented for Montana combat; all but four went to the Fifth Infantry. All the awards merely cited "gallantry in action," but it was a long, hard campaign. In fact, the Sioux had counted on the Army's usual routine of retiring to winter quarters, but the Fifth's aggressive commander had other plans. Colonel Nelson Miles, a Civil War medal recipient, had trained and equipped his men for prolonged marches on the snow-swept northern plains. He remorselessly pursued the Indians, alternately harassing and sending Crazy Horse entreaties to return to the agency. The campaign climaxed at Wolf Mountain on January 8 when soldiers captured or destroyed most of the Sioux food and equipment. By spring, the effort was ended.

Meanwhile, farther west occurred one of the saddest events in frontier history: displacement of the Nez Perce from their home in the beautiful Wallowa Mountains of northeastern Oregon. In June 1876, while reluctantly moving to Idaho, some of Chief Joseph's braves killed several whites. Knowing that retribution was coming, Joseph embarked upon a thousand-mile trek over mountainous terrain with some eight hundred of his people and as many as 2,000 horses. In a series of well-fought actions, the Nez Perce, with perhaps two hundred warriors, held off persistent efforts by the army and militias to overtake them. The most notable battle occurred on June 17 at White Bird Pass in northern Idaho.

First Sergeant Michael McCarthy of the First Cavalry survived an epic ordeal at White Bird. Leading a detail of six men, he held a defensive position against the Nez Perce but became isolated when members of Troop H withdrew. McCarthy shot his way out of trouble, rejoined part of his troop, and conducted a fighting retreat. In the process, he lost two horses and was overwhelmed. Taken captive, the resourceful Newfoundlander escaped and spent three days alternately hiding and wandering in the mountains. Finally, he regained Troop H and reported for duty. The soldiers suffered thirty-three dead, third-highest toll for a single engagement of the Indian wars.

The Nez Perce were trapped within forty miles of their Canadian goal; some eighty were killed, a few hundred escaped, and Joseph led the rest into exile in Kansas.

WOUNDED KNEE

A flurry of medals for actions in South Dakota arose during late 1890 and early 1891. Even at that late date the U.S. government remained nervous about a resurgence of Indian activity, and moved to quell the emerging "ghost dance" movement in the Dakotas. On December 29, two weeks after Sitting Bull's death during an attempted rescue, a force of nearly five hundred soldiers oversaw the return of about 350 Sioux to their agency. Stopping for the night at Wounded Knee Creek, the Seventh Cavalry, with elements of the First and Second Artillery, established a position overlooking the Indians, with four Hotchkiss cannon in place. While troopers were collecting Indian weapons, someone (probably a Sioux called Black Coyote) discharged a rifle. The cavalrymen, mindful of Custer's fate fourteen years before, immediately opened fire. A century later, the phenomenon acquired a name: firing contagion.

When the smoke cleared in the frigid winter air, scores of Indians lay dead. Figures vary between 126 and nearly 300 Sioux braves, squaws, and children. Twenty-five troopers were killed and nearly forty wounded, many by "friendly" fire.

For Wounded Knee, eighteen Medals of Honor went to the Seventh Cavalry and attached artillery. A dozen more medals were presented for actions at White River and White Clay Creek over the next few days.

The Dakota citations make poor reading. The large majority refer only to bravery or gallantry, and one reference to killing a hostile Indian. A few instances mention rescuing a comrade or continuing to fight when wounded.

Ironically, the first and last medals for the Indian wars went to members of the medical corps. Beginning with Bernard Irwin in 1861, surgeons and hospital stewards demonstrated their devotion to duty and loyalty to comrades in a variety of climes and circumstances.

The medical recipients included contract surgeon John Skinner in Oregon in 1873; Hospital Steward William Bryan at Powder River,

Wyoming, in 1876; Major Henry R. Tilton at Bear Paw, Montana, in 1877; and Assistant Surgeon Leonard Wood in Arizona during 1886.

Wood's action brought widespread acclaim. Though a surgeon, he volunteered to carry dispatches through Apache territory, keenly aware of the gruesome penalty for failure. By horse and on foot, he made one hundred miles in two days in a remarkable feat of endurance. Subsequently, he commanded an infantry detachment lacking an officer, demonstrating capability in the field as well as in hospital. His

*Asst. Surgeon Leonard Wood,
4th Cavalry*

Medal of Honor was awarded in 1898 shortly before he left for Cuba with the Rough Riders.

The last Medal of Honor of the Indian wars went to Private Oscar Burkard of the Hospital Corps. He was decorated for his valor at Leech Lake, Minnesota, during a Chippewa uprising in October 1898. Though six soldiers were killed, German-born Burkard retrieved and tended wounded men under fire.

CHANGING STANDARDS

The medal underwent major revision between 1876 and 1905. After the Custer debacle, large numbers of recommendations were forwarded to the War Department, which finally decided that enough was more than enough. The deluge of nominations was pared to twenty-four, and for the first time the concept of more than "soldierly qualities" appeared. The Army board stated that henceforth the medal would only be awarded for "gallantry and intrepidity."

In 1876, the first reference to service beyond "the simple discharge of duty" appeared, paving the way to the now familiar criterion of "above and beyond." As of 1897, soldiers could no longer nominate themselves for the medal, and at least one witness was necessary. A time limit also was imposed, leading to a spate of additional nominations before the cutoff. Thereafter, a statutory requirement of one year from action to nomination was implemented, and though later expanded, it would be widely ignored for reasons of political patronage.

CHAPTER THREE

WARS OF EXPANSION

■

I N the late nineteenth and early twentieth centuries, the United States
emerged as a significant player on the global stage. With internal
concerns approximately concluded in the Reconstruction era, and the
West fully settled, the nation looked outward. The period included the
Spanish-American War, the Philippine Insurrection, and the Boxer Rebellion in China, often characterized as proof of American imperialism.

Perhaps a definition of terms is necessary. In a European context, the
United States was a third-tier imperial power. It possessed few colonies
worth the name, and gained precious little use from them. In fact, the
prevalence of Medal of Honor awards from 1898 to 1913 would indicate otherwise. Following the short, "splendid little war" with Spain,
America easily could have annexed Cuba but chose not to. Puerto Rico
and Guam proved of limited benefit. By far the greatest acquisition, the
Philippines, became an exercise in nation building—the same sort of
folly that led to the Vietnam morass. Eventually, of course, the Filipino
people became staunch allies against the Japanese.

■ *Spain, the Philippines, and the Boxers: The Numbers*

Thirty-one soldiers received Medals of Honor for the Spanish-American War: seventeen privates, seven non-coms, and seven officers. All lived to receive their medals, except Theodore Roosevelt, whose award was made a century later.

Four men were decorated for the Boxer Rebellion: two officers and two enlisted men (one posthumously).

Seventy awards in the Philippines went to twenty-eight privates, thirteen NCOs, and twenty-nine officers.

SPANISH-AMERICAN WAR

On February 15, 1898, the American battleship *Maine* blew up in Havana Harbor, killing more than 260 sailors, three-quarters of the crew. Spain, which ruled Cuba, was immediately blamed. Though later investigation indicated that the blast was internal (probably caused by accumulation of coal dust), U.S. newspapers, and the public at large, beat the drum for war. They got their wish. Relations between the United States and Spain already had been deteriorating over the issue of Cuban independence. Congress declared war on April 25; an expedition was hastily assembled to punish the "dons" and liberate Cubans from European oppression.

The Army fielded 280,500 men and sustained very small combat losses: 369 killed and 1,600 wounded. (The Navy and Marines together lost just sixteen.) Nearly six times as many soldiers were lost to disease, as some 2,000 succumbed to fever and other maladies.

As a result of the easy victory, the United States acquired concessions from Spain in the form of Puerto Rico and Guam, and purchased the Philippines.

The force that sailed to Cuba in the summer of 1898 was top-heavy with experience and Medal of Honor recipients. General William Shafter and Theodore Roosevelt's brigade commander, Colonel Leonard Wood, both had the medal: Shafter as an engineer lieutenant in 1862; Wood fighting Apaches as a surgeon in 1886. Shafter's award had been presented in 1895, while Wood only received his a week before the

---

■ *U.S. and Spanish Comparisons*

From the perspective of more than a century later, it's almost a marvel that the U.S. Army defeated Spain in Cuba. America's hastily mobilized force of more than a quarter million enthusiastic men was opposed by some 150,000 Spaniards, though only a portion of the U.S. force reached Cuba. Still, the Spanish enjoyed significant advantages. Their German-designed Mauser Model 1893 rifles fired high-velocity 7.7mm bullets from smokeless cartridges. Many American units were armed with obsolete single-shot Springfields with black powder, which immediately gave away the Yanks' position.

Spain, with long experience in the tropics, dressed its troops in pinstriped white cotton. Though the color provided no concealment in jungle or foliage, it was lightweight and comfortable. In contrast, the Americans arrived in heavy, scratchy wool shirts with no option available.

Maine exploded. The commander of the Second Division also was a medal man, as Henry W. Lawton had captured a Confederate position and then defended it near Atlanta in 1864.

Thirty-one medals eventually were awarded for a period of thirty days between June 24–July 23, 1898. Only two involved direct combat while the huge majority were presented for saving wounded men. More than three-quarters (twenty-four) occurred east of Santiago on July 1.

The Army's first Medal of Honor action in Cuba occurred on June 24, when Doctor James R. Church of the First U.S. Volunteers rescued wounded troopers under fire.

Six days later, four troopers of the Tenth Cavalry did the same. Fifty men from A, H, and M troops had been detailed to a supply mission aboard two transports escorted by a gunboat, intending to deliver matériel to Cuban *insurrectos* fighting the Spanish. The initial landing attempt on June 29 was repulsed, but the next day a successful beachhead was established near Tayabacoa. However, the Spanish quickly responded, and were only prevented from overrunning the landing beach by shelling from the gunboat USS *Peoria*.

With only twenty-eight men ashore, the small party remained in peril. After dark, Lieutenant George Ahern (last in the West Point class of 1882) took Sergeant William H. Thompkins, Corporal George Wanton, and troopers Dennis Bell and Fitz Lee ashore in a longboat. They located the survivors and prepared to return to the ships with the seven wounded when the Spaniards attacked again. Ahern's men got away safely and briefly considered an attempt to retrieve the body of one man still ashore. However, with the enemy fully alerted, the effort was called off. The four cavalrymen received identical twenty-eight-word citations.

SAN JUAN AND ALL THAT

The July 1 drive toward Santiago involved attacks on Kettle Hill and San Juan Hill east of town as well as combat at El Caney to the northeast. Six regiments were represented among the two dozen medals awarded for that day.

At El Caney, the Seventeenth Infantry received nine awards for lifesaving: First Lieutenant Benjamin F. Hardaway and Second Lieutenant Charles D. Roberts; corporals Ulysses G. Buzzard, Norman W. Ressler, and Warren J. Shepherd; privates George Berg, Oscar Brookin, T.J. Graves, and Bruno Wende.

Undoubtedly the most dramatic award went to Captain Albert L. Mills, a career officer (West Point class of 1879) serving as assistant adjutant general of the U.S. Volunteers near Santiago. He took a Mauser bullet to the head, which blinded him, but he continued encouraging soldiers nearby. Mills regained the use of one eye and became superintendent of West Point. He retired as a major general.

Fifteen awards eventually were presented for the San Juan Heights action. Sergeant Major Edward Baker of the Tenth Cavalry set the tone in preventing a wounded trooper from drowning. Meanwhile, Sergeant Andrew J. Cummins and four F Company privates of the Tenth Infantry braved Spanish gunfire to retrieve wounded from the ground before the U.S. lines.

Sergeant Alexander Quinn, Thirteenth Infantry, "gallantly assisted

2nd Lt. Charles D. Roberts, 17th Infantry   *Capt. Albert L. Mills, U.S. Volunteers*

in the rescue of the wounded from in front of the lines and under heavy fire." Likewise, Corporal Thomas M. Doherty with five privates of the Twenty-first saved wounded men.

While the infantry attacked the dominant feature—San Juan Hill— Colonel Leonard Wood's dismounted cavalry brigade assaulted Kettle Hill: the First and Tenth (Colored) Cavalry plus the First Volunteer Cavalry (aka Rough Riders). The other three regiments of General Samuel Sumner's cavalry division secured the opposite flank.

Theodore Roosevelt, erstwhile assistant navy secretary, assumed command of the First U.S. Volunteer Cavalry shortly before the storied attack on San Juan Heights.

Except for officers and couriers, the cavalry had been forced to leave its mounts in Florida. Roosevelt rode "Little Texas" within forty yards of the crest, then dismounted. By the time the footsore cavalrymen

---

■ Rifles of Expansion

The .45–70 Trapdoor Springfield remained in service well beyond its prime, equipping state volunteer units in the Spanish-American War. Most common was the Model 1888, which remained in production to 1893.

Meanwhile, Regular Army regiments received the bolt-action Danish Krag-Jorgensen design, adopted as the Model 1896 and 1898. Some 330,000 were procured, nearly half of which remained in stock in 1917. Weighing 9.3 pounds, the Krag was a .30 caliber repeating rifle shooting a 220-grain bullet at 2,000 feet per second. Its nitro-cellulose powder was generally smokeless, making it more or less comparable to Spain's German-designed Mausers. The Krag fed from an unusual latch on the right side, permitting easy "topping off" of the magazine, and its smooth bolt lent itself to rapid fire. However, the .30–40 cartridge lacked the range and penetration of the 7mm Mauser, and the Krag was soon replaced by the immortal M1903 Springfield.

Owing to the criteria of the time, no firearms figured prominently in Spanish-American War Medals of Honor. Of thirty-one Army awards, only two involved direct combat.

---

reached the top, the Spaniards were nearly all gone, though Roosevelt reportedly shot one with a revolver salvaged from the *Maine*. Professional soldiers noted that the enemy positions were poorly sited: they prevented a clear view of the slope below. Still, the Spanish killed 124 *Americanos* and wounded nearly 1,000.

Roosevelt never concealed his ambition for the medal, but after the war his political enemies ensured that his nomination was declined. Reportedly, his adverse comments about the Army's lamentable preparedness reflected poorly upon Secretary of War Russell Alger and others. Nevertheless, a century later the wheel turned full circle. In 2001, four days before leaving office, Bill Clinton presented the coveted decoration to Roosevelt's great grandson.

Roosevelt's citation said, "His leadership and valor turned the tide of battle." That seems an overstatement, as by then the issue was no longer in doubt. Four or five other Rough Riders reached the top at the same time but none were decorated.

Any objective reading of the citation demonstrates that Roosevelt did nothing "above and beyond" that historic day: he was a regimental commander who successfully led his regiment. Nevertheless, retroactively, he and his namesake (who received the medal for directing men off Utah Beach in June 1944) became the second set of father and son to receive the award, after the MacArthurs.

On July 2, the day after San Juan, Second Lieutenant Ira Welborn of the Ninth Infantry voluntarily aided a wounded private near Santiago.

The last of the original Spanish War awards was the most unusual. On July 23, Lieutenant John W. Heard of the Third Cavalry was aboard the *Wanderer* at the mouth of the Manimani River. His is an excellent example of how narrowly focused some Medal of Honor citations have been.

Lt. Col. Theodore Roosevelt, 1st Vol. Cavalry

Heard was a seasoned professional from the West Point class of 1883. While supervising unloading ammunition for Cuban rebels west of Havana, his small party was attacked on the beach. By one estimate, the area was defended by a thousand Spaniards. Nevertheless, with only a dozen troopers and forty or so laborers, he repulsed a cavalry charge and executed an orderly withdrawal to the ship.

As the *Wanderer* paralleled the shore, it came under fire by Spaniards, and conning the vessel became difficult. One man was hit on the bridge while relaying orders to the engine room. His replacement lasted a few minutes, then fell victim to enemy riflemen. Nevertheless, Heard stepped into position, fully knowing the risk. There the Mississippian continued passing engine orders until the *Wanderer* was out of range. He received the medal eleven months later, but the citation only mentioned his shipboard valor.

■ Long War in the Philippines

The treaty ending the Spanish-American War ceded the Philippines to U.S. control. American forces occupied Manila, but the rest of the archipelago remained in the hands of Filipino nationalists.

In February 1899, Emilio Aguinaldo opened hostilities near Manila, and though originally his larger force was defeated, he proved durable and skillful. He was finally captured in 1901 and swore allegiance to the United States.

The high (or low) point of the war occurred on the island of Samar in 1901. Americans had been massacred by guerrillas, prompting the U.S. commander General Jacob Smith to retaliate in kind. The ensuing atrocities resulted in widespread horror in America, leading to Smith's court-martial.

After 1902, U.S. authorities regarded remaining guerrillas as outlaws, but sporadic fighting occurred until 1906.

Meanwhile, serious problems with the Moro population in the southern islands began in 1902. Largely Muslim, they proved themselves sometimes fanatic, always resilient, enemies with an awesome reputation for toughness. Occasional fighting continued until 1913.

As in Cuba, the U.S. Army was ill prepared for the environment. Sweltering heat was endured in heavy wool shirts that quickly grew sweaty and clammy, sticking to the skin, causing perennial rash. The soldiers' original weapons were identical to those in the Spanish-American War, but eventually the Model 1903 Springfield appeared.

Because Moros often used drugs or tied off pressure points on their bodies, the Army discovered a deficiency in its weapons. The modern .38 caliber double-action revolver was a poor man-stopper, even at point-blank range, which prompted partial reissue of .45 Colt single-actions.

Between 1899 and 1913, over 125,000 U.S. troops were committed to the Philippines; some 4,200 were killed. Seventy soldiers received Medals of Honor, but only one posthumously. The Army recognized eleven battle and campaign streamers for regimental honors, but Samar is conspicuously absent.

PHILIPPINE INSURRECTION

Hard on the heels of the U.S. victory over Spain, American troops in the Philippines found themselves in combat with the people recently freed. From the Filipino perspective, the islands had merely exchanged one white master for another. The ensuing dispute lasted until the verge of World War I, and proved militarily and politically complex. Among other factors, it involved Christian Filipinos and Muslim Moros fighting U.S. rule, though not in alliance.

The first forty-six awards were made for 1899 actions, perhaps reflecting the enthusiasm for the Philippine venture. Thereafter, decorations fell off markedly: eleven in 1900 and only thirteen over the next thirteen years.

Among the earliest recipients was Webb Cook Hayes, son of Rutherford B. Hayes, nineteenth president of the United States (1877–81). Hayes was an Ohio veteran of the War Between the States, and in 1899, his son was an Army officer in the Philippines. At Vigan, Luzon, Lieutenant Colonel Hayes of the Thirty-first U.S. Vol-

Lt. Col. Webb Cook Hayes, 31st U.S. Volunteers

unteers distinguished himself on December 4, 1899. Fighting Filipino rebels, he "pushed through the enemy's lines alone, during the night, from the beach to the beleaguered force at Vigan, and returned the following morning to report the condition of affairs to the Navy and secure assistance."

On April 27, 1899, a detachment of the Twentieth Kansas Volunteers faced a hazardous river crossing led by Colonel Frederick Funston, who led a charmed life. He joined the Cuban rebels in 1896 and, never having fired a cannon, was made an artilleryman. He learned his trade by reading a manual en route and, by one reckoning, he lost seventeen horses in twenty-two firefights. He was severely wounded leading a cavalry charge but recovered and returned to duty in the U.S. Army.

During the march on the rebel stronghold at Calumpit, Luzon, Funston found a way across the Rio Grande de la Pampanga. With privates William B. Trembley and Edward White, he managed to cross the river by raft, securing a position on the far bank and permitting the rest of the force to cross. Funston's bold action was credited with leading to victory at "the important strategic position."

Col. Frederick Funston, 20th Kansas Volunteers

A week later, Funston was jumped to brigadier general commanding a brigade. He was thirty-five years old.

On May 13, Brigadier General H. W. Lawton ordered a reconnaissance of San Isidro, a rebel stronghold. Guided by a civilian scout, Arthur Young, twenty-five picked men set out. The trek was exhausting, and by the time the group reached the town of San Miguel de Mayumo only a dozen remained.

Captain William E. Birkhimer, a forty-one-year-old attorney in the Third Artillery, had joined the group the day before. Though supporting units had not arrived, he decided that time was crucial and attacked with eleven scouts from the First North Dakota, Second Oregon, and Fourth Cavalry.

Sending five soldiers around the left flank, Birkhimer led five others in a series of short rushes, providing mutual support. They took thirty minutes to cross 150 yards, taking shots at the *insurrectos* as chances afforded. Their marksmanship was excellent: on reaching the rebel lines, the Americans found forty-nine dead.

With his full "command" intact again, Birkhimer proceeded another two hundred yards to the bridge through town. The soldiers engaged in a short firefight, killing six rebels and repulsing others, but Young was shot. He was carried back into town, where reinforcements arrived that afternoon following a four-hour standoff. The gallant Young died, ineligible for the medal that went to Birkhimer and the five who had joined his headlong rush at the barricades.

Birkhimer retired as a brigadier general and is buried at Arlington National Cemetery as are both his grandsons, themselves four-star generals.

Another scouting expedition brought similar results on May 16, when an advance party surveyed Aguinaldo's fortress at San Isidro. If Army accounts are to be believed, the twenty-two scouts - attacked across a burning bridge to rout 600 entrenched enemy. Seven privates from the First North Dakota and Second Oregon received the Medal of Honor, though it is not clear how their actions were distinguishable from the other fifteen.

Capt. William E. Birkhimer, 3rd Artillery

Three Medical Corps officers earned Medals of Honor during the insurrection, all in 1899. Surgeon George F. Shiels served with the U.S. Volunteers at Tuliahan River that March. He exposed himself to the enemy and went with four men to retrieve two Filipinos lying wounded 150 yards beyond the lines. There, he picked up one of the men and personally carried him to safety.

In October, George W. Mathews, assistant surgeon of the Thirty-sixth Infantry, came under attack on Luzon. While tending wounded under heavy fire, he picked up a carbine and fought off an attack upon injured soldiers. Two months later, the regimental surgeon, Paul F. Straub, took up a pistol to help repel an insurgent attack and, at "great risk of his own life," dashed to a wounded officer and evaded enemy fire.

Corporal Robert Lee Gillenwater, a Virginian, set new standards of modesty. His medal was authorized in 1902, but apparently he did not receive it until 1927. In either case, his family never knew until some papers were found after he died in 1946. As a corporal in the Thirty-sixth Infantry, he was scouting on Luzon when attacked by rebels. With another man, he rescued a seriously wounded soldier and retrieved the body of another.

Following cessation of hostilities with Aguinaldo's followers, action focused on the southern islands of Mindanao and Jolo, home of some incredibly tough Muslim warriors. Fighting flared up intermittently for years before an estimated 900 Moros were killed in a three-day battle at Bud Dajo in March 1906.

A Filipino decorated during the war was Private Jose Nisperos of the Philippine Scouts. On Basilan in September 1911, he was badly wounded by Moros; his left arm was broken, and he was repeatedly stabbed in the torso. Though unable to stand, he continued firing his rifle one-handed until the rebels were driven off. Testimony to the bitterness of the fighting was the final sentence of his citation: Nisperos aided "in preventing the annihilation of his party and the mutilation of their bodies."

From January to June 1913, some 5,000 Moros defied U.S. authority at Mount Bugsak on Jolo. A week of fighting in mid-June resulted in 300 Moro dead; it was the final battle of the long campaign. It also involved the last Medal of Honor action for the insurrection period. On June 11, Lieutenant Louis C. Mosher of the Philippine Scouts risked his life to rescue a wounded man. Running within twenty yards of Moro lines, the thirty-three-year-old officer exposed himself in an open area to retrieve the soldier and return him to U.S. lines. Mosher died in 1958.

■ *Boxers*

The McKinley administration supported the "open door policy" toward China, which encouraged Western trade with the internally fractious Peking government. However, simmering resentment toward "foreign devils" from as far afield as Japan, Russia, and Europe erupted into violence in 1900. The Boxers, named for their clenched-fist emblem, aimed to end outside exploitation of their nation. The dowager empress disavowed the Boxer violence while tacitly supporting it; hundreds of Chinese Christians were murdered, then the German ambassador. Fearful Europeans and others concentrated in Peking, besieged by Boxers and imperial troops. The garrison barely held on, awaiting deliverance or gruesome capture.

The China Relief Expedition was quickly formed, involving some 2,500 American soldiers, sailors, and Marines. Ships sailed from the Philippines and the United States and, with troops from other nations, arrived outside Tientsin in mid-July.

BOXER REBELLION

Fifty-nine medals were awarded for action against the Boxers, but only four went to soldiers—three from the Ninth Infantry. At Tientsin on July 13, 1900, Captain Andre W. Brewster, under fire, rescued two of his men from drowning. The thirty-seven-year-old officer retired as a major general and died in 1942.

A New Yorker, First Lieutenant Louis B. Lawton, carried a message and led reinforcements across a fire-swept open area. Though hit by three Boxer bullets, he completed his assignment. Reportedly, the Boxer "marksmen" believed that elevating their sights increased muzzle velocity, and most of their rounds went high.

That same day, Private Robert H. von Schlick was wounded while carrying an injured man to safety. Nevertheless, the German-born soldier returned to Company C of the Ninth Infantry in an exposed position atop a dike. When the company was withdrawn, Schlick covered the retreat, maintaining a steady fire with his rifle. As the lone occupant, he was targeted by every Boxer in range; he was swept off the dike by multiple bullet impacts. Incredibly, von Schlick survived his wounds and retired in Los Angeles, where he died in 1941. Apparently, his medal was awarded after he died, but the Army seems to have no record of the process.

Capt. Andre W. Brewster, 9th Infantry

In August, a force of some 19,000 troops was ready to take Peking. Americans, Britons, French, Austrians, Germans, Italians, Russians, and Japanese sortied from Tientsin for the seventy-mile trek to the capitol, where the foreign legations had been besieged in the Outer City. On August 13, the first allied effort was repulsed, but the multinational force returned the next day.

Musician Calvin P. Titus of the Fourteenth Infantry was cited for "gallant and daring conduct" at Peking. A call went out for volunteers to climb the "Tartar Wall," gaining a response from the twenty-one-year-old trumpeter. Titus had no ropes or scaling ladders but inched his way up the thirty-foot precipice, finding occasional purchase on projecting stones. Somehow surviving the Boxers' close-range fire, he held the top while other soldiers followed, providing cover for British troops entering the city.

For his exceptional courage, Titus received the Medal of Honor and a presidential appointment to West Point. He graduated in the upper one-third of the Class of 1905 and retired as a lieutenant colonel.

Thus ended the famous fifty-five days at Peking, later the title of a Charlton Heston film. Lawton's and Titus' Medals were authorized in 1902; Brewster's in 1903.

MORE CHANGING STANDARDS

More changes were implemented in the wake of the Spanish-American War. "Risk of life" appeared in the September 1898 regulations, adding the requirement of recommendation by the commanding general or responsible officer, plus two witnesses.

In September 1901, the War Department appointed Major General Arthur MacArthur, a Civil War medal recipient, to oversee a board for selection of Spanish-American War nominations and any additional nominations from the continuing Philippines insurrection. Three years later, General George Gillespie, another medal recipient, suggested the addition of the green laurel wreath to the Army version, with a pale blue ribbon worn about the neck.

Musician Calvin P. Titus, 14th Infantry

By then, most Spanish War awards already had been made. Of those originally allowed, twenty-seven had been presented in 1899. Two more were approved in 1902 and one in 1906. Ironically, the latter was chronologically the first, as Dr. James R. Church's action at Las Guasimas occurred in June 1898. Theodore Roosevelt's award came more than a century later.

Other changes occurred early in the new century. In 1916, with the Great War raging in Europe, the Army reviewed the 2,625 medals previously awarded and determined that one-third were not merited,

Dr. James R. Church, 1st Volunteer Cavalry

mainly because of a clerical error involving most of a Civil War regiment. Some 900 were rescinded, including those awarded to civilians such as Dr. Mary Walker and scout William F. Cody (subsequently reinstated). Similarly, the combat requirement was further stipulated, requiring acts "above and beyond the call of duty," though some later awards were made in violation of that policy.

CHAPTER FOUR

THE GREAT WAR

■

W ORLD War One represented an organizational and technological landmark for the U.S. Army. For the first time since the
Civil War, divisions were fielded in numbers, now supported by automatic weapons, rapid-fire cannon, and airplanes. Also, for the first time
in a century, America fought a first-class foreign opponent.

Following the declaration of war in April 1917, war fever swept the
nation as Teutonophobia swirled down Main Street, USA. Sauerkraut
was renamed "liberty cabbage," and dachshunds (the Kaiser's favorite
pets) were abused. Young men rushed to the flag—and were appalled at
what they found. By April 1917, the nation had squandered two years
of preparation time since the loss of the *Lusitania*. America's tiny army,
previously concerned with Indians and the brief set-to with Spain, was
woefully unprepared. The first American soldiers arrived in Europe that
summer, but not until mid-1918 were they sufficiently trained and experienced to launch major offensives. When they did, they went over the
top with optimism and enthusiasm.

In Europe, American infantrymen (and Yanks generally) became

■ *Why Over There?*

America fumbled the geopolitical football in the Great War and nearly lost possession on the kickoff.

Originally, most Americans saw no reason to become embroiled in the European family feud involving cousins astride the thrones of Britain, Germany, and Russia. Despite traditional sympathy for Britain and France, the United States also possessed a large Germanic population, especially in the Midwest. Certainly the 1914 assassination of Austria-Hungary's archduke in Sarajevo seemed of little concern to the Yanks.

However, over the next three years, events in Europe exerted increasing influence as Britain, France, Belgium, Italy, and Russia fought Germany, Austria, and Turkey. British ships carrying American nationals were torpedoed in European waters, notably the *Lusitania*

sinking in May 1915. The liner probably was carrying munitions for Britain, and objective Americans realized that sailing into a war zone involved serious risk. However, the ultimate straw on the proverbial camel's back was the Zimmermann Note in 1917. Germany's foreign minister proposed that his government support return of major portions of the Southwest to Mexico in exchange for Mexican military pressure along the border. It was an absurd concept, even granted the U.S. Army's fruitless 1916 expedition to catch *bandito jefe* Pancho Villa. The nominally pacifist President Woodrow Wilson was outraged; he requested the Senate to declare war on Germany and got his wish.

After the war, Wilson's own naïveté was squandered on the doomed League of Nations. The harsh Allied terms at Versailles only ensured that Germany would arise again, more capable and more vengeful than before.

known as "doughboys." The origin is unclear, though the term originated before the Civil War, alluding to doughnuts that were popular with soldiers. Presumably, the troops who ate the treats were called "doughboys." Another theory refers to the adobe clay barracks frequently found in the prewar Southwest.

America had enormous resources, not least of which was manpower. Some 4 million men served in the Army during the Great War, but only half of the American Expeditionary Force reached France before the armistice. Even so, the logistical "tail" to support the AEF was substantial, with 650,000 men in the Service of Supply alone.

The AEF eventually involved forty-three divisions, with the first eight composed of Regular Army troops and volunteers. The Twenty-sixth through Forty-second were National Guard divisions or units from the same regions, though the latter was an exception, representing twenty-six states. The "national divisions" (Seventy-sixth to Ninety-first) included draftees from all over the United States. The Ninety-second and Ninety-third were Negro divisions, though the latter's four regiments were distributed among French divisions.

American divisions were huge by European standards, and large by comparison with World War II organizations. Comprising some 28,000 men, the doughboy divisions were nearly as large as many Allied corps. The standard format was four infantry regiments with three field artillery battalions and a machine gun battalion.

The AEF was organized into two subordinate commands. The First Army was formed in August 1918 prior to the St. Mihiel offensive; the Second Army became operational in October, working east of the River Meuse. The Third was reserved for occupation duty.

It took time to deploy the AEF to Europe, but some units made good progress. The first doughboys arrived in France in June 1917, and the first combat casualties fell in November 1917, seven months after the declaration of war. They belonged to the First Division, entrenched near Bathelemont in the British sector. In an expertly conducted raid for prisoners, the Germans killed three Americans and dragged off eleven others. Over the next twelve months, 116,700 more died of all causes (just over half in combat), and 204,000 were wounded.

At the end of the shooting match, the AEF occupied eighty-three of the 392 miles along the Western Front; the British, seventy. The French were responsible for nearly all the rest.

It was a ragtag army in some respects, caught in America's early-twentieth-century transition from an agricultural to an industrial economy. Some 52 percent of the doughboys were from rural areas, and more than one-third were functionally illiterate. Barely 20 percent of the draftees had any education beyond grade school.

But they could fight. Lord, could they fight.

The doughboys' fighting tools covered the gamut for the Great War. Rifles were specifically fired in only eleven Army Medal of Honor actions, but many more citations imply the use of rifles.

Though there were notable exceptions, most of the infantry fighting

■ Doughboy Medals

Excluding fliers, Medals of Honor went to eighty-six Army men: twenty-one enlisted, forty NCOs, and twenty-five officers. Twenty-one of the Great War awards were posthumous, one-quarter of the ground force total.

Demographically, eleven recipients were foreign-born including two from Norway. Others had emigrated from eight more European nations; one man was born in China. The Medal of Honor doughboys came from twenty-six states, paced by New York with fourteen and Illinois with nine. Other leaders were California, South Carolina, New Jersey, and Tennessee, with six or more.

Medal recipients ranged from an eighteen-year-old corporal to a forty-seven-year-old major. In between were long-service men who became captains at forty-one and lieutenants at thirty-five. A few privates were well over thirty, but there were also captains at twenty-three and sergeants at twenty.

Medals of Honor went to members of twenty-one infantry divisions and the tank corps; four Army aviation awards are beyond the scope of this study.

If Medals of Honor are any indication, the fightingest outfit in the American Expeditionary Force was the Thirtieth Infantry Division, with twelve awards. Next were the Thirty-third and Eighty-ninth, with nine each. Five other divisions garnered five or more. The most decorated regiments were the Thirtieth Division's 115th Infantry, with six, followed by the 132nd (Thirty-third Division) and 308th (Seventy-seventh), with five each.

Second Division infantrymen received eight Medals of Honor, but only two went to soldiers. The balance were presented to members of the Marine Brigade, whose two regiments comprised half the division—and got nearly all the press.

in France was at close range, as expected in trench warfare. Pistols and revolvers were wielded, if not always fired, in more than a dozen Medal of Honor actions, while grenades featured nine times, including use of German *grenaten*.

Automatic weapons featured in at least nine Medal of Honor actions, with the execrable French Chauchat far outweighing tripod-mounted guns. At least two soldiers used pump shotguns to good effect.

Edged weapons were freely issued and somewhat less employed, but still there were seven or more uses of the bayonet and one trench knife. Improvisation also counted when the chips were down: one soldier wielded a mortar shell as an oversized grenade, which proved more useful at intimidation than actual use. Another warrior took up a pick when he ran out of rifle and pistol ammo.

FIRST BLOOD

The first seven Army awards of the Great War all were earned in July 1918, fifteen months after America declared war on Germany.

A Chicago man received the first Army medal of the war, Corporal Thomas A. Pope of the Thirty-third Division's 131st Infantry. Appropriately, his action near Hamel, France, occurred on the Fourth of July. While Company E advanced behind French-built tanks, German machine guns opened fire and drove the doughboys to ground. Pope crawled forward by himself, reached an advantageous position, and rushed the nearest Maxim gun. In a brief, vicious tussle, he bayoneted several of the gun crew and drove off the others. Standing his ground, his feet astride the gun, Pope fought off more Germans until other E Company men arrived and took them prisoner. Pope contributed to the Prairie Division's tally of 4,000 enemy captured, fourth-highest total in the AEF.

The next Medal of Honor action provided a dramatic contrast to the technological advancement represented by the tanks in Pope's citation. First Lieutenant George P. Hays was a China-born officer in the Third Division, which, except for the Seventy-seventh, spent more days on the front lines than any AEF outfit.

On July 14 (Bastille Day in France), Hays' Tenth Field Artillery Battalion was taken under bombardment by German guns, destroying the telephone lines he had seen laid. The twenty-five-year-old Oklahoman mounted a horse and galloped to the nearest command post to coordinate counter-battery fire. He then spurred his way toward two French batteries, established relations with the senior officers, and returned to his own headquarters. Throughout that day and the next, Hays went through one mount after another, keeping contact with the neighboring units so that maximum effectiveness was maintained. Much of the time he was exposed to enemy shells; six horses were killed in the process. The next day, his seventh mount was shot from beneath him

Cpl. Thomas A. Pope, 131st Infantry

and Hays was badly wounded. He recovered to receive the medal after the war.

Of the Army's first seven medals in the European war, one was posthumous. Private First Class George Dilboy of the Twenty-sixth Division was born in Greece but called New Hampshire his home. Scouting with his platoon near Belleau on July 18, Dilboy and his lieutenant were spotted by an enemy machine gun crew and fired upon. Dilboy stood upon a railroad embankment, coolly returning fire in an offhand position from a hundred yards away. Then he dashed forward through waist-high wheat, intending to put the Germans to the bayonet. He was closing the last twenty-five yards when 8mm bullets nearly severed his right leg above the knee. Dilboy tumbled to the ground with bullet wounds in the body as well. Nevertheless, he rolled into a prone position and opened fire, killing two gunners and forcing the others to flee. Dilboy succumbed to his wounds thereafter.

PFC Daniel R. Edwards of the First Division's Third Machine Gun Battalion didn't know when to quit. The twenty-one-year-old Texan had recently been released from the hospital, but he was badly injured again on July 18. Despite a shattered arm, he crawled alone into a German trench intending to capture prisoners for interrogation. Single-handedly, he killed four and nabbed four more, herding them to friendly lines. A German shell exploded nearby, killing one prisoner and nearly

■ *"The Damned Marines"*

Six Marines fighting with the Second Army Division received the Medal of Honor in the Great War, leading to no end of confusion. The Fifth and Sixth Marine Regiments were brigaded in the "Indian Head Division," fighting with notable success in Belleau Wood and beyond—thereby earning the undying enmity of a generation of Army officers such as George C. Marshall and Harry S Truman. Gunnery Sergeant Charles F. Hoffman (aka Ernest A. Janson); sergeants Louis Cukela and Matej Kocak; Corporal John H. Pruitt; and Private John J. Kelly received both the Army and Navy awards for their actions. For reasons that probably will never be known, Gunnery Sergeant Fred W. Stockham got only the Army medal.

Just to confuse things further, three Navy medical corpsmen were awarded the medal while serving with the Marines, as were three Navy doctors. Those six men received the Navy Medal of Honor, though they also were operating under Army auspices.

Logic and consistency have never been requirements for the awards and decorations process.

severing one of Edwards' legs. He was immediately sent back to the hospital, but his commanding officer attributed the private's example with raising unit morale "to high pitch."

The second officer awarded the medal was Second Lieutenant Samuel I. Parker of the Big Red One's Twenty-eighth Infantry. Near Soissons the same day as Edwards' feat, Parker noticed a gap developing with the French unit on his left. The Twenty-eighth's exposed flank rendered the doughboys vulnerable to grazing fire from high ground, so Parker took his bobtailed platoon to correct the matter. En route, he found a leaderless group of French colonial infantry and convinced them to go with him. The North Carolinian's improvised command took the German position by direct assault, seizing six guns and some forty prisoners.

The following day, Parker was nearly the only officer remaining on his feet. He took command of the remnants of the regiment's second and third battalions, successfully supporting the first battalion. Despite a painfully wounded foot, Parker declined evacuation and completed his task by crawling on hands and knees, being unable to walk.

Another fighting Southerner was Corporal Sidney E. Manning of the

Forty-second "Rainbow" Division. The Alabaman had just turned twenty-six when he found himself leading his platoon on July 28. Toting a cumbersome Chauchat automatic rifle, he ignored repeated wounds to gain a foothold on the heights overlooking the Ourcq River. He consolidated his men's position, then opened fire on the inevitable German counterattack. Firing short, aimed bursts at fifty yards, he helped repulse the enemy effort, taking additional hits in the process. At length, he was able to crawl to cover for treatment of nine gunshot wounds.

Two days later, the Rainbow Division garnered another medal as Sergeant Richard W. O'Neill (variously O'Neil) also survived repeated wounds to accomplish his objective. As his battalion approached the Ourcq River, he was scouting ahead when his platoon clashed with two dozen Germans at close range. The fight became hand-to-hand, with the nineteen-year-old New Yorker taking hits from pistol bullets. Nevertheless, he continued advancing but was wounded again. Shaking off the pain and growing fatigue, O'Neill continued directing his detachment until struck a third time and collapsed. However, he had the stretcher bearers take him to battalion headquarters before the aid station in order to provide current information on German defenses. He received the Medal of Honor from Marshal Ferdinand Foch in the Bronx three years later.

Corporal Jake Allex knew about Europe. The Chicagoan had been born in Serbia in 1887, and perhaps he appreciated the irony of fighting in a war that had been started by a Serbian. In any case, the Thirty-third Division noncom took over his platoon when the officers and senior NCOs had fallen during an assault at Chipilly Ridge on August 9. When his advance faltered against heavy machine gun fire, he fixed bayonet and set out alone. Somehow surviving the trek, he leapt into the machine gun nest and put his bayonet to work. He killed four Germans, then broke the blade on a fifth. Undeterred, Allex applied the butt stroke as taught in basic training. His one-man onslaught convinced fifteen more Germans to surrender.

Two days later, another European-born doughboy earned his adopted nation's highest award. Sergeant James I. Mestrovich of the Twenty-eighth Division emigrated from Montenegro to Pittsburgh, where he enlisted. Near Fismette, France, Mestrovich and others took cover behind a stone wall during a German "hate session," but he glimpsed his company commander lying wounded thirty yards away. Risking artillery and automatic weapons fire, Mestrovich crawled to the captain's side, placed him on his back, and slowly began the tedious trip back. Once under cover again, he provided first-aid and was credited with saving the officer's life. Mestrovitch was killed on November 4, a week before the armistice, and buried in his native Cma Gora, in what became Yugoslavia.

Sgt. Richard W. O'Neill, 165th Infantry

September 1918 was a stellar month for Medals of Honor. Twenty-nine eventually were awarded for actions during those thirty days, including nine on September 26 and ten on September 30.

SEPTEMBER 26

Before addressing the record days of medals awarded, at least one previous action demands attention. On September 14, the Seventy-seventh division was trying to push across the Aisne Canal. Commanding one company was forty-five-year-old Captain Louis Wardlaw Miles, Ph.D., a

■ Guns of the Doughboys

America produced nearly 4 million military rifles from 1917 to 1919, notably the M1903 "Springfield" from the government arsenal. Based on the German Mauser action, it was one of the finest infantry weapons of its time but could not be produced in quantity to meet the total need. Some 600,000 had been delivered prior to 1917, and another 1.26 million were made during hostilities. The '03 equipped the early divisions sent to France, mainly Regular Army and National Guard units, at least up to the Twenty-sixth.

However, more than half the AEF's rifles were the British-designed Enfield. Faced with an acute shortage of everything (many rookies learned the manual of arms with brooms), the Army adapted the Pattern 1914 .303 British weapon to the standard U.S. .30-06 cartridge and turned them out like the proverbial hotcakes. Over 2.4 million were manufactured, and they equipped about three-quarters of the U.S. divisions in France.

America relied on its allies for most automatic weapons, though latecomers were John M. Browning's excellent M1917 machine gun and M1918 automatic rifle. The standard infantry machine gun was the tolerable 8mm French Hotchkiss augmented by the Chauchat ("Show-show") automatic rifle, chambered in 8mm and .30-06 but arguably the worst piece of ordnance ever inflicted upon the U.S. Army. The vastly better British Vickers heavy and Lewis light machine guns were not available in comparable numbers.

American divisions relied on the Allies for heavier weapons as well, including the British three-inch Stokes mortar and the lightweight French 37mm field gun. The famous French 75mm cannon was a world-class artillery piece, so much so that it lent its name to a popular cocktail, the French 75 ($\frac{1}{2}$ oz. gin, 2 oz. lemon, champagne, 2 tsp. sugar, 1 cherry).

Doughboys received nearly 650,000 M1911 pistols and some 300,000 revolvers from Colt and Smith & Wesson. Large-caliber sidearms were especially valued in trench warfare, where agility and stopping power were crucial. There were also 30,000 shotguns and more than 4 million edged weapons: bayonets, daggers, and trench knives.

Johns Hopkins professor in his civilian life. Recognizing a German trench line as the key element of the defense, Miles offered his company of the 308th Infantry to seize the position. His men immediately came under heavy automatic fire that remained undiminished owing to a lack of American artillery. The literature professor crawled ahead of his first wave, cutting a way through the German wire despite repeated gunshot wounds. The Germans hit him five times, breaking both legs and an arm. Nevertheless, Miles ordered some doughboys to carry him to the trench line where he could brief his surviving platoon leaders on the German disposition. After two pain-wracked hours without treatment, Miles endured the jolting, jostling trek by "agony wagon" to a field hospital.

Miles lived to see Americans fighting in France once more, passing away at age seventy-seven in June 1944.

Sergeant Lloyd M. Seibert of the Ninety-first Division provided a lesson in determination and stamina on September 26. Though he already was suffering a bad cold, he remained with his platoon. He grabbed his shotgun and, with two others, went ahead of the company, scouting for Germans. The trio found a Maxim nest that Seibert reduced with his twelve-gauge, capturing two gunners. He was wounded in the fight but helped a more seriously injured

Capt. Louis W. Miles, 308th Infantry

doughboy to the rear. That evening, he offered to continue fetching casualties until exhaustion overtook him. Seibert fainted and finally received treatment.

Another Ninety-first NCO was Sergeant Phillip C. Katz, who learned that a wounded soldier had been left at a spot now two hundred yards in enemy territory. Nevertheless, the Californian took it upon himself to return to the withdrawal point, where he found the missing man and carried him to safety.

A third medal to the Ninety-first that day went to Lieutenant Deming Bronson for inspirational leadership and uncommon devotion to duty. Over the course of two days, he was repeatedly wounded by gunfire and artillery but remained with his company, personally taking one gun position and directing the seizure of others. Despite pain and shock, he re-

mained overnight and was the last man to leave the line when German artillery dropped a major barrage on September 27. In the shelling, Bronson lost the use of both arms but insisted on remaining until the
withdrawal was complete. Fortunately, he survived his multiple wounds.

Elsewhere on September 26, the Thirty-fifth Division's 138th Infantry received two posthumous awards while attacking the Hinden-
burg Line near Chepy. Captain Alexander R. Skinker took an automatic
rifleman and his ammo bearer through a gap in the enemy wire, suppressing machine gun fire along the way. When the "number two" was
killed, Skinker picked up the extra magazines, passing them to the gunner until the officer was shot down.

In the same advance, a Minnesotan, Private Nels Wold, with another
soldier, knocked off three machine gun nests, returning with eleven prisoners. Resuming the advance, he leapt from a trench and saved a fellow
doughboy from being shot by a German officer. Attempting to take a
fifth nest, Wold was killed.

That same day, the Thirty-third Division's 132nd Regiment logged
two Medals of Honor. Captain George H. Mallon and nine men became
separated from their battalion in heavy fog. Nevertheless, they continued
in the assigned sector, attacking nine German machine guns and capturing
all without sustaining a loss. With their strength intact, they pressed
ahead, finding four 155mm howitzers whose crews never suspected the
Americans' presence. Mallon led his doughboys in storming the battery,
subduing one gunner with his fists. Subsequently, he sent his men around
both flanks of another Maxim gun while he charged head-on—and survived. Mallon's tiny detachment had done a regiment's work, capturing
one hundred prisoners, eleven machine guns, four howitzers, and an antiaircraft gun.

Meanwhile, a Kentucky sergeant, Willie Sandlin of Company A,
went about reducing machine gun nests single-handedly. The twenty-
eight-year-old noncom was a veteran, having chased Pancho Villa with
Black Jack Pershing two years previously. Now, in the close cover of

Bois-de-Forges, he used grenades, pistol, and bayonet to take three machine gun nests, killing two dozen Germans in the process. Gassed and slightly wounded, as Kentucky's only Medal of Honor man, Sandlin sailed home to much acclaim but was sent back to France to help supervise the return of soldiers' bodies to American soil. Thereafter, he settled in East Kentucky, bought a farm, and raised a family. But he died of lingering complications from the German gas he inhaled in the Argonne, a victim of the Great War, in 1949.

Sgt. Willie Sandlin, 132nd Infantry

On September 27, the Twenty-seventh Division was attacking near Rossnoy and received two medals: one for aggressiveness; one for lifesaving. First Lieutenant William B. Turner of the 105th Infantry exercised leadership and skill at arms to reduce three German trench lines. He led his company across successive enemy defenses, shooting and stabbing his way until he was killed holding his ultimate objective.

Meanwhile, Sergeant Reidar Waaler, a Norway-born New Yorker, served as a machine gunner near Ronssoy. His battalion was supporting an Anglo-American drive against artillery and small arms fire when he noted a British tank afire with some crewmen trapped inside. Waaler ignored the flames to pull two men to safety. Then, although he knew that ammunition could explode, the NCO crawled into the burning vehicle to search for other survivors. Finding none, he climbed out and rejoined his unit.

Second Lieutenant Albert E. Baesel was a twenty-six-year-old officer in the Thirty-seventh Division. Like many Buckeye Division men, he was an Ohioan with a genuine concern for his fellow soldiers. On September 27, he learned that one of his squad leaders had been severely wounded attacking a machine gun position some two hundred yards ahead of the American line. Baesel asked permission to retrieve the NCO but was refused three times, owing to heavy artillery, small arms fire, and a gas attack. Finally, the company commander relented and Baesel took another soldier with him. They reached the critically injured corporal, and the lieutenant raised him for the trek back when German fire killed them.

SEPTEMBER 28

On September 28, Corporal Freddie Stowers' company of the Ninety-third Division advanced on Hill 188 in the Champagne sector. The black soldiers got within a hundred yards of the German trenches when well-laid Maxim guns opened fire, cutting down half or more of the Americans. Stowers crawled forward, leading his squad over the fire-swept ground, until close enough to rush a German gun crew. A brief fight ensued, but Stowers' men prevailed. He then led them toward the next trench line and was severely wounded. Nevertheless, the South Carolina noncom shouted directions to his men, still leading by example until he died. The medal was presented to Stowers' sisters in 1991.

A Ninety-third officer also was decorated for action that month. Thirty-one-year-old Lieutenant George Robb, a Kansan, was badly wounded while leading his platoon against dug-in machine guns near the objective of Sechault. He returned from the aid station in less than an hour, stood watch that night, and early the next morning he was hit again. Later in the day, an explosion killed Robb's CO and two other officers, wounding the Jayhawker twice more. Yet he assumed command

and became the only officer of his battalion to advance beyond Sechault, directing maneuvers against German defenses.

If some Germans were eager to march into captivity that late summer, others were not. Lieutenant Dwite H. Schaffner learned that lesson, leading his Seventy-seventh Division platoon through gunfire and artillery on September 28. Reaching the enemy lines near Saint Hubert's Pavilion—a lavish compound deep in the Argonne—the Yanks fought hand to hand and man to man. Schaffner's men repelled two counterattacks while he personally dealt with a troublesome Maxim gun. Then a small group of Germans approached, apparently intending to surrender. When some doughboys climbed from the trench to round up the supplicants, other Germans stunned the Americans with calculated treachery, sweeping the khaki ranks with close-range gunfire and grenade blasts. Schaffner, just back from clearing the machine gun nest, seized a Chauchat and cut down several offenders, then used his .45 on the enemy captain. The Pennsylvania officer dragged his prisoner into a trench and convinced the officer to part with some useful information before the man expired. Subsequently, Schaffner's depleted platoon held out for five hours, though assailed from three sides. Schaffner died an Ohio lawyer, succumbing to a heart attack while walking to court in 1955.

SEPTEMBER 29

Of ten awards for September 29, half went to the hard-fighting Twenty-seventh Division. East of Ronssoy the regiments encountered dug-in Germans and proceeded with the dangerous task of rooting them out.

PFC Frank Gaffney, an automatic rifleman in the 108th Infantry, found himself alone during the advance near Ronssoy. Though his squad members had been killed, the New Yorker continued walking ahead and found a German machine gun crew setting up a Maxim gun. Gaffney used his Chauchat on the crew, captured the gun, and tossed grenades into nearby dugouts. He then used his Colt to kill four more Germans and occupied the position until help arrived. Subsequently, eighty enemy soldiers surrendered.

Sergeants John C. Latham and Alan L. Eggers, and Corporal Thomas E. O'Shea of the 107th Infantry's machine gun company heard calls for help from a disabled tank thirty yards off. Despite exploding mortar rounds, they left cover to lend a hand. O'Shea was hit and fell, mortally wounded, but the two sergeants ran ahead through increasing gunfire. They pulled the three-man crew from the tank and helped the casualties into a trench, then risked more German fire to retrieve the tank's machine gun. They put the Hotchkiss to work for the rest of the day, holding off German efforts to dislodge them, and returned to friendly lines after dark.

Meanwhile, Italian-born Private Michael Valente and an unidentified partner cleaned out two Maxim nests, killed five gunners, and captured twenty-one other Germans. Valente was wounded later that day but recovered and received the British Military Medal for the same action. The other doughboy's identity apparently is lost in swirling mists of smoke and time; efforts to trace him have failed. It is possible that Valente did not know the other soldier.

Also on September 29, two Thirtieth Division Tennesseans earned medals for tackling machine guns near Bellicourt. First Sergeant Milo Lemert of the 119th Infantry took the initiative to deal with machine gun nests inflicting casualties on Company G. He single-handedly wiped out three positions, then with Sergeant Joseph B. Adkinson of Company C charged a fourth. Lemert was killed upon reaching his final objective, but Adkinson reached the muzzle of the Maxim gun, kicked it into the bottom of the trench, and took three prisoners.

OCTOBER HARVEST

Doughboys received forty-one Medals of Honor for actions during October 1918: nearly as many as the rest of the war combined. Nine were awarded for actions in the first seven days of October, representing seven divisions. But not all were infantrymen.

Two tankers received Medals of Honor in Europe, both from the 344th Tank Battalion, equipped with tiny two-man Rhinolith machines. On September 26, Corporal Donald M. Call was supporting an attack against German positions near Variance. An artillery shell scored a direct hit, destroying half the turret and forcing Call to bail out. He scurried to cover in a hole about thirty yards away, choking from gas. Then he realized that Lieutenant John Castles had not appeared. Call, a twenty-five-year-old New Yorker who had entered service in France, risked the dash back to the wrecked vehicle, dodging gunfire and artillery. He found Castles temporarily pinned and, despite growing flames, pulled him from the tank and dragged him to cover before the seven-ton Rhinolith exploded. Call then carried Castles more than a mile to safety.

Barely a week later, on October 4, eighteen-year-old Corporal Harold W. Roberts was driving his tank in an advance near the Montrebeau Woods. He halted to check on a stranded doughboy, was assured the man was safe, and pressed ahead. But Roberts' "track" slid into a tank trap about ten feet deep and filled with water. The little Renault overturned and rolled to a halt, inverted. With precious little time, Roberts realized that only one man could escape. He told his gunner, Sergeant Virgil Morgan, "Only one of us can get out, so out you go." With that, he pushed his gunner through the rear hatch. Morgan turned to lend help but was forced back by heavy gunfire. When he was able to return, he found that the San Franciscan had drowned.

In 1941, Camp Roberts in California became the only Army facility named in honor of an enlisted man.

Another tank action occurred shortly thereafter when PFC John L. Barkley of the Third Division turned tanker near Cunel on October 7. Though presumably restricted to an observation post near Hill 25, he repaired a Maxim machine gun and placed it on an immobile French tank. When the Germans counterattacked, Barkley hunkered down in his armored hideout until enemy infantry approached. The Missourian opened fire at close range, bringing the attack to a halt. In response, the Germans moved up a 77mm field gun and blasted the Renault, knocking off one drive wheel. Nevertheless, Barkley stuck it out and had ammunition remaining to repel a follow-up attack. He was cited with much of the credit for the eventual capture of Hill 25.

Unquestionably the most famous Medal of Honor action involved the "lost battalion" of the 308th Infantry, Seventy-seventh Division. In truth, it was elements of two battalions totaling some six hundred men who knew where they were. Their position, however, remained unknown to higher command for days.

The "Metropolitans" advanced more miles than any doughboy division, but inevitably there were reverses. The tangled, choked terrain of the Argonne Forest swallowed Major Charles Whittlesey's men. Cut off and surrounded from October 2–8, Whittlesey's troops were killed and wounded almost hourly. Attacked by *Sturmtruppen* with flamethrowers, pounded by enemy and friendly artillery alike, the doughboys tenaciously hung on. Fewer than 200 walked out of the weeklong horror.

The bookish, bespectacled Whittlesey had refused German invitations to surrender and held his diminishing command together thanks to experienced soldiers such as Captain George McMurtry, a forty-one-year-old former Rough Rider who received the medal. Another was Captain Nelson Miles Holderman, who, like McMurtry, ignored multiple wounds to continue leading his men and retrieving casualties. Holderman, aptly enough, was named for the Medal of Honor man from Chancellorsville in 1863.

Two AEF fliers, lieutenants Eugene Bleckley and Harold Goettler, received posthumous medals for their courageous support of the "lost command." In all, five medals were awarded for the action.

After the war, Whittlesey grew despondent over unfounded accusations of glory hunting. In 1921, he booked passage on a cruise to Cuba and disappeared at sea.

OCTOBER 8: BAKER'S DOZEN

Thirteen actions resulted in medals for October 8, the most for one day in the twentieth century. One of them passed into legend in the Eighty-second Division—and across America.

Corporal Alvin C. York, a Tennessee mountaineer, became an American icon for his action west of the River Aire. His epic battle against elements of the Second Wurttemberg *Landwehr* Division placed a premium on close-range snap shooting in tangled, broken terrain, and quick pistol work. It was a story crammed with imagery beloved of early-twentieth-century Americans: a lone rifleman—in this case, a former conscientious objector—shooting down two dozen enemy soldiers in order to preserve the lives of his remaining comrades. Twenty-three years later Gary Cooper won an Oscar for his portrayal in *Sergeant York*, wetting his front sight and "tetching off" twenty-five Germans, then capturing 132 others with remnants of his squad.

That same day, five medals went to the Thirtieth Division; three to the 118th Infantry, recruited mainly from South Carolina.

Advancing near Montbehain, Lieutenant James D. Dozier (aka Doshier) of Company G was wounded early in the attack. However, he continued ahead until his platoon was halted by heavy machine gun fire. With one soldier, Dozier crept up on the nest, scoured it with grenades, and finished off the defenders with his pistol.

Sergeant Thomas L. Hall, also of Company G, led a platoon in

■ Gas Warfare

Military use of chemical agents brought a wretched new dimension to a wretched war. At least 1,462 American troops died from gas exposure on the Western Front and 71,345 became casualties. The proportion of gas victims among combat deaths was small (2.7 percent) but the ratio among other battlefield losses was significant (nearly 35 percent). Doughboys sustained early losses to gas and learned how to survive in the process. In May, the Forty-second Division had heavy gas casualties, as did the Eighty-ninth at Flirey in August.

The Germans introduced gas to the battlefield in 1914, but the irritating tear gas proved ineffective. The following year, Germany deployed chlorine at Ypres, Belgium, and gained a local advantage. However, the attackers lacked sufficient reserves to exploit the breach in the allied line, and the entente forces soon retaliated.

Gas could be dispensed from frontline containers or in artillery shells. Neither side gained much advantage: gas made life more miserable for the frontline troops, but that was about all. Soldiers had to carry bulky, uncomfortable gas masks wherever they went.

Two types of gas were generally used: asphyxiants and blister agents. Chlorine and phosgene caused death by asphyxiation: the former could kill in about four minutes; the latter in as little as forty seconds. Mustard gas raised painful blisters on exposed skin, but mainly it affected the throat, lungs, and eyes. Experience proved the first four hours or so as crucial for a gas victim. If he showed no serious effects in that period, he was likely to return to duty. Otherwise, even if he survived, he was susceptible to greater risk from pneumonia.

knocking out two Maxims. However, resistance increased and the Palmetto soldiers stopped eight hundred yards from their halt line. Hall ordered his men to cover in a sunken road, advanced alone, and bayoneted the five-man gun crew. His action was cited as enabling the advance to continue.

F Company was ably represented by Sergeant Gary E. Foster, who accompanied an officer to attack machine gun nests. The officer was wounded, but Foster continued alone with grenades and pistol, killing several Germans and capturing eighteen.

The division's fourth and fifth medals that day were awarded to a pair of Tennesseans: Sergeant James E. Karnes and Private Calvin J. Ward of the 117th Regiment. Advancing against machine guns near Estrees, they killed three gunners and captured seven.

Elsewhere on October 8, Private Henry G. Costin of Baltimore ably represented the Twenty-ninth Division. He answered a call for an automatic rifle squad to eliminate a stubborn machine gun nest and proceeded with his team. Despite fire from artillery, machine guns, and mortars, he continued after all the others were hit and he was seriously wounded. Nevertheless, he fired his Chauchat until he collapsed from loss of blood. Other doughboys exploited Costin's success, taking one hundred prisoners. Henry Costin died shortly thereafter.

Informed that the 116th Infantry had hit a snag, another Twenty-ninth doughboy had a plan. Sergeant Earl D. Gregory merely said, "I will get them." The Virginian took a rifle and a mortar shell, left his weapons platoon, and stalked into the Borne de

Cpl. Alvin C. York, 328th Infantry

Cornouiller. There he tossed his improvised ordnance into a machine gun nest and nabbed three surviving Germans. Prodding them with his bayonet, he approached a 75mm howitzer, seized control of the field-piece, and convinced nineteen more to emerge from hiding. His twenty-two prisoners were well received as stretcher-bearers for "Blue and Gray" casualties.

Certainly courage and tenacity were exhibited in all these actions and more. But in objectivity, the German Army was whipped. Outnumbered, worn down, and unable to match the enormous Allied resources, more and more of the Kaiser's soldiers decided to quit. Time and again, one or two doughboys captured twenty or thirty Germans, most of whom appeared all too eager to see an end to the fighting.

Though York's feat quickly became legendary, other lone riflemen faced equally perilous odds and turned the course of other engagements with exceptional marksmanship. None were more notable than First Lieutenant Samuel Woodfill, a career soldier and former noncom.

Woodfill was a dedicated shooter, a match competitor with a wealth of experience that provided the bedrock for his awesome marksmanship. He was probably the finest field shot in the U.S. Army; perhaps in the war. Though not given to boasting, allegedly he had once killed a caribou with an unscoped rifle at more than a mile. He enlisted in 1901, soldiered in the Philippines, Alaska, and Texas, and was commissioned in 1917. That year, he married a descendant of Daniel Boone. In 1918, he was thirty-five; experienced, confident, and lethal.

On October 10, pinned down by Maxim fire, Woodfill had hugged the earth, scratching a farewell note to his wife while 8mm bullets punctured his backpack. The Indiana veteran reflected the conventional attitude of the era, referring to his impending death "on the Field of Honor." In truth, he was about to bring great honor to a sanguinary field.

On October 12, Woodfill was a company commander in the 60th Infantry, Fifth Division, at Cunel, four days after York's feat. With his men pinned down by machine guns, Woodfill used his extensive hunting and competition experience to solve the problem. When a Maxim gun dominated the area from a church tower at an estimated three hundred yards, Woodfill held above the muzzle flash and squeezed off five rounds. His first clip eliminated the five-man crew; he reloaded and moved forward.

Methodically, stealthily, Woodfill made his way across the fire-swept terrain. He silenced another machine gun with one round, then crawled within perhaps forty yards of a third. His remaining four rounds finished the affair, flushing out a sixth German. Woodfill drew his Colt and killed the man with a running head shot at forty yards. Upon clearing the nest, Woodfill found a seventh German and dispatched him with the pistol as well.

By now, some of Woodfill's men caught up with him, and one spotted a camouflaged tree hide. Woodfill threw his Springfield to his shoulder, squeezed the trigger, and dropped the sniper.

Moving through the Bois de la Pultiere, the stalker eliminated another five-man gun crew and captured three ammo bearers. He thumbed another clip into his '03 and went forward again, hunting more targets while crawling through mud a foot deep. He came upon a fifth Maxim position and killed all five soldiers, then leapt into an occupied trench. Confronted with two Germans at close range, Woodfill got off a snap shot with his pistol, hitting the nearest

1st Lt. Samuel Woodfill, 60th Infantry

man in the stomach. Later, Woodfill called it "the worst shooting I did all day." With his Colt jammed by mud, Woodfill grasped an entrenching tool and slew the second opponent, then turned it on the first man who was ineffectually shooting a Luger.

Sam Woodfill had destroyed five machine gun positions, killing twenty-one enemies with twenty-one .30-06 rounds and three pistol rounds.

It has been stated—factually—that the officers who composed Woodfill's citation did not appreciate the magnitude of his feat. While it credits him with reversing a dangerous tactical situation, overcoming automatic weapons by precision rifle fire, it does not include the conditions under which he fought. The text does not mention that he crawled through shell craters where gas had settled, stinging his eyes and fogging his vision. Yet he shrugged off the debilities, forced himself to focus on his front sight, and repeatedly scored long-range head shots on enemy gunners. General John Pershing, chief of the AEF, considered him America's greatest soldier. In a galaxy of warrior heroes, none shone brighter than Sam Woodfill.

After the war, Woodfill reverted to NCO rank and spent much off-duty time working at day jobs to meet expenses. He was commissioned again in World War II, serving as an infantry instructor, and finally retired to his Indiana farm, where he died in 1951.

Unlike Woodfill and York, other doughboys shunned the rifle in favor of the shotgun. Less than two weeks after Sergeant Seibert's exploit, another scattergun featured in First Sergeant Johannes S. Anderson's award on October 8. Evading artillery and machine gun fire, the Finnish-born Chicagoan used his sawed-off pump action to announce his presence via the rear door of a concrete pillbox. There, he encountered twenty-five *soldaten* busily engaged in serving a clutch of Maxims; he reduced their number by two and marched the others back to the Thirty-third Division lines.

It's doubtful whether these actions were known to the German high command, but during the war a formal protest was lodged with the U.S. Department of State over American use of shotguns. The Kaiser's government contended that they were banned by the Hague Convention, but in truth only lead shot was prohibited. Copper-plated shot was no different than jacketed rifle bullets; the Yanks continued toting their "street howitzers."

One thing seems clear: the exploits of Seibert and Anderson were unknown to the esteemed jurists of the United States Supreme Court who, in 1939, deemed sawed-off shotguns illegal because "they have no militia use."

By mid-October the end was near—though it wasn't clearly seen as so at the time. Certainly the Germans facing the Forty-second Division near Landres did not evidence any inclination to concede the match prematurely, as a Rainbow battalion commander learned. Lieutenant Colo-

nel William J. Donovan was skip-
per of the 165th Infantry, ironically
known as "Wild Bill" for a namesake big-league pitcher rather than
his actual demeanor. A quiet, gen-
tlemanly graduate of Columbia, he
was, according to a contemporary,
"a killer with a calm bearing."
Leading his men against heavy resistance, the thirty-five-year-old attorney reduced himself to platoon
leader and company commander,
deploying squads where necessary
and leading fast, desperate rushes
to close with the gunners. When
Maxim bullets cut him down,
Donovan intrigued the orderlies
eavesdropping on his debate with

Lt. Col. William J. Donovan, 165th Infantry

the regimental chaplain as to who would live long enough to bury whom.
Donovan, of course, survived to prominence as Franklin Roosevelt's spy-
master in the next German war.

On October 31, the Eighty-ninth Division's 354th Infantry was
engaged near Bois de Bantheville. A pair of stretcher bearers—PFCs
Charles D. Barger and Jesse N. Funk—learned that two patrols had
been caught between the lines in daylight. Despite the obvious danger, Barger and Funk resolved to do something. Twice they ventured
five hundred yards beyond the American lines, under constant gunfire, to rescue two wounded officers, apparently lieutenants Ernest G.
Rowell and Beverly C. Ohlandt. Funk was a thirty-year-old South
Carolinian; Barger a Missourian. They were the only Army medical
personnel to receive the medal in the war; both men died young, in
the mid-1930s.

As the Great War entered its final days, the AEF had enough institutional experience to draw some conclusions. Tackling dug-in machine guns was the doughboy's stock in trade, and nearly two-thirds of the Army Medals of Honor involved one or two soldiers assaulting Maxim guns. Major General Bullard of the First Division put great store in the feat, establishing his elite "Solo Club" for men who did so unassisted. However, not until mid-October did the AEF produce a field manual on the subject, emphasizing the traditional solutions: artillery, mortars, automatic rifles, and grenades. Use of the bayonet was not among the preferred options.

Eight medals were awarded in the last nine days of hostilities; six went to soldiers of the Eighty-ninth "Midwest" Division. Two men from different regiments displayed courageous initiative on November 1 in an advance around Bois de Bantheville. Near Remonville, Sergeant Arthur J. Forrest's company was halted by a half dozen machine guns, but the Missourian wriggled across the terrain, approaching the closest position without being seen. At fifty yards, he leapt to his feet and charged alone, driving the gunners away.

Nearby, First Lieutenant Harold A. Furlong saw his company commander shot down by Maxims; several doughboys also fell dead or wounded. Furlong took charge and scurried across several hundred yards of open ground, weaving between the "seams" of the defense. Then, from the rear, he took four machine gun nests in succession and brought back twenty prisoners.

Two days later, Captain Marcellus H. Chiles faced a challenge as a new battalion commander. Halted by automatic weapons to the front and left, he picked up a dead man's Enfield and led his doughboys across a waist-deep stream. Despite more machine gun fire, Chiles made the opposite bank and was deploying his men when he was shot in the stomach. Before being evacuated, he insisted on briefing his second in command, who completed the attack. Chiles was taken to a field hospital but died that day.

Twenty-eight miles northwest of Verdun's ossified fields, the River Meuse makes a hard double bend. At the base of the first curve is the tiny village of Pouilly, where the Eighty-ninth and Second Divisions were committed to crossing without bridges. Consequently, on the evening of November 7, volunteers were requested to swim the river, scout the German lines, and return. It was certainly a voluntary mission: the Meuse was not wide at that point, but the current was swift; the water extremely cold.

Two men responded from the First Battalion, 356th Infantry: B Company's Sergeant Waldo M. Hatler and Corporal John McAfee of D Company. During the crossing, McAfee developed severe cramps, lost his strength, and drowned, but Hatler returned with the desired information. Though Hatler's Medal of Honor citation states November 8, the battalion history is clear about the seventh, but perhaps the crossing was made after midnight. In any case, it seems peculiar that McAfee did not receive equal recognition.

The last three medals of the war were presented for two actions on November 9. PFC Harold I. Johnston of Chicago and Private David B. Barkley, a Texan, volunteered to swim the Meuse near Pouilly as Hatler and McAfee had done. The river was no less treacherous during the second effort. The two soldiers made the difficult crossing, scouted the terrain a quarter mile deep on the east bank, then returned to the river. It was an exhausting struggle: the nineteen-year-old Barkley developed severe cramps and drowned. Ironically, he had concealed his mother's Mexican background for fear it would prevent a combat assignment.

The young Texan's surname was spelled "Barkeley" on his citation but his gravestone in San Antonio is "Barkley." In some politically correct circles, he has also been identified by his mother's maiden name, Cantu. (Just to confuse things further, as previously noted, PFC John L. Barkley earned the medal near Cunel four weeks previously.)

Johnston, seven years older than Barkley, was exhausted; he had to be

Sgt. Waldo M. Hatler, 356th Infantry

pulled to safety. After regaining his strength, he provided the information to his company commander, and the operation proceeded. The 356th Regiment had received four Medals of Honor in six days.

That same day, five miles north at Mouzon, Sergeant Ludovicus M. M. Van Ierstel also conducted a dangerous river crossing. A native Hollander, the Second Division noncom volunteered to take a patrol across a damaged bridge but met heavy resistance. Under rifle and machine gun fire from as close as seventy-five yards, he crawled along the structure until he found an access to the river. Van Ierstel plummeted into the water and fought the rapid current in the chilling November darkness but, incredibly, he struck out for the far shore. There he found cover from enemy gunfire and noted the defense before recrossing. The fact that he could eavesdrop on German conversations was an additional bonus. He personally reported his reconnaissance to his battalion commander in the Ninth Infantry.

Germany agreed to the armistice two days later.

AFTERWARD

In 1918–19, legislation changed the warrant, limiting one Medal of Honor per recipient. The change occurred in the wake of the First World War, which raised the number of double recipients to nineteen.

Pvt. David B. Barkley, 356th Infantry   *PFC Howard I. Johnston, 356th Infantry*

Most of the second awards went to Navy and Marine Corps men who were eligible for the Army as well as Navy versions by virtue of serving under Army command.

The Distinguished Service Cross and Distinguished Service Medal were proposed before entry into World War I, and gained presidential as well as congressional support. The Distinguished Service Medal remained a noncombat award, but a lesser decoration emerged in the Citation Star. Originally a small silver star worn on the appropriate campaign ribbon, it was elevated to medal status in 1932 with retroactive presentation to the Spanish-American War. Thus, the pyramid of valor was nearly complete: only the Bronze Star remained to be added in World War II.

In 1935, Congress decided to ignore the law and awarded the Medal

---

■ *Who Were Those Men?*

For all the glory, very few Medal of Honor recipients are well known to the public. Usually only those with star power remain in the limelight. What, then, of the supporting players? All too rarely do official documents, let alone citations, mention "the rest of the cast."

Three of the four soldiers who swam the Meuse opposite Pouilly received the Medal of Honor. John McAfee lost his life in the attempt, but his name appears only in the battalion record. Did he ever receive a medal?

Who was Private Valente's "companion" east of Ronssoy? Neither the United States nor the British citations mention that other courageous soldier; the Italian-born hero himself may not have known him.

Who was the volunteer accompanying Lieutenant Baesel in the attempt to rescue the wounded noncom near Ivoury? For that matter, who was the injured man?

Who were the automatic riflemen that Captain Skinker selected to plug the gap in the wire? Skinker and the ammo bearer were both killed; we don't know what happened to the gunner, let alone his name.

Perhaps the answers may yet be found in musty archives long hidden from view; the names were unobtainable via the sources for this volume.

---

of Honor to retired Major General Adolphus W. Greely at age ninety. His citation remains the most curious ever, simply stating that he was born in 1844, enlisted in 1861, and retired on his sixty-fourth birthday. Though a former arctic explorer, his citation merely lauded "a life of splendid public service."

Greely's award violated almost every requirement for the medal. In approximate order of precedence, his citation mentioned no combat action (it did not even allude to risk of his life), and by its nature had no witnesses. Nor was it endorsed by a superior officer, since Greely had been retired twenty-seven years and the statutory limits had lapsed. Greely's award was an insult to every combat soldier ever nominated for the Medal of Honor, let alone those who received it.

The only other Army award between the wars went to Charles Lindbergh, who likewise received the medal for noncombat service, though he certainly risked his life on his transatlantic flight.

CHAPTER FIVE

WAR AGAINST JAPAN

■

W AR came to America on a Sunday, borne on wings "made in Japan." It was breakfast time in Hawaii; dinnertime in Washington, D.C. Two hours later, the raiders departed, leaving the wreckage of the Pacific Fleet in their slipstream. And something more:

A visceral desire for revenge.

The numbers tell the tale: 350 Japanese aircraft sank two battleships and destroyed or damaged seven other warships, destroyed 198 planes and killed 2,400 Americans. Eventually, thirteen Medals of Honor were awarded for Pearl Harbor; all went to Navy men.

Far across the International Date Line it was Monday, December 8. Yet General Douglas MacArthur, supreme commander in the Philippines, was caught by surprise. Hours after the calamity on Oahu, most of his air force was destroyed on the ground. His confidence that no invasion force could seize the islands was disproved with violent finality. Many felt he should have been court-martialed. Instead, he was given the Medal of Honor, escaping the accountability visited upon Admiral Husband Kimmel and Major General Walter Short in Hawaii.

■ *"The Greatest Generation"*

As of 2003, some 287 Medals of Honor had been awarded to the Army Ground Forces in World War II. More than two hundred were presented for action against Germany; the seventy or so in the Pacific represented about one-quarter of the total. Nearly 150 were posthumous awards, or more than half. Statistically, fighting the Japanese was more dangerous than the western Axis, as nearly two-thirds of the Pacific Theater awards were posthumous, compared to "only" 48 percent of the Mediterranean and European actions.

Medals went to soldiers in fifty-one infantry divisions, four airborne, and nine armored divisions.

MacArthur coveted the Medal of Honor, as his father had received it in the Civil War. His Philippine citation specified his leadership on the Bataan Peninsula, but apparently he spent only one day there: January 10, 1942. Various explanations have been offered for his professional survival, including his status as a former Army chief of staff. MacArthur resisted the president's order to evacuate from the Philippines, stating that he would resign his commission and remain as a private soldier. Whether he meant it or not is problematical; essentially, he received the medal for overseeing the worst defeat in American history.

MacArthur left the Philippines with his family on March 11 and received the medal from a U.S. diplomat in Melbourne at the end of June.

Following MacArthur's departure, command passed to Jonathan M. Wainwright IV. The Bataan Peninsula fell on April 19 and Corregidor Island on May 7. More than 100,000 Filipino and American troops were taken into brutal captivity.

Wainwright was promoted to lieutenant general shortly before the capitulation. Known as "Skinny" during his thirty-five-year career, the rail-thin veteran sadly decided to surrender in hope of saving some American and Filipino lives. MacArthur was livid. Already sensitive to Axis criticism (which may have partly explained his own medal), he regarded Wainwright as custodian of his Philippine legacy. MacArthur felt that Wainwright's medal could lead to "embarrassing repercussions," an atrocious statement considering that his own medal remains the most political of all. Nevertheless, MacArthur declined to endorse Chief of Staff George

Marshall's Medal of Honor recommendation for Wainwright. Marshall withdrew the nomination but revived it in 1945; that time MacArthur offered no objection.

Whatever controversy attended his 1945 citation, Wainwright certainly was more deserving than MacArthur. He too was urged to evacuate but replied, "We've been through so much together that my conscience would not let me leave before the final curtain." Wainwright became the senior American POW of the war and was sixty-two when released.

The old cavalryman was photographed carrying an issue

2nd Lt. Alexander R. Nininger Jr., 57th Infantry Rgt.

M1911 pistol, but he favored his single-action Colt revolver made in 1906, the year he graduated from West Point. Wainwright was a shooter: reportedly he picked up an '03 rifle and fired at Japanese troops on at least one occasion. With the end in sight, he gave his Colt to a subordinate to carry to Australia, but the plane crashed on Mindanao. Therefore, the vintage revolver was wrapped in oilcloth and stashed in a tree. It was retrieved in 1946 and eventually donated to the West Point Museum. Wainwright probably never saw it again; he died in 1953 at the age of eighty.

The first combat awards to Army men in World War II all occurred in Bataan Province. On January 12, 1942, Second Lieutenant Alexander R. Nininger Jr., of the Fifty-seventh Infantry insisted on joining another company under Japanese attack. In close combat, Nininger repeatedly overcame enemy infantry in prepared positions, using rifle and

■ *Pacific Geography*

Of the Army's Pacific awards, by far the greatest number were presented for liberation of the Philippines. Thirty-six of the seventy medals earned against Japan (just over half) were awarded for action there in 1944–45. Another five had been awarded for the 1941–42 defense of the islands, including those of MacArthur and Wainwright. Some soldiers remarked that presenting 40 percent of the campaign's Medals of Honor to the losing generals spoke of politics more than valor, and though MacArthur was excoriated as "Dugout Doug," Wainwright retained the respect of his troops.

Other Pacific combat arenas were Okinawa/Ryukyus (nine awards), New Guinea (eight), the Solomons (seven), Marshalls (two), plus the Admiralties, Alaska, and Burma with one each.

Often overlooked is the Aleutian campaign. Stretching westward from Alaska, the chain generates some of the worst weather on earth, yet Japan controlled Attu Island for almost a year. On May 26, 1943, a Thirty-second Infantry Regiment attack to clear ridge lines overlooking Chichagof Harbor was halted by heavy Japanese fire. By exhortation and example, Private Joe P. Martinez led other soldiers in an uphill assault, using his BAR and grenades to take one position after another. Approaching the vital pass over the hills, he ignored fire from both flanks to reach the crest, firing into the last Japanese trench when he was killed.

grenades. The Floridian was wounded three times but pressed ahead until far beyond help, and was killed. Other soldiers found his body amid three Japanese corpses.

Four days later, Sergeant Jose Calugas was a mess attendant attached to the Eighty-eighth Field Artillery. He took it upon himself to sprint more than a half mile to a battery whose crew had been killed or wounded. There, he formed a squad of volunteers to repair the gun and return fire, though under frequent enemy barrage. He died in 1998, age ninety-nine.

On February 3, First Lieutenant Willibald C. Bianchi of the Philippine Scouts was in action. He volunteered to join another platoon in seizing two Japanese strongholds and, though shot in the left hand, he dropped his rifle and persisted with his sidearm. He found a camouflaged machine gun nest and destroyed it with grenades. Though struck by two bullets in the chest, he climbed atop an American tank and fired its machine gun until mortally wounded.

SOLOMONS SLUGFEST

Guadalcanal is often regarded as a Marine Corps operation, but the Twenty-fifth Infantry Division was committed in December 1942, resulting in three Medals of Honor.

On January 10, 1943, M Company, Thirty-fifth Infantry, was attacked by determined Japanese forces along the Matanikau River. Perimeter defense fell to Sergeant William G. Fournier's machine gun section, but one crew was killed and two other men wounded. Though his flankers were repulsed, Fournier refused to quit and rushed to the second gun with Tech/5 Lewis Hall. Unable to engage approaching Japanese in defilade, Fournier raised the second Browning on its tripod to improve the field of fire while Hall did the shooting. They kept firing until both men were killed.

Two days later, Captain Charles W. Davis, Seventh Infantry, led a charge that gained a prominent hill for the division.

Also part of the Solomons campaign was the New Georgia, farther up "the Slot" from Guadalcanal. New Georgia was a pest hole of brutal heat, swarming insects, tangled vines, and insufficient water. But it had one thing worth gaining: Munda airfield.

Lieutenant Robert S. Scott of the Forty-third Division used grenades to blast his way toward the airstrip on July 29. Despite wounds to the head and hands, he took the initiative and led his platoon against entrenched Japanese in a succession of attacks. At length, he reached the crest of the hill overlooking the field, which was seized four days later. Summarizing his leadership philosophy, Scott has written, "I was awarded the Medal of Honor for deeds one day as a second lieutenant infantry platoon leader, deeds that I initiated at least in part from the conviction that I ought to have enough guts to do what I was authorized to order a soldier to try to do. And I wanted the enlisted men and the officers to respect me and to judge me as a man."

Two days after Scott's action, one of the famous events of the war oc-

Sgt. William G. Fournier, 25th Division

curred. Private Rodger Young of the Thirty-seventh Division's 148th Regiment was a thin, bespectacled Buckeye who had been promoted to staff sergeant. However, a serious hearing impairment concerned him about his suitability to command, so he requested reduction to private. His company commander compromised at PFC.

On July 31, Young's platoon was pinned down by a Japanese bunker seventy-five yards away. Though wounded, he crawled toward the position, trying to reach grenade range. Other Japanese spotted him and fired, hitting him again. Young pressed forward, firing his rifle, until he could throw grenades at the pillbox. In doing so, he was struck a third time and killed, but his platoon disengaged safely.

"The Ballad of Rodger Young" became one of the war's anthems. It was written by Frank Loesser, best known for *Guys and Dolls:*

> *On the island of New Georgia in the Solomons*
> *Stands a simple wooden cross alone to tell*
> *That beneath the silent coral of the Solomons*
> *Sleeps a man, sleeps a man remembered well.*

Another Thirty-seventh soldier, PFC Frank J. Petrarca, was a medic awarded a posthumous medal for repeatedly tending wounded amid enemy small arms and mortar fire during July 1943.

Bougainville was the largest of the Solomon Islands, and there Staff

Sergeant Jesse R. Drowley earned the last Army medal of the campaign. On January 30, the Americal Division NCO ran through enemy fire to help three wounded GIs but spotted a camouflaged bunker. He boarded a tank, climbed on the turret, and offered to direct its fire with tracer rounds from his Thompson. Within twenty feet of the emplacement, Drowley was struck in the chest but remained aboard to ensure the tankers had the target. He was then shot off the vehicle with a round to his left eye, but remained alongside to direct fire against another bunker. Only then did the resolute NCO return to his lines for treatment.

PFC Rodger Young, 37th Division

NEW GUINEA MEAT GRINDER

The hard-fought New Guinea campaign produced nine Army Medals of Honor.

Christmas Eve 1942 was a day of bitter combat for the Thirty-second Division, resulting in two posthumous medals for the 127th Infantry in southeastern New Guinea. Driving for Buna on the north coast, the regiment encountered heavy opposition. First Sergeant Elmer J. Burr dived on a grenade that landed near his company commander, absorbing the explosion to save his comrades.

That same day, Sergeant Kenneth E. Gruennert attacked enemy pill-

Pvt. Junior Van Noy, Engineer Boat & Shore Rgt.

boxes and destroyed the first by himself with grenades and rifle fire. He paused to bandage his own shoulder wound, then singly advanced against the next objective. Again he used grenades to flush out the defenders, who were then shot down by his soldiers. But before his platoon could reach him, he was killed by enemy rifle fire.

On March 8, 1943, Private George Watson of the Twenty-ninth Quartermaster Regiment was aboard the army transport *Jacob* near Porlock Harbor. Bombed by Japanese aircraft and clearly sinking, the Dutch ship was abandoned, but Watson remained to help some nonswimmers reach a life raft. The suction of the sinking vessel pulled him under, and he drowned. Watson's medal was authorized by congressional waiver owing to statutory limitations, and presented in 1997.

Private Junior Van Noy distinguished himself with the Engineer Boat and Shore Regiment near Finschafen on October 17, 1943. Previously wounded, Van Noy had refused evacuation and manned a machine gun opposing two Japanese landing craft. The enemy beached within yards of his position and threw grenades that wounded both team members. The loader was evacuated, but Van Noy stubbornly remained. Repeatedly hit, he refused to be moved and kept firing until he died. Comrades credited him with killing nearly twenty of thirty-nine Japanese in the attack.

July 1944 brought a heightened amount of combat to New Guinea. On the 11th Staff Sergeant Gerald L. Endl's company of the Thirty-second Division's 128th Infantry was advancing along a jungle trail when the lead platoon was ambushed. With his lieutenant wounded, Endl assumed command and scouted in dense foliage. He found eight Japanese machine guns supporting an envelopment of his platoon. But twelve of Endl's men were wounded, including seven who were separated from the rest. Realizing they would quickly be overrun, he attacked head-on, fighting vastly superior numbers for ten minutes. He then dragged four soldiers to safety but was killed as he delivered the last to cover.

Second Lieutenant Dale E. Christensen of the 112th Cavalry received the medal for four days of combat in mid-July. In prolonged fighting, Christensen personally destroyed a Japanese machine gun nest with grenades. Later, he crept up on another position, had his rifle shot from his hands, and again used grenades. Gathering his soldiers, he led them in overrunning four mortars and ten machine guns. He was killed on August 4 within a few paces of his objective—another automatic weapon.

Two medal actions occurred near Arufa on July 22–23. The first involved Private Donald R. Lobaugh, 127th Infantry of the Thirty-second Division. With his platoon surrounded and pinned down, Lobaugh volunteered to attack a machine gun position blocking the only escape route. He crossed thirty yards of open ground, drawing heavy fire, and was shot while throwing a grenade. Despite mortal wounds, he charged the position, killing two gunners, and opened a breach for his platoon.

The next day, another cavalryman, Second Lieutenant George W. Boyce, was leading his platoon toward a surrounded unit. Boyce took his men within yards of a Japanese position, when the enemy launched a grenade barrage. One grenade rolled between Boyce and the men behind him; he unhesitatingly smothered it and absorbed the blast with his body.

That same day, a paratrooper earned the medal on Noemfoor Island, Dutch New Guinea. In an incredible display of determination and self-sacrifice, Sergeant Ray E. Eubanks of the 503rd Parachute Infantry led his squad in flanking an enemy position, then he took a BAR within fifteen yards of the Japanese. He opened fire but quickly drew heavy fire that jammed the automatic rifle. Eubanks charged and beat four Japanese to death with his heavy Browning before he was killed. He became the first paratrooper to receive the medal in the Pacific.

SAIPAN

Three Twenty-seventh Division men received medals for Saipan in the Marianas, the vital air base that put Tokyo in range of B-29s. Two are addressed in Chapter Ten; one was a much belated award.

Captain Benjamin L. Salomon, twenty-nine, was the dentist for the Second Battalion, 105th Infantry, on Guam's northern coast. Salomon was no ordinary medico; he'd been drafted as a GI, and friends called him "the best infantryman you ever saw."

Early on July 7, at least 3,000 Japanese swarmed through a three-hundred-yard gap between the regiment's two advance battalions. Thirty or more casualties quickly filled Salomon's tent behind the line. As he squatted over one man, Salomon saw a Japanese bayoneting another patient and immediately shot the offender. Six more Nipponese entered the tent, and Salomon used a rifle to shoot one and bayonet another. Then he knifed one and grappled with others until they too were shot.

Salomon advised the wounded to withdraw to the regimental aid station, saying he would provide cover. Then he grabbed a rifle and exited the tent, finding a machine gun with its crew dead. The surgeon perched behind the Browning and opened fire, covering the wounded men's withdrawal until he was killed. When the area was secured, ninety-eight Japanese bodies were found nearby. Survivors reckoned that Dr. Salomon had killed most of them. Physical evidence showed he had been shot repeatedly but still moved the heavy M1917 three times to gain better fields of fire around the heaped bodies.

Salomon was recommended for the Medal of Honor, but the division commander, though sympathetic, erroneously felt it illegal for a doctor to engage in combat. Salomon's admirers tried to reverse the decision in 1951 and 1972 and had to wait until 2002. Finally, presentation was made to the USC School of Dentistry, Salomon's alma mater.

RETURN TO THE PHILIPPINES

Capt. Benjamin L. Salomon, 27th Division

The Philippines campaign of 1944–45 became a slugging match: as close to conventional warfare as the Army found in the Pacific. On Leyte, between Mindanao and Samar, the fighting was especially hard: ten of the twelve medal awards were posthumous.

American forces landed on Leyte in October 1944, two and a half years after the collapse of Corregidor. The first medal for the campaign went to twenty-three-year-old Private Harold H. Moon Jr., of the Twenty-fourth Division. He was killed defending a newly won beachhead at Pawig during the early morning of October 21. Exhibiting exceptional skill and determination, Moon killed scores of Japanese who repeatedly attacked his advanced foxhole during a four-hour standoff. Though wounded and with little support, he called for mortar fire that broke up persistent enemy attacks. Finally, a Japanese platoon launched a bayonet charge against his position, and he calmly, coolly cut down the enemy with his Thompson. He was killed throwing a grenade at a ma-

■ The Greatest Guns

"The greatest generation" that fought World War II did so with some of the greatest infantry weapons of all time. At the beginning of the war, the revolutionary M1 rifle was standard issue, but production had not caught up with need. Consequently, most line units were armed with M1903 Springfields almost identical to their fathers' rifles in the "war to end all wars." The irony could not have been lost on many, though some GIs reportedly said, "If it was good enough for my old man, it's good enough for me!"

The .30 caliber M1, designed for the United States by Canadian-born John M. Garand, was the result of nearly fifteen years of development. When accepted for service in 1936, it was the world's first standard issue semiautomatic rifle, firing eight rounds loaded into the top of the receiver. At nine pounds it was rugged, reliable, and reasonably accurate.

Three other weapons also were veterans of World War I, all from the prolific John M. Browning. His legendary M1911 .45 caliber pistol remained standard long after 1945, only enhancing its matchless reputation. The Browning Automatic Rifle (BAR) and M1917 water-cooled machine gun saw very limited use in 1918 but were universally employed from 1942 through 1945. After World War I, Browning also developed the much lighter M1919 air-cooled model, a handier infantry weapon but less capable of long-range, sustained fire. All three Browning automatics fired the standard .30-06 rifle cartridge.

Yet another Browning contribution was his M2 .50 caliber machine gun, the standard American aircraft weapon and favorite of heavy weapons companies. Possessing awesome range, power, and accuracy, the "Ma Deuce" was also mounted on tanks and other vehicles, often as an antiaircraft gun.

One of the most produced World War II weapons was the M1 carbine, with 6 million delivered in barely three years. Feelings about the "war baby" were ambivalent. Infantrymen liked its fifteen-round magazine, light weight, and portability, but its .30 caliber round was found too anemic for reliably stopping a determined enemy. It was often issued to officers and NCOs, a fact not lost on enemy snipers.

Two primary submachine guns were produced during the war: the M1 Thompson, derived from the famous "Chicago typewriter" of gangster fame, and the M3 "grease gun," named for its resemblance to that tool. Both fired the M1911 pistol's .45 caliber cartridge, proving reliable and decisive in close-quarter combat.

Across the globe, GIs used hand grenades in Medal of Honor actions more than anything else. At least 121 citations mention grenades, including enemy weapons. Rifles were cited seventy-four times, though the total is unquestionably higher. Meanwhile, the growth of automatic weapons is evident in 109 cases: varying along machine guns, automatic rifles, and submachine guns.

chine gun crew that had flanked his line. Almost two hundred Japanese bodies were found within a hundred yards of his position, testament to his forward observation and exceptional skill with his Thompson.

A UCLA athlete, Captain Francis B. Wai, also of the Twenty-fourth, retroactively, and posthumously, received the medal for his action the day before Moon's. Landing in the fourth wave at Red Beach, he found hundreds of GIs pinned down, leaderless and confused. Wai organized a

movement inland, identifying camouflaged positions by exposing
himself to draw fire until he was
killed. In 2000, Wai's award was
made in recognition of the fact that
no Asian American had received
the medal in the Pacific Theater.

Another Twenty-fourth soldier,
Sergeant Charles E. Mower, was
posthumously decorated for continuing to lead his squad despite
mortal wounds on November 3.

Three men gave their lives protecting comrades from enemy
grenades on Leyte, including PFC
John F. Thorson of the Seventh Division on October 28. Two
Thirty-second Division men acted

Pvt. Harold H. Moon Jr., 24th Division

in December: PFC William A. McWhorter and Sergeant Leroy Johnson,
who jumped on two grenades.

Personal initiative counts for a great deal in combat. The Seventh Division's PFC Leonard C. Bostrom proved the point on October 28,
when his platoon ran into a well-designed Japanese defensive line. Positions were so well camouflaged that they were often invisible beyond
twenty yards. Without orders, Bostrom dashed forward to throw
grenades into a pillbox. He survived the maelstrom of gunfire only to be
met by a bayonet charge. Bostrom killed one Japanese soldier and repulsed the others with his rifle. He turned back to the pillbox, throwing
more grenades, and was shot down. Somehow, he rose again, tossed another grenade, and the enemy survivors fled. Leonard Bostrom died of
his wounds a long way from his home in Preston, Idaho.

Two medals were awarded for actions on December 8, including

PFC Leonard C. Bostrom, 7th Division

Private Elmer E. Fryar, 511th Parachute Infantry. While covering his company's withdrawal under heavy fire, Fryar was wounded but shot nearly thirty Japanese. Hastening to rejoin his squad, he found a wounded trooper and picked him up to continue with his platoon leader and another casualty. Along the way, a Japanese light machine gunner aimed at the lieutenant, but Fryar instantly leapt into the line of fire. He absorbed the 6.5mm burst but killed the Japanese soldier with a grenade before dying.

Assaulting Buri Airstrip, Company A of the Ninety-sixth Division's 382nd Infantry met heavy resistance. Private Ova A. Kelley from Missouri saw that American mortars were largely ineffective and, on his own initiative, left cover with a stash of grenades. His initial barrage forced Japanese infantry to scatter and, in the words of Nathan Bedford Forrest, he decided to "keep up a 'skeer'." He picked up a Garand, killed three fleeing enemy, then found a carbine and dropped three more. Thus inspired, Kelley's friends destroyed an enemy platoon. Advancing to the airstrip, he was mortally wounded by snipers and died two days later.

In the Seventy-Seventh Division, Lieutenant Robert B. Nett led his company in assaulting enemy positions near Cognon on December 14. Leading from the front, he used his rifle and bayonet to root out entrenched Japanese, personally killing seven. Despite multiple wounds, he organized for the advance to continue before consenting to medical assistance. Like many medal recipients, Nett accepted the accolade on be-

half of his men, saying, "I have the Medal of Honor with all the courageous soldiers in E Company, 305th Infantry, Seventy-seventh Division."

As a youth, PFC Dirk J. Vlug of the Thirty-second Division enjoyed
building birdhouses in the Midwest. Yet on Leyte, he set a record when
he destroyed five Japanese tanks on December 15. Near Limon, a roadblock of the 126th Infantry was attacked by Japanese armor. Packing a
pistol and bazooka, Vlug left cover, sprinting alone through machine
gun and 37mm fire. His first round destroyed the first enemy tank,
prompting the second three-man crew to dismount and rush him. He
shot one Japanese with his pistol, and when the others scampered back
to their tank he reloaded and destroyed it with his second rocket.

When three more tanks clanked up the road, Vlug moved to the
flank and dispatched the leader with his bazooka. The others had seen
him and directed close-range fire, but he destroyed the nearest. With his
final rocket, he knocked the fifth tank off the road, careening down an
embankment. He had destroyed five tanks with six 2.36-inch rockets.

The last medal for Leyte went to PFC George Benjamin of the
Seventy-seventh Division, on December 21. Though a radio operator
stationed in the rear of his platoon, Benjamin dashed forward when a
Stuart light tank met increased opposition. Benjamin saw a way through
the enemy defenses and waved the other soldiers to follow him. Still
packing his bulky radio, he drew his pistol and quickly killed a Japanese
rifleman and a machine gun crew. Now exposed to much of the enemy
gunfire, he pushed ahead, killing two more before he was shot down.
Despite the pain of mortal wounds, Benjamin insisted on telling an officer the enemy disposition. He died shortly thereafter, age twenty-five.

LUZON

Things were only slightly better on Luzon, with twelve of twenty-five
posthumous awards.

Several Luzon awards were presented for life saving, and the circumstances varied widely. A Twenty-fifth Division medic, Tech/4 Laverne Parrish, received a posthumous medal for valor January 18–24 at Binalonan, Luzon. Over a period of a week, Parrish repeatedly risked his life to assist wounded GIs. He frequently entered the kill zone of automatic weapons to retrieve fallen soldiers, each time taking them to safety. He treated all thirty-seven casualties sustained by his company in that period before he was fatally stricken by mortar fire.

Another Tropic Lightning soldier, Master Sergeant Charles McGaha, carried wounded men through heavy gunfire on February 7. Two days later, PFC Joseph J. Cicchetti, Thirty-seventh Division, became a volunteer stretcher bearer south of Manila. For four hours he helped carry wounded men to safety over hundreds of yards, and continued even after sustaining a mortal head wound.

On Luzon, two soldiers received Medals of Honor for jumping on enemy grenades, but the Thirty-seventh Division's Lieutenant Robert M. Viale sacrificed himself on his own weapon. In Manila on February 5, he was climbing a ladder to throw his grenade at Japanese outside his building, but his injured arm weakened and he lost his grip. The spoon ejected and the armed grenade fell to the floor in a room crowded with men. Viale dropped off the ladder, scooped up the grenade and turned toward the wall. The explosion eviscerated the Californian, who died within thirty seconds.

In a similar incident later that month, Staff Sergeant Raymond A. Cooley, Twenty-fifth Division, held a grenade to himself amid closely grouped friendlies and enemy troops.

Luzon's terrain and foliage lent itself to defense in depth, but courageous GIs consistently found ways around the Japanese.

As an acting platoon leader, Technical Sergeant Donald E. Rudolph's company of the Twentieth Infantry, Sixth Division, was held up by Japanese fortifications near Munoz on February 5. Munoz was a tough nut: the entire division was needed with tanks and artillery. Rudolph was treating casualties when he noticed gunfire from a nearby culvert. He crawled to a favorable position and used his rifle and grenades to kill three Japanese soldiers inside. The Minnesotan then crossed open ground to approach a pillbox close enough to toss in a grenade. Before the dust settled, he scrambled atop the structure, tore off the roofing, and dropped in another grenade, killing the gunners.

Tech. Sgt. Donald E. Rudolph, 6th Division

Gathering some riflemen for support, Rudolph took a pick to attack the next pillbox in line. He chopped a hole in the roof, fired several rifle rounds, and heaped dirt inside.

Don Rudolph was just getting started.

Taking each position in turn, Rudolph silenced six more pillboxes with grenades and rifle fire. Nor was that all. Later in the day, his platoon was approached by a Japanese tank, but the NCO leapt atop the vehicle and dropped a phosphorous grenade inside. In addition to the Medal of Honor, Rudolph was subsequently commissioned a second lieutenant.

On February 9, two privates of Company B, 148th Infantry, Thirty-seventh Division, took Paco Railroad Station in Manila. The platoon of twenty-two-year-old Oklahoma PFC John N. Reese and Private Cleto Rodriguez, a twenty-one-year-old Texas BAR man, was held up a hundred yards from the station. On their own, they advanced to a house sixty yards from the objective and spent an hour there, killing thirty-five Japanese. With the defenses thinned out, they resumed their advance but clashed with enemy reinforcements. The deadly duo killed more than forty, preventing a strengthening of the Japanese line. Reese then covered Rodriguez, who destroyed a 20mm cannon and heavy machine gun with grenades. Understandably low on ammo, they hopscotched back toward their lines, intending to load up and get on with the war. However, Reese was killed at that point. In two and a half hours, Reese and Rodriguez killed more than eighty Japanese, playing a major role in seizure of the important station.

Two medals went to Eleventh Airborne troopers during the campaign. At Fort McKinley on February 13, PFC Manuel Perez staged a one-man attack on Japanese defenses. He killed eight enemies with his rifle and tossed grenades into concrete bunkers. He had shot down four more, when a Japanese soldier threw his bayoneted rifle at Perez. The trooper blocked the toss but dropped his Garand and, grasping the enemy rifle, used it to kill two more opponents. With the Arisaka in hand he killed three with the butt, then entered the pillbox and bayoneted the one remaining. His onslaught removed the major impediment to his company's advance. But combat continued, and Perez was killed a week later.

From February 16–19, Private Lloyd G. McCarter distinguished himself as a scout on Corregidor. In four days of almost constant combat, he used a rifle, submachine gun, and grenades to seize enemy positions and kill snipers. He also hazarded several risky trips to obtain more ammunition. His single-handed defense of his portion of the line resulted in some thirty Japanese dead, and he was wounded while standing erect to locate enemy positions.

The First Cavalry's PFC William J. Grabiarz, a twenty-year-old New Yorker, gave his life in Manila on February 23. With his troop commander lying wounded in a street, Grabiarz sprinted through close-range fire and was hit in one arm. He reached the captain but, unable to lift him, used his good arm to drag the officer toward a tank. Grabiarz realized he could not reach safety in time, so he fell upon his captain to afford the protection of his own body. Japanese gunfire killed him on the spot, but the captain survived. Buffalo, New York, honored its self-sacrificing son.

Some lifesaving involved shooting. On March 10, PFC Thomas E. Atkins, Thirty-second Division, survived prolonged combat on the Villa Verde Trail. Atkins and his machine gun crew occupied a forward position, when an estimated two Japanese companies attacked in the dark. Though the men with Atkins were killed and he was wounded, he kept firing and helped repulse the Banzai charge. For four hours he remained in place, exhausting his Browning's four hundred rounds. He then seized three rifles in succession and fired them until they jammed from overheating.

After daylight, with thirteen enemy corpses around his position, Atkins went for more ammunition but was detained by medics. While awaiting treatment, he spotted a Japanese infiltrator and shot him, then agreed to lie on a stretcher. Despite serious wounds he defended other casualties at the collection point, firing from his litter to kill or repel other infiltrators. The tireless Carolinian received the Medal of Honor seven months later.

On March 31, another machine gunner made an exceptional contribution. PFC William R. Shockley was a twenty-seven-year-old veteran of the Thirty-second Division who had been wounded at Saidor. Now, with his company under heavy fire prior to a Japanese infantry attack, Shockley called for his friends to withdraw. Some of them heard him exclaim that he would stay to the end. He was as good as his word.

Despite two stoppages, Shockley kept his gun in action, blunting a frontal attack and then shifting to protect the left flank. By now, the enemy had nearly blocked the egress route, so Shockley ordered his squad to pull out. He kept firing to cover their withdrawal. Later, when the ground was reoccupied, Shockley was found dead at his gun with Japanese bodies in front of his fighting hole.

Grenades were the favored weapon of the Fortieth Division's Staff

Sergeant John C. Sjogren. On May 23, near San Jose Hacienda on Negros Island, the Michigander led his platoon uphill against an extremely well-defended position. In a double envelopment, two squads made the rush, when the leader on the other flank was shot. Sjogren sprinted across twenty yards of open terrain, dodging gunfire and explosions, to drag the man to cover and apply first aid.

Resuming his advance, Sjogren killed eight Japanese in spider holes guarding the approach to the pillbox dominating the crest. With his soldiers firing into the embrasure, Sjogren tossed in several grenades. The Japanese returned two or three, and Sjogren was wounded by fragments. Nevertheless, he continued depositing "pineapples" inside faster than the defenders could eject them, and the position was silenced.

Sjogren continued his assault, taking one position after another. He stealthily approached one pillbox, grasped the exposed muzzle of a light machine gun, and pulled it out through the firing port. He then returned to his preference, grenades.

At the end of the action, Sjogren had overcome nine pillboxes, killing forty-three enemy soldiers.

PFC Dexter J. Kerstetter of the Thirty-third Division hailed from Washington State. Leading his squad forward of the U.S. lines near Galiano on Friday, April 13, he used his Garand and hand and rifle grenades to take one position after another. Out of ammo, he returned to his squad for resupply and treatment of a hand blistered from the heat of his rifle. He then led a fresh platoon into position to resume the assault. His citation stated, "In all, he dispatched sixteen Japs that day. The hill was taken and held against the enemy's counterattacks, which continued for three days." He was "largely responsible for the capture of this key enemy position."

PFC William H. Thomas, Thirty-eighth Division, died fighting in the Zambales Mountains on April 22. The automatic rifleman had both legs blown off below the knees while attacking a wooded ridge, but he declined all aid. Refusing evacuation, he continued firing until his BAR was hit by enemy fire. Still refusing to be moved, he used his last two grenades to kill three Japanese. His exceptional tenacity prevented repulse of his platoon and enabled capture of the position.

Private John McKinney earned the respect of the Thirty-third Division on May 11. Japanese soldiers expertly infiltrated McKinney's company before dawn, and he was attacked in his foxhole near a machine gun position. A sword stroke clanged off his helmet, and the twenty-four-year-old Georgian used his rifle to beat his assailant to the ground. McKinney shot another enemy, then saw the Browning gunner hauling his wounded partner to safety. The gun was seized by ten Japanese, who began turning it on the Americans, but McKinney took the initiative. He jumped into the position, killed seven with the remaining rounds in his Garand, and beat the others to death.

Though the gun was inoperative, McKinney stood his ground. Amid exploding grenades and mortar rounds, he fired his M1, moving in the dark to confuse successive enemy attacks. When he was unable to reload, he used butt strokes and sheer physical strength. When the hand-to-hand battle ended, the determined Southerner was the last man standing. Forty enemy corpses lay strewn within forty-five yards of his position; McKinney was promoted to sergeant.

On June 6, Staff Sergeant Howard E. Woodford coordinated with a guerrilla battalion attached to the Thirty-third Division. Near Tabio, Woodford organized the Filipinos in seizing a hilltop against determined opposition. Though recalled to his own unit, he decided to remain with the guerrillas through the night and bolster their position. Before dawn, the Japanese launched a "suicide attack" with supporting mortars and automatic weapons. Woodford called down friendly mortar fire until his radio was destroyed. Then he plugged a gap in the Filipino line, fighting largely alone in the dark. After daybreak, his body was found with thirty-seven enemy dead at his position. Barberton, Ohio, was justly proud of its citizen.

The Army's last Pacific Theater medal went to Corporal Melvin

Mayfield for July 29, 1945, combat on Luzon. Fighting with the Sixth Division in the Cordillera Mountains, Mayfield noted two Filipino companies pinned down from ridges overlooking the area. Mounting a one-man assault, the NCO sprinted from one shell hole to another, flanking four Japanese-occupied caves. Frequently under fire, he attacked each cave in turn with carbine and grenades. When his carbine was shot out of his hand, he obtained more grenades to destroy a final position in a headlong rush through close-range gunfire.

Mayfield's medal was approved in 1946.

OKINAWA

Okinawa and the Ryukyus were the last significant islands before Japan itself. The campaign produced medals for nine soldiers, twelve Marines, and four Navy men.

The assault troops landed against minimal opposition on Easter Sunday, April 1, and moved inland. The first days ashore were deceptive, as the Japanese had planned a defense in depth. Okinawa turned into a prolonged meat grinder.

PFC Edward J. Moskala was the first of four medal recipients in the Ninety-sixth Division. On April 9, the twenty-three-year-old Chicagoan was ahead of his squad, when Japanese small arms and mortar fire stopped the advance on Kakazu Ridge. Without awaiting support, Moskala sprinted forty yards through gunfire to destroy two machine gun nests with grenades and his BAR.

With enemy pressure building, Moskala and eight others volunteered to cover the company's withdrawal. In a three-hour holding action, he was credited with twenty-five or more kills before the group retreated through chemical smoke. At the rendezvous, the GIs realized that one man had been left behind, so Moskala and others went back for him, returning under fire.

Moskala then set up a protective position covering the casualty assembly area after retrieving another man. Aware that Japanese were infiltrating the area, probably to kill the wounded, Moskala shot down four, then turned to help another soldier. At that point, he was shot and killed. His citation properly acknowledged "his complete devotion to his mission and his comrades' well-being."

Another Ninety-sixth soldier, Technical Sergeant Beaufort T. Anderson, fought a medal action five days later. A large Japanese force rushed the 381st Infantry before dawn on the 13th, forcing Anderson's men to seek cover in a tomb. He remained at the entrance, firing fifteen carbine rounds into the mad rush, but had no time to reload. Thinking fast, the Wisconsin NCO picked up a dud mortar round and flung it at the enemy. It exploded, killing several and giving him time to find more shells. Anderson pulled the safety pins, armed the shells by pounding them on a rock, and used them as oversized grenades. Though wounded by shrapnel, he continued tossing shells and firing his carbine until the Japanese withdrew, leaving two dozen corpses behind. Anderson ignored his bleeding wounds to report to his company commander before receiving treatment.

On April 28, PFC Alejandro R. Ruiz's squad from the Twenty-seventh Division was pinned down by a well-camouflaged pillbox. Amid bursting mortar rounds, Ruiz grabbed a BAR and ran to the top of the bunker, dodging constant fire. A Japanese soldier attacked the New Mexican, who turned and fired. His rifle jammed, but he bludgeoned his opponent, then ran back to his squad through more automatic weapons fire. Ruiz grabbed another BAR and again survived a dash across the fire-swept terrain, regaining the top of the pillbox. There, he emptied several magazines through firing ports, silencing all opposition. When the position was taken, it contained twelve dead enemy. His commanding officer considered Ruiz's survival "miraculous" after four dashes through small arms fire and grenades and prolonged exposure atop the pillbox.

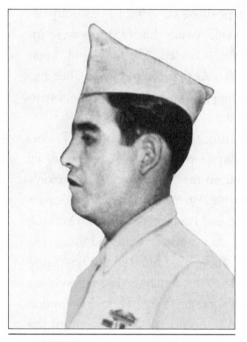

PFC Alejandro R. Ruiz, 27th Division

From April 19–21, PFC Martin O. May of the Seventy-seventh Division fought a three-day action on Ie Shima, off the Okinawa coast. A machine gunner, May fought off successive Japanese efforts to dislodge the Americans from a rugged mountain slope, remaining at his M1919 despite mortar and small arms fire. He even used grenades to break up an enemy attack when mortar explosions reduced visibility with swirling dust and smoke.

On the morning of the third day, a mortar shell badly wounded May and disabled his water-cooled Browning. Nevertheless, the New Jersey soldier remained in the fight, throwing more grenades at charging Japanese until he was wounded again. The second wound proved fatal, but he was credited with killing sixteen Japanese in his final defense.

At least ten Army medics received Medals of Honor during World War II, exemplified by slender PFC Desmond T. Doss of the 307th Infantry Regiment, a veteran of Guam and Leyte. Like many medics, Doss was a conscientious objector, accepting combat duty for the purpose of lifesaving. His medal is unusual in that his actions covered a three-week period in April and May. During that time, the devout Adventist repeatedly risked his life to retrieve wounded men from extreme danger against an enemy that often targeted medics. On April 29 alone, he dealt with seventy-five casualties, taking many of them down the steep, fire-swept slope of Urasoe-Mura one at a time. On other occasions he ventured as much as two hundred yards beyond American lines to bring back injured soldiers; once he treated casualties within a few paces of an enemy-occupied cave. On the night of May 21, he was wounded in a Japanese attack but treated his own injuries, waiting five hours for evacuation. When Japanese tanks attacked, Doss selflessly crawled off his stretcher in favor of a more seriously wounded man. Hit again, he crawled three hundred yards to the aid station. His citation concluded, "His name became a symbol throughout the Seventy-seventh Infantry Division for outstanding gallantry far above and beyond the call of duty."

PFC Desmond T. Doss, 77th Division

Lieutenant Seymour W. Terry of the Ninety-sixth Division became the only Army officer to receive the medal on Okinawa. On May 11, he was leading Company B, 382nd Infantry, in an attack against an enemy line on Zebra Hill, when five well-sited pillboxes halted his advance. In an awesome solo effort, the Arkansas soldier repeatedly braved automatic fire over expanses of a hundred yards, carrying satchel charges and grenades to reduce one position after another. When Japanese emerged to confront him, he methodically shot them down with his rifle, then pressed on to the next pillbox. Later in the day, he led Baker Company against a ridgeline and directed a flanking maneuver. When that tactic met more opposition, he again handled the situation with grenades. Terry's personal example led to seizure of the ridge, but he was killed in a mortar barrage. In addition to the Medal of Honor, Terry was posthumously promoted to captain.

Sergeant Joseph E. Muller of the Seventy-seventh Division directed

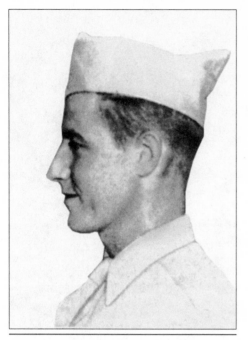

PFC Clarence B. Craft, 96th Division

his men against a defended ridgeline on May 15, taking one position single-handedly. The next morning, following a close-range firefight, he shared a foxhole with two other men, when a Japanese soldier rose up. He had been "playing possum" amid the corpses of his comrades and threw a grenade into the hole. Muller rolled onto the grenade, shielding his friends from the explosion at the cost of his life.

PFC Clarence B. Craft demonstrated that one soldier can make a difference. On May 31, elements of the Ninety-sixth Division had been stalled nearly two weeks against the Japanese line at "Hen Hill." It turned into a grinding, bloody slugfest, with no end in sight. Craft and five others were sent to scout the ground ahead of their company and met heavy fire that wounded three GIs and pinned down the others. Nevertheless, Craft rose to his feet and methodically began killing Japanese wherever he saw movement. His fast, accurate shooting allowed him to advance alone to the crest, where he stood silhouetted against the sky. There he tossed grenades at nearby enemy positions while other GIs formed a human chain to pass boxes of grenades uphill. Subsequently, the lone Californian extended his solo charge downhill, reducing enemy positions and routing more defenders. As if that weren't enough, when he threw a satchel charge into a cave, it failed to explode. He crawled into the cave, relit the fuse, and threw it back in, where it sealed the tomb. Later, he said, "I just kind of saw red when my buddy got hit, and I turned and took off for those damned Japs."

Clarence Craft's initiative had broken a prolonged stalemate around Shuri Castle. Few individual soldiers ever made so great a contribution to winning a battle, but he continued supporting veterans, with 8,500 hours of volunteer work at a VA hospital in Arkansas before he died in 2002.

Sheer determination marked the action of Technical Sergeant John Meagher on June 19. During a Seventy-seventh Division attack, he leapt aboard a Sherman tank to direct the gunner's fire, ignoring 7.7mm rounds banging off the armor. The New Jersey noncom glimpsed a Japanese approaching with an explosive charge, dismounted, and bayoneted the sapper. An explosion then knocked Meagher unconscious and destroyed his rifle, but he shook off the effects, obtained a light machine gun, and advanced on foot. Shooting from the hip, he strode through a crossfire that holed his clothes and, at close range, he killed six enemies in the closest pillbox. Meagher continued his solo assault through more gunfire and grenades, suppressing fire from the next pillbox. Now out of ammo, he reversed the thirty-pound Browning and, swinging it by the barrel, used it as a giant shillelagh to bludgeon the enemy crew to death. His platoon then continued its advance. Meagher died in 1996, age seventy-eight.

The soldiers who earned their Medals of Honor against Japan fought the toughest enemy in American history. Their opponents were among the hardiest soldiers of all time: imbued with a religious devotion to their emperor, whom they believed was a living god. The Japanese Army was characterized by brutal discipline that no Western nation could match—and few would want to.

GIs respected Japanese soldiers' fighting skills, recognizing them as nearly unstoppable on the offensive and fanatical in defense. Many armies speak of fighting to the last man; only Japan's practiced what it preached.

Yet few GIs ever expressed regret about killing "Japs." In pre-combat surveys, far more U.S. soldiers wanted to kill Japanese than Germans, and it had little to do with race. In the years leading up to war, Tokyo's calculated atrocities in China shocked the world: mass murder, rape, and pillage. In the stunning aftermath of Pearl Harbor, continuing outrages such as the Bataan Death March only solidified many Americans' resolve. By 1943, the variety of most Japanese excesses was known: prisoners used for bayonet practice; beheading contests among officers; institutionalized cannibalism. Eventually, the Imperial Army reaped what it had sown; many GIs didn't bother taking prisoners.

Almost sixty years after VJ-Day, a Medal of Honor officer said, "I don't hate the Japanese anymore, but I did then. Time changes that, I guess. But during the war they were 'Japs,' and to me, that wartime bunch will always be Japs." P.F.C. Joe M. Nishimoto

CHAPTER SIX

GERMANY, AGAIN

■

A S of 2003, three-quarters of the Army's World War II Medals of Honor went to soldiers in North Africa, the Mediterranean, and Western Europe. By far the greatest number was bestowed upon the Fifth Army's Third Division, with thirty-eight awards. The "Big Red One" garnered sixteen, while the Thirty-second, Thirty-fourth, and Thirty-sixth all received a dozen or more. In some cases, an accurate divisional count is difficult owing to units being transferred in and out as needed. The 442nd Regimental Combat Team, famous as the Niesi "Go for Broke" unit, alternately served in the Thirty-fourth, Thirty-sixth, Eighty-eighth, and Ninety-second Divisions.

The 442nd received more than 18,000 awards and decorations including 9,486 Purple Hearts and seven Presidential Unit Citations. It received one wartime Medal of Honor and, in 2000, twenty more upgraded DSCs and Silver Stars.

Among infantry regiments the Third Division's units led the list: the Fifteenth Infantry with sixteen, the Thirtieth with eleven, and the Seventh with five. However, attached units with Medals of Honor included the engineers, reconnaissance troop, and 756th Tank Destroyer Battalion.

TUNISIA: FIRST BLOOD

The first Medal of Honor against the Western Axis in the new war was presented to Colonel William H. Wilbur for his efforts to contact Vichy French officials in Morocco on November 8, 1942. After splashing ashore, he made his way sixteen miles through hostile territory, dodging random fire, and delivered his documents to officers in Casablanca. Upon returning to his command, he learned of a Vichy stronghold at Camp de Fedala and pulled together an impromptu command. Combining elements of two units, he led his improvised tank platoon against the Frenchmen, who surrendered after a twenty-minute set-to. With the hostile battery neutralized, the advance could continue.

The Tunisian landscape, often bleak and barren, represented a training arena for the U.S. Army. Generals and privates alike learned necessary lessons at the hands of veteran Germans, then absorbed the knowledge and applied it with growing confidence and power. But first came the blooding against a world-class enemy.

Near Fondouk on April 9, 1943, Private Robert D. Booker served as a Thirty-fourth Division machine gunner. Despite direct fire from enemy machine guns and mortars, the courageous Nebraskan carried his light Browning over two hundred yards of open ground. Ignoring artillery fire called on his position, he silenced one enemy gun and was engaging the second when mortally wounded. He became the first Medal of Honor recipient to die fighting Germany in the Second World War.

Two weeks later, another posthumous award went to Sergeant William L. Nelson of the Ninth Division. The Delaware NCO set up his heavy mortar section northwest of Sedjenane, then proceeded alone to a vantage point to direct fire. His commands stopped a mounting counterattack, but he was mortally stricken. Nevertheless, he crawled forward to a better position, directing additional fire until killed by grenade blasts.

Private Nicholas Minue was the first member of an armored division to receive the medal. Born in Poland, he enlisted in New Jersey and was assigned to the First Armored. On April 28, he found himself facing the same army that had conquered his native land three and a half years before. When his company was held up by automatic fire from one flank, he fixed bayonet and charged. Somehow he survived the gauntlet, closed on the position, and killed as many as ten Germans. He persisted in his solo assault, forcing Germans from dugouts, but was killed in the process.

SICILY

The Allies landed in Sicily under Operation Husky on July 10, 1943. It was the largest amphibious operation to date: 160,000 Allied troops supported by nearly 1,400 ships plus thousands of landing craft. Husky lasted five weeks, costing 19,000 U.S. and British casualties, but it trapped 100,000 Germans.

On the second day ashore, Second Lieutenant Robert Craig voluntarily offered to locate a well-concealed machine gun nest holding up his company in the Third Division. The Scottish-born Craig proceeded alone despite knowledge that three other officers had returned wounded without finding the German position. He low-crawled in the likely direction, snaking his way within thirty-five yards of the nest. At that point, knowing he had been seen, Craig leapt to his feet and ran headlong at the machine gun, firing his M1 carbine at close range. With the three-man crew dead, Craig directed his platoon forward.

Unexpectedly, the GIs collided with as many as a hundred Germans. Outnumbered on a barren slope, Craig immediately ordered his men back to the crest. Again he dashed toward the threat, only stopping within twenty-fire yards of the enemy company. He took a kneeling position and began firing his carbine, drawing the Germans' attention onto himself. His troops rallied at the crest and drove off the enemy, finding Craig's body with five German corpses and three wounded. His sacrifice was credited with saving his platoon from annihilation.

At the end of the month, near Gagliano, Sergeant Gerry H. Kisters was one of ten soldiers of the Second Armored Division filling a crater that blocked vehicles from entering town. It was the sort of job Kisters knew well; the plainspoken GI had been a private for the full eighteen months permitted by law. But now, two German machine guns opened fire, forcing most of the GIs to take cover. However, Kisters and his lieutenant flanked the nearest gun and captured the crew. With suppressing fire aimed against the second machine gun, Kisters crept forward alone, but he was seen by the Germans. They turned on the Indiana soldier, who was hit five times in the right arm and both legs. Nevertheless, he pressed ahead and took the second gun after killing three men and routing a fourth. Kisters recovered and was commissioned, receiving the medal in February. Thus he became the first living recipient fighting the Germans in World War II: the son of German immigrants, no less.

The Third Division collected another medal on July 17, when First Lieutenant David C. Waybur volunteered to take three vehicles into German territory to find an overdue Ranger patrol. That night, his jeeps stopped at a destroyed bridge over a dry streambed. Abruptly, the Americans were surrounded by four Mk IV tanks. Waybur would have been justified in surrendering, but the young Californian determined to fight. He deployed his vehicles and ordered his machine gunners to open fire. In the nocturnal gunfight, three of his men were wounded and Waybur also was hit. Nevertheless, he grabbed a Thompson and fired at the lead tank only thirty yards away. Almost incredibly, he killed the crew and the panzer crashed into the streambed. Waybur's stunning success gave him time to place his men under cover while one soldier ran for help. The besieged GIs kept firing, holding off the Germans until help arrived. Waybur's medal was approved barely three months later.

Another mortar man like Sergeant Nelson in Africa was Private James W. Reese of the First Division. On August 1, his company occupied a position near Mt. Vassillio, which came under heavy enemy pressure. As acting section leader, Reese took his 60mm mortar squad forward to a better position, directing rounds to stop the German advance. But only temporarily. Counterattack was gospel with the German Army, and the assault resumed. The Pennsylvanian told his crew to seek cover while he remained. Somehow, without assistance, he lugged the heavy tube, bipod, and base plate to another position to engage an automatic weapon. With only three rounds remaining, Reese dropped a shell on target and destroyed the gun. Then he scooped up a rifle and took an exposed position permitting him to fire at the remaining Germans. He stood his ground until killed. There was no doubt about his action: the medal was authorized before year end.

ITALY 1943

The Allies wasted little time invading Italy. On September 3, only three weeks after Operation Husky, British forces transited the three-mile Strait of Messina from Sicily to Italy. Just six days after that, Anglo-American troops went ashore in Operation Avalanche on the Gulf of Salerno. It was the beginning of a long slogging march that lasted until the end of the war.

Eventually, the Italian campaign produced more than sixty Medals of Honor. The Third Division received fourteen medals in Italy; the Thirty-fourth got six. The Forty-fifth, Eighty-fifth, and Eighty-eighth received three each.

The first award of the campaign came at Salerno. On September 9, Sergeant James M. Logan's company of the Thirty-sixth Division waded ashore in the first wave and moved almost a half mile inland. There, the advance was stopped at an irrigation canal, opposed by Germans behind a rock wall some two hundred yards away. The enemy, confident of fire superiority from MG.34 and MG.42 machine guns, launched an attack to repel the Americans. Logan ignored 8mm bullets smacking the ground around him and shot the first three Germans rushing through the wall.

With a temporary advantage, the Texan crawled along the base of the rock wall until directly opposite a chattering machine gun. Taking the crew by surprise, the former squirrel hunter popped up, shot both gunners, and hurdled the wall to seize their weapon. He turned the machine gun on other Germans as they fled. Then he smashed the gun on the rocks and pressed ahead, capturing two Germans en route. Later that day, he continued his heroics by single-handedly killing an enemy sniper.

Much later, Logan said, "People always ask me how I dodged all those bullets. I just tell 'em there weren't many bird, squirrel, or rabbit hunters among that bunch we were fighting."

Eleven more Medal of Honor actions were recorded up to the year's end. Five came in the wake of the Salerno landings and five more in November, including three retroactive awards to Niesi soldiers of the 442nd Regimental Combat Team, two posthumously.

The most-reported Medal of Honor action was that of Corporal Charles E. Kelly near Altavilla on September 13. The Thirty-sixth Division rifleman volunteered for two patrols that day, and on the second returned for extra ammunition. At the distribution point, he found Germans attacking the storehouse and held his position through the night. The next morning, he conducted a solo defense using two BARs, hand-armed mortar shells, and a bazooka. In the process, he covered his friends' retreat and eventually rejoined his unit. At twenty-three, "Commando Kelly" became a Pittsburgh icon. A stretch of highway was named in his honor, but he died in a VA hospital in 1985, largely unheralded by his hometown.

Nine days after Kelly's action, Second Lieutenant Ernest Childers made excellent use of the hunting and stalking skills he learned near Broken Arrow, Oklahoma. After his father died, the young Creek provided the family's only meat, learning the philosophy of "one shot, one kill."

Despite a broken instep, Childers took eight men from his Forty-fifth Division platoon up a hill, scouting for German emplacements at Olivetto. His group reached a rock wall, where he deployed his GIs to cover his lone approach across an open field. When two German riflemen fired on him, the experienced hunter dropped both with precision marksmanship, then located the machine gun positions and circled behind them. Attacking alone, he killed the crew of the closest gun but could not draw a bead on the second. Needing a target, he tossed some rocks at the position, prompting two curious Germans to peek over the berm. Childers put a .30-06 round through one man's head while the squad dropped the other. At that point he might have called a halt, but he pressed ahead and, unaided, captured a German forward observer.

Ernest Childers became the first American Indian to receive the Medal of Honor in World War II. He was not the last.

On September 23, another Forty-fifth Division soldier used multiple weapons. Corporal James D. Slaton was scouting ahead of his squad, searching for a way around German defenses. The thirty-year-old Southerner inched his way close enough to a machine gun nest to charge with his bayonet, skewering the gunner. When he was unable to extract the blade, he detached the bayonet from his rifle and shot the next gunner in line. Slaton then was fired upon from his left and scampered across open ground, closing the distance. He tossed two grenades: the first was short; the second was on target. Another machine gun then opened up on Slaton, who coolly shot the crew from a hundred yards away. That evening, his platoon leader finally ordered him to safety out of mortar fire. In killing six enemies at three machine gun positions, Slaton had taken serious pressure off two platoons.

On November 10, Lieutenant Maurice L. Britt of the Third Infantry Division became the first soldier to receive the Medal of Honor in addition to the Distinguished Service Cross and Silver Star. A member of the much-decorated Thirtieth Regiment, he received his medal for a close-range battle near Mignano, Italy. Britt's men were forced onto the defensive by a determined German counterattack of approximately one hundred Wehrmacht troops. The Germans came in firing automatic weapons and throwing grenades. Britt was repeatedly hit: his canteen and binoculars were destroyed; he was shot in the side and suffered grenade fragments to the chest, face, and hands. He shrugged off the medics' attention in order to remain in the fight, emptying his carbine five times and seizing an M1 rifle to kill a machine gun crew. With ammunition running low, the combat descended into a grenade fight. Britt threw an astonishing thirty-two fragmentation grenades in the course of the action. When it ended, he had killed five or more Germans, helped capture four, and permitted some of his men to escape captivity. Britt only stopped for medical attention when ordered by his battalion commander, who credited him with saving Love Company. His medal was authorized four months later.

ITALY 1944

The first medal of the new year went to Sergeant Joe C. Specker of the Forty-eighth Engineer Battalion on January 7. Owing to heavy casualties in the Sixth Armored Division, the battalion was attached as infantry to resume the advance up Mount Porchia. Specker's unit was halted by enemy automatic weapons and sniper fire, but the Missourian gained approval to place one of his own guns to engage the Germans. He took an M1919 and a box of ammo, and proceeded alone. However, he was seen and shot through the legs. Nevertheless, he crawled up the slope, pulling his load as he went. He then set up his gun, spotted the enemy positions, and opened fire. As his company advanced, it was free to maneuver without sustaining further casualties. Specker was found dead at his gun, age twenty-two, and the medal was authorized barely six months later.

Another posthumously decorated machine gunner was Staff Sergeant Thomas E. McCall of the Thirty-sixth Division. Near San Angelo on January 22, the 143rd Infantry was forcing a crossing of the Rapido River in the face of concentrated machine gun and mortar fire. McCall's two gun crews were knocked out of action, with one Browning destroyed. He pulled the wounded to cover, then picked the second gun off its tripod. Firing from the hip, McCall advanced alone on two German nests, killing the enemy gunners in succession. Incredibly, he survived heavy return fire to approach a third position, where he was last seen firing .30 caliber rounds. He was posted missing, presumed dead, and his medal was presented to his parents. Incredibly, McCall survived the war as a prisoner, but he died in 1965, only age forty-nine.

Two Thirty-fourth Division GIs were honored for their actions on February 3. With his platoon pinned down, Second Lieutenant Paul F. Riordan crawled through crossfire to attack a machine gun nest, while PFC Leo J. Powers went for a bunker on the right. Both men had to expose themselves to throw grenades, but Riordan made an amazing toss, landing on target from forty-five yards to destroy the nest. Meanwhile, Powers destroyed three pillboxes or machine gun nests with four grenades, prompting the survivors to surrender to the Montanan, who was now unarmed. The two-man onslaught broke the German line, permitting the 133rd Infantry to continue its advance on Cassino. However, five days later, the twenty-three-year-old officer was cut off from his men and died fighting a solitary battle in town.

On the day Riordan died, a paratrooper survived a seemingly fatal ordeal. Corporal Paul B. Huff of the 509th Parachute Battalion was attached to Darby's Rangers, operating near Carano on February 8. The Tennessean volunteered to take a patrol toward gunfire on his company's right flank, but the scouting party was seen and drew heavy resistance. Huff was already taking fire from three machine guns and a 20mm cannon, when he dashed through a minefield to approach the closest German nest. At that point, he had to crawl seventy-five yards under direct fire, somehow escaping injury. He killed the gunners with his Thompson, then reared up to engage another gun, confirming its position. Huff then returned through the minefield, led his patrol to safety, and guided a stronger group back to the area. The latter sweep killed twenty-seven Germans and captured twenty-one more, losing just three GIs in the process.

At sunset on April 23, PFC John C. Squires was a combat rookie. That changed quickly as he adapted to a variety of enemy weapons. Squires was a runner who realized that his company's attack at Spaccasassi Creek had bogged down near Padiglione. He found that an anti-tank mine had slowed the lead platoon, but the young Kentuckian pressed forward through bursting shells to suggest an alternate route to his platoon leader. Squires then pulled together a disparate group of GIs to hold a position along the creek. With casualties mounting and few NCOs on their feet, he continued directing the defense, twice returning through gunfire and minefields to bring reinforcements in the dark. Squires stood off three German counterattacks, using his Garand, a BAR, and a German MG.42 to good effect. Later, he shifted to the flank, engaging twenty-one Germans with his captured machine gun, forcing their surrender.

The next night, bolstered by thirteen captured MG.42s, Squires' pickup platoon again held fast. The teenager used German "potato masher" grenades as well as his "Spandau," personally killing three more enemy. Squires was promoted to sergeant before he was killed on May 23, four days past his nineteenth birthday.

May of 1944 involved furious combat during the breakout from Anzio to Rome. Fifteen medals were awarded for actions that month, more than the previous four months combined. On the day John Squires was killed, seven soldiers earned the award: three from the Third Division; two from the Thirty-fourth; and one each from the Forty-fifth and First Armored.

The Third Division's soldiers fought a tough battle on May 23.

Oddly, all were privates first class and all used the classic Browning Automatic Rifle. PFC John Dutko (I/30th) used grenades and a BAR to eliminate two enemy machine gun positions and the crew of an 88mm fieldpiece. Despite wounds, he advanced on a third nest, firing his Browning as he went, and fell dead atop the gun he had silenced.

PFC Patrick Kessler (K/30th) was an antitank grenadier who saw five of his friends killed by German machine guns near Ponte Rotto. After organizing covering fire, he ran across open ground, snaking his way to confound the enemy's tracking. He arrived at the lip of the machine gun position, shot two gunners with his '03 rifle, and beat the third into submission. Returning with his prisoner, he saw more GIs shot down and decided to get an automatic weapon for himself. He picked up a BAR and magazines, then braved minefields, artillery shells, and machine guns to neutralize successive machine gun positions, capturing fifteen prisoners in the process. The Ohioan was killed before his medal could be awarded.

PFC Henry Schauer (E/15th) was a superb automatic rifleman. When his patrol was fired upon, the GIs dived for cover, but Schauer left the ditch and spotted five German riflemen in succession. Walking in the open, he killed them with five well-aimed bursts at varying ranges. Subsequently, he ignored gunfire and shell bursts to cut down two machine gun crews with two bursts at some sixty yards. Schauer reloaded, adjusted his sight, and then engaged another machine gun at an estimated five hundred yards. He killed four men with twenty rounds—an incredible piece of shooting. The next morning, despite the presence of enemy armor, Schauer again demonstrated his exceptional skill by killing four more machine gunners with one steady burst. He had killed seventeen Germans in as many hours.

The Thirty-fourth Division men were Technical Sergeant Ernest H. Dervishian and Staff Sergeant George J. Hall, both of the 135th Infantry fighting near the Anzio beachhead.

Near Cisterna, Dervishian and four men spotted a platoon-strength group of Germans along an embankment. The Virginian advanced alone and, firing his carbine, compelled ten to surrender. When his soldiers joined him, they rooted out fifteen more. In later firefights, Dervishian used a German machine gun, grenades, and "Schmeisser" machine pistol in clearing a defended vineyard. Dervishian had personally captured at least twenty-eight enemy soldiers and supervised taking many more. He was later commissioned and, after the war, pursued a law practice like his brother and father.

Hall, like Dervishian, favored enemy weapons. After using four of his own grenades to destroy a machine gun nest, he found a stash of German "potato mashers" and put them to use. He killed five gunners and captured as many more at the next position, then low-crawled toward a third. At that point, the Germans dropped artillery on the area, and a steel shard nearly sliced off Hall's right leg. Since the limb was only hanging by two tendons, Hall completed the amputation and related "I could crawl again after that."

Hall received the Medal of Honor in January 1945 but died thirteen months later.

Technical Sergeant Van T. Barfoot showed exceptional versatility in his action with the Forty-fifth Division. He used grenades and a Thompson submachine gun to take several machine gun positions, single-handedly capturing seventeen Germans in the process. Then he consolidated the position, deploying his men for the next enemy attack. Hearing tanks approaching, he grabbed a bazooka and made a seventy-yard shot on one of three Tigers attacking his position. With a thrown tread, the fifty-six-ton panzer lurched to a stop and the crew bailed out. Barfoot shot three with his "Tommy gun." Faced with unexpected opposition, the other two tanks turned away.

Proceeding alone, Barfoot found an operable German artillery piece and disabled it with a satchel charge. Then he returned to his lines and somehow found the energy to assist two wounded men almost a mile over broken terrain. Barfoot, a Choctaw from Mississippi, was commissioned a lieutenant soon afterward. Remarkably, of four American Indian soldiers awarded the medal in World War II, three were members of the Forty-fifth Division. The previous two were from Oklahoma: Lieutenant Ernest Childers in September 1943; and Lieutenant Jack C. Montgomery, a Cherokee, in February 1944. PFC John Reese, another Oklahoman, received a posthumous award for action in the Philippines in February 1945.

A tanker was the seventh man to receive the medal on May 23. Lieutenant Thomas W. Fowler of the First Armored Division was engaged in a combined-arms attack near Carano when he found two infantry platoons slowed down by mines. The Texan organized the confused soldiers, then began probing his way through the mine belt, scooping the devices out of the ground by hand. Satisfied that he had cleared a path, Fowler led the GIs through seventy-five yards of dangerous ground, then brought up supporting tanks.

With his impromptu command, Fowler continually scouted well ahead of friendly forces, working dismounted to find the best route for his Shermans. Along the way, he captured several Germans, then plugged a growing gap on his right flank. However, the Germans promptly counterattacked and one of his tanks was struck by a panzer's shell. The former Aggie (class of 1943) sprinted through artillery explosions to reach the stricken tankers and remained for thirty minutes, applying first aid. Forced to abandon that effort by more enemy pressure, he treated nine wounded riflemen amid additional shellfire. Fowler was killed only ten days later, leading another armored attack.

Five more men earned medals before the month was out; three from the Thirty-fourth Division and two from the Third. Captain William W. Galt of the former was credited with killing forty Germans while firing the machine gun on a tank destroyer that he commandeered. He was finally killed when an 88mm shell destroyed the vehicle.

In 2000, another Third Division man received a retroactive award as Staff Sergeant Rudolph Davila's Distinguished Service Cross was upgraded along with awards to twenty-one additional Niesi or veterans of Asian extraction. The former machine gunner had been commissioned after his action near Artena on May 28, 1944. "I don't remember being afraid or timid," he said. "It just happened."

Sergeant Christos H. Karaberis was of Greek descent and, like many immigrant families, demonstrated his devotion to his nation. A native of Manchester, New Hampshire, he enlisted in 1942, and by late 1944 he was a thirty-year-old veteran. In the first two days of October 1944, his Eighty-fifth Division company assaulted toward the Casoni di Remagna near Guignola. With his platoon pinned by small arms, automatic weapons, and mortars, he climbed around the Germans' left flank, dodging ricochets off the rocky slope. Karaberis worked into the enemy rear and, with a burst from his Thompson, he surprised eight Germans, whom he subsequently delivered to his squad.

The aggressive GI then returned to work. For the most part single-handedly, he seized four more nests, taking a toll of eight enemy soldiers and twenty-two prisoners. His citation credited him with his battalion's success in opening a gap in the enemy line and occupying a commanding position overlooking the ancient Appian Way.

Subsequently, the New Hampshire soldier anglicized his name to Chris Carr. He remained in the army, served in Korea, and retired as a sergeant first class.

Lieutenant John R. Fox was one of the few artillerymen to receive the medal in World War II. On Christmas Day, the Ninety-second Division forward observer was positioned at Sommocolonnia with much of the 366th Infantry. But during the night, Wehrmacht troops expertly infiltrated the town, and by dawn Sommocolonnia was in enemy hands. Outnumbered, the GIs withdrew, but Fox and his forward observation crew volunteered to remain, calling down defensive fire. From their vantage of a second-story window, they directed artillery rounds progressively closer as the Germans continued advancing. Fox's last call was to fire on his position. When the town was retaken, approximately one hundred enemy bodies were found around the gallant observer's last vantage point, with members of his fire-control party. His Distinguished Service Cross, awarded in 1982, was upgraded along with those of six other black soldiers in 1997.

On April 14, 1945, PFC John D. MacGrath became the only member of the Tenth Mountain Division to earn the Medal of Honor. The Connecticut soldier volunteered to reconnoiter an area containing German machine gun nests holding up his company's advance. Seeing his chance, he dashed at the first enemy position, shooting the five-man crew and capturing their gun. Like many other GIs, he was impressed with the MG.42's 1,200-round-per-minute cyclic rate and picked up the weapon. He used it on two more nests, evading gunfire in open terrain, then circled behind a fourth position. The four-man crew was absorbed in shooting at MacGrath's comrades and probably did not realize the peril until he killed them from behind.

At that point, MacGrath might have withdrawn, but he spotted yet another nest and took it on. The automatic weapons duel continued until two Germans were killed and two wounded, permitting George Company, 85th Infantry, to occupy the ground.

With German artillery now ranging in, MacGrath risked exploding shells to obtain a casualty report. In the process, the courageous, self-taught machine gunner was killed.

Throughout the Italian and southern France campaigns, the 442nd Regimental Combat Team was constantly in combat. Its members, of Japanese ancestry, accepted appalling casualties while earning an unexcelled fighting reputation. The 442nd became a sort of fire brigade, transferred among several divisions wherever the need was greatest.

PFC Sadao Munemori was the first member of the 442nd Regimental Combat Team to receive the Medal of Honor. Near Seravezza on April 5, Company A of the 100th Battalion was pinned down by automatic weapons fire from commanding terrain. With the squad leader wounded, Munemori took the initiative. In a series of solo frontal at-

PFC Sadao Munemori, 442nd RCT

tacks, he destroyed two machine gun nests with hand grenades. The Californian then pulled back through heavy gunfire and enemy grenades, one of which bounced off his helmet. Seeing the "potato masher" rolling toward his friends, Munemori smothered it before detonation, saving two other soldiers from harm.

In July 2000, twenty members of the 442nd received retroactive awards from the Clinton administration. The actions occurred between November 1943 and April 1945 in Italy and France. Nine of the men were killed in action, while four survivors died in the subsequent fifty-five years. The upgrades, mostly of Distinguished Service Crosses, were made because only Munemori had received the Medal of Honor among the 442nd's soldiers. The assumption was that Niesi troops were discriminated against, though as already noted, the "Go for Broke" outfit was the most-decorated regiment of the war. *Stars and Stripes* cartoonist Bill Mauldin spoke for thousands of GIs when he said, "No unit in the army could match them for loyalty, courage, hard work, and sacrifice . . . We were proud to be wearing the same uniform."

The twenty-one Medals of Honor awarded the 442nd exceeded the totals of all but one division (the Third) in the Second World War and easily outmatched any from the First. Notable among the upgraded awards was that of Lieutenant Daniel Inouye, in 2000 a ranking Senate Democrat from Hawaii. The congressional assessment of the discrimination issue was instigated by Daniel Akaka, Hawaii's other Democrat senator, and appended to an appropriation bill.

NORTHWEST EUROPE

From June almost to the end of 1944, more than sixty medals were awarded soldiers fighting in France. The total included those advancing inland from Normandy and those who landed on the Riviera under the Mediterranean Theater of Operations. Twenty-three were killed in action.

The medal count began on D-Day, with three awards for actions on June 6. Two recipients served in the First Infantry Division, landing on bloody Omaha Beach. Private Carlton W. Barrett waded ashore in neck-deep water, surviving concentrated machine gun and mortar fire. Though he reached the dubious safety of the beach, he returned to the cold, blood-spumed water time and again to save other Big Red One men who were wounded or in danger of drowning. The young New Yorker realized that taking casualties to the beach offered only marginal safety, so he towed many GIs to rescue boats standing offshore. Once back on land, he tended more wounded, then carried messages up and down Omaha Beach, where 2,500 GIs were shot down. Barrett's heroism was exceptional: his medal was awarded not for one act, but for dozens during "the longest day." In his CO's words, the private became a leader.

The other Big Red One recipient was a Southerner, First Lieutenant Jimmie W. Monteith. From the moment he splashed ashore, the Virginian brought some order to the noisy, violent chaos, led soldiers across the fire-swept beach, and established a position at the base of the bluff. Then he dashed back to the waterline to guide two Sherman tanks through a minefield and directed their fire against nearby defenses. Next, he led his GIs uphill, establishing a foothold on the heights, which

Pvt. Carlton W. Barrett, 1st Division *1st Lt. Jimmie W. Monteith, 1st Division*

drew a German counterattack. Eventually, the enemy succeeded, surrounding the Americans and pouring gunfire into their position. Monteith was killed, but his efforts led to victory.

West of Omaha Beach was Utah, far less heavily defended. In fact, the Fourth Division took only about one-tenth the casualties inflicted on Omaha. The assistant division commander was a solid veteran, Brigadier General Theodore Roosevelt Jr., son of the former president, cousin of the current one, and a veteran of the First World War, North Africa, and Sicily. Widely admired by his soldiers, Roosevelt was described by another officer as "the most beat-up looking GI you ever saw." "Teddy Junior" recognized that the tide had placed his advance element a mile or more east of the designated spot, but he was unperturbed, saying, "We'll start the war from here." He organized the dispersed GIs and headed inland. However, Roosevelt succumbed to a heart attack five weeks later, age fifty-six. His medal was popular with many men but also was widely regarded as politically inspired, since he did no more than was expected of an assistant division commander, especially against light opposition.

Eight more medals were awarded for subsequent actions in June. On D-Plus Two, Technical Sergeant Frank D. Peregory of the Twenty-ninth Division recorded an epic solo effort, killing eight Germans with grenades and bayonet, and capturing thirty-five more. He was killed six days later.

June 9, D-Plus Three, produced two more awards, including a glider-borne BAR man, PFC Charles N. DeGlopper of the Eighty-second Airborne. Advancing along the Merderet River, DeGlopper's platoon lost contact with its company and was attacked by Wehrmacht troops. The Virginian offered to provide withdrawal support while the troopers pulled back, then he walked in full view of the enemy, firing his Browning. He was hit but continued assault-firing until knocked down, then he emptied another magazine before being killed. DeGlopper was credited with saving the lives of his friends, who later retrieved his body.

Meanwhile, the devout Staff Sergeant Walter D. Ehlers began a two-day spree with the First Division. Already a four-year veteran, including North Africa, the young Kansan led his squad from the point position. On D-Day, he eliminated a German patrol, two machine gun nests, and led a successful attack on a mortar position. The next day, he covered his squad's withdrawal from an untenable position, drawing enemy fire upon himself and sustaining a wound. Nevertheless, he carried his wounded BAR man to safety before returning to fetch the automatic rifle. Only then did he allow a medic to treat him. Subsequently, Ehlers was commissioned but learned that his brother Roland had been killed on June 6.

Months later, Ehlers was wounded in Germany and lost his backpack containing his New Testament. He mourned the loss of the scripture but gave it little thought until about 1955, when his mother received a pack-

Staff Sgt. Walter D. Ehlers, 1st Division

age from a German woman. Her children had found the Bible near her house, and she returned it to the wartime address, assuming it would comfort a bereaved mother after the loss of her son.

Up-front leadership was widespread in Normandy that month. On June 10, Staff Sergeant Arthur F. DeFranzo of the First Divsion was repeatedly wounded in attacks against German defenses but would not be stopped. Alternately firing his M1 and throwing grenades, he enabled his soldiers to advance in the face of automatic crossfire. Unable to continue, he rose up and, with his dying strength, threw a grenade into the last enemy machine gun nest.

Lieutenant Colonel Robert G. Cole was a battalion commander in the 101st Airborne. The aggressive Texan led his paratroopers in a bayonet charge against German positions near Carentan on June 11, seizing a vital bridge across the Douve. Three months later, Cole jumped into Holland in Operation Market Garden, where he was killed by a sniper.

Unusual among all Army awards during the war was Captain Matt Urban's, for action between June 14 and September 3. The Ninth Division officer was cited for events on six days in that period, and despite multiple wounds returned to his battalion in the 60th Infantry. At different times he used a bazooka, directed a tank attack, and ultimately had to whisper orders owing to a throat wound. During that period, he became a lieutenant colonel on his twenty-fifth birthday. His 713-word citation necessarily is one of the longest ever compiled; a typical Army text was less than three hundred words. Perhaps he held another record as well: among his twenty-nine decorations were seven Purple Hearts.

The assault on the Douve featured another Ninth Division award. Second Lieutenant John E. Butts earned his medal in ten days from June 14 to June 23, leading his platoon despite repeated bullet wounds. On the last day, he was shot down again but directed one squad in a flanking move against an automatic weapon while he charged head-on to his death.

The last award in June went to First Lieutenant Carlos C. Ogden

Capt. Matt Urban, 9th Division

as the Seventy-ninth Division approached Cherbourg. The platoon leader took it upon himself to get his company out of trouble while under 88mm artillery and machine gun fire. He grabbed a Garand equipped with a grenade launcher and proceeded alone up the slope toward the German guns. Though an 8mm bullet bounded off his helmet, he fitted a rifle grenade to his M1 and fired one round to knock out the cannon. Though wounded again, the Illinois officer used hand grenades to destroy two machine gun nests.

The first Medal of Honor awarded to a tank formation in France went to Sergeant Hulon B. Whittington of the Second Armored Division's Combat Command B. On July 29, not yet twenty-three, Whittington assumed command of his platoon during a German attack because the lieutenant and platoon sergeant were missing in action. Whittington organized his soldiers on either side of the unit's roadblock

near Grimesnil, coordinating the defense and directing fire when necessary. He climbed on a Sherman and coached the gunner onto an approaching Panther, which was destroyed. With the narrow road
blocked, scores of other enemy vehicles piled up, and Whittington's men
destroyed more with grenades, bazookas, and 75mm tank weapons.
The panzer grenadiers dismounted to continue the attack but were dispersed by a bayonet charge. Whittington then turned to his casualties,
treating as many as possible after his medic had been shot. The young
Louisianan remained in the Army, retiring as a major. He also became
the model for the "G.I. Joe" statue in Washington, D.C., and died in
1969.

Following the breakout from the beachhead, the Allied armies
pressed full ahead. Nearly 50,000 Germans were trapped in the Falaise
Pocket, though for reasons still unexplained, General Omar Bradley's
First Army permitted 35,000 to escape before the encirclement was
complete.

Meanwhile, Operation Anvil Dragoon placed U.S. amphibious
troops ashore on the exotic Riviera, expanding the scope of the Mediterranean theater. The veteran Third Division received two medals that
month, while the Red Bulls of the Thirty-sixth added another.

On "D-Day South," the Third Division's Seventh Infantry landed on
Red Beach at Cape Cavalaire. Sergeant James P. Connor's platoon was
assigned to eliminate fortified positions providing artillery observation
from the peninsula. Approaching the area, a hanging mine detonated,
killing Connor's lieutenant and wounding the Delaware NCO. However, Connor declined first aid and continued advancing with the platoon along the mine-strewn beach. When the senior noncom was killed,
Connor took over, leading the dwindling number of GIs through gunfire
and a heavy mortar barrage. Along the way, he shot two enemy riflemen
but was himself wounded twice more. Nevertheless, though unable to
walk, he directed the final assault on the German position, killing or
capturing nearly fifty Wehrmacht troops.

Two days later, the Seventh Infantry garnered another Medal of Honor when Staff Sergeant Stanley Bender demonstrated that thirty-four was a prime age for a dogface. When Easy Company's advance stalled, Bender climbed atop an immobile tank, ignoring incoming rounds, to spot the German positions. He dismounted, gathered two squads, and led the GIs down a shallow irrigation ditch. Enemy gunfire struck four men, leaving Bender alone as others took cover. But he calmly walked some forty yards through aimed small arms fire, eerily cool among bursting grenades, and destroyed the first of two machine gun nests. Apparently unconcerned, he survived two close-range bursts from another gun and killed its crew. Bender then motioned his soldiers forward to reduce the remainder of the enemy defenses, including two antitank guns. The NCO subsequently led Easy Company into La Lande, seizing three bridges over the Maravenne River and opening a route to advance farther.

Back in northern France, the Falaise Pocket was closing on August 20. The Ninetieth Division was one of those trying to slam the "back door" on the German Fifteenth Army, and a strong enemy effort was made to break out near Chambois. Sergeant John D. Hawk had a light machine gun sited to engage German infantry, separating the soldiers from their armor. However, his position was spotted and received artillery fire that destroyed the M1919 and wounded Hawk. Undaunted, the Westerner obtained a bazooka and, with his loader, fired at the panzers, forcing them to seek protection in a copse. When the Germans launched another effort, Hawk ignored his leg wound to climb a knoll, serving as a human aiming stake for indirect fire from two tank destroyers. The Hellcats, firing from defilade, required verbal orders that Hawk provided by twice running through more explosions. His "forward observation" resulted in two panzers stopped and one repulsed.

Looking back on his combat career, Hawk said, "There are no winners in the game of war, and to call me a 'hero' suggested I had done something more than the people I served with—and that I never could

Sgt. John D. Hawk, 90th Division

accept. To this day, I still talk of 'what happened to me' rather than 'what I did' with regards to the award . . . I consider the medal as not a personal thing, not belonging to me. It is a symbol of honorable service in defense of my country. I hold it in trust for all who have served."

Near Montereau on August 25, the Fifth Medical Battalion, Fifth Division was evacuating casualties to the south shore of the Seine. Private Harold A. Garman, a twenty-six-year-old Illinois soldier, was a stretcher bearer helping transfer casualties from the boats to ambulances. But he saw a boat in midstream take machine gun fire, forcing the GIs into the water except one man unable to move. Garman dashed into the river and struck out for the boat, ignoring bullet impacts to reach the craft. Two other men, nonswimmers, were clinging to the sides, unable to help, so Garman towed the boat to shore. His citation, approved seven months later, lauded his "great courage and heroic devotion to the highest tenets of the Medical Corps."

Eleven medals were earned in September, including five more for the Third Division in the south of France. One went to a sergeant named Harold O. Messerschmidt, whose surname differed only slightly from the German aircraft designer. Whatever ribbing he may have taken from his friends, the Pennsylvanian conducted a desperate fight against the odds. Faced with a strong assault in the Vosges Mountains, his squad held a hillside under persistent small arms fire. The twenty-year-old noncom was knocked off his feet by a burst of gunfire but arose, firing his Thompson at little more than arm's distance. He killed five Germans, shot down several more, and ran out of ammo. With his position now overrun, he swung his weapon as an awkward club, saving another GI from death. Rather than retreat, Messerschmidt continued fighting hand-to-hand before dying, and in the process held his ground until reinforcements arrived.

Before the war, Technician Fifth Grade Robert D. Maxwell of the Third Division yearned to become an aviator, but as he later quipped, "I chickened out and waited to be drafted." Whatever fear he experienced was tempered by his profound trust in God and the Colt Model 1911, most notably near Besancon on September 7. With two other men of the Seventh Infantry he manned an observation post, armed only with pistols to save weight. It was a wholly lopsided fight, as Germans attacked in platoon strength, supported by automatic weapons and even 20mm flak guns. The Wehrmacht troopers sensed an easy mark, pressing to close range with rifles, machine pistols, and grenades. Finally, a German tossed a "potato masher" from ten paces out, and Maxwell leapt upon it, grasping a blanket as his only protection. The observation post was evacuated under heavy pressure, but the critically injured Maxwell survived.

Early in the morning of September 12, Second Lieutenant Almond E. Fisher led his platoon forward to seize a defended hill for the Forty-fifth Division near Gramont. In the dark, the GIs were fired upon from twenty yards, but Fisher closed to twenty feet to kill the enemy gunners with his carbine. Later that night, he destroyed four more positions with the carbine and grenades, then had his men dig in before daybreak. Shortly, the Americans were attacked from three sides as the Germans came on in repeated rushes. Fisher took 9mm wounds in both feet but wriggled from hole to hole, checking on his men and lending encouragement. When the situation stabilized, the New Yorker crawled three hundred yards to an aid station rather than weaken the thinly held line by seeking help to walk.

Pvt. John R. Towle, 82nd Airborne Division

MARKET GARDEN

Private John R. Towle was among the Eighty-second Airborne troopers dropped into Holland during Operation Market Garden that September. Near Oosterhout on the 21st he was a bazooka gunner near the Nijmegen bridgehead facing a company of German infantry with two tanks and a halftrack. Without asking permission, Towle left his company lines and advanced two hundred yards through small arms fire to take advantage of a dike overlooking the enemy advance. Though he realized his rockets could not defeat German armor, he scored two hits on the panzers' side skirts, compelling them to withdraw. By then, the Buckeye was the focus of German attention, but he remained uninjured and took aim on an occupied house. His next projectile removed the threat, killing all nine Germans inside. With ammunition remaining, Towle dashed more than a hundred yards, hunched over to avoid grazing fire, and confronted the halftrack. He was preparing to fire from a kneeling position, when a mortar shell knocked him over; John Towle was mortally wounded but repelled the attack threatening his company's front.

Meanwhile, by mid-September, U.S. forces were closing on Brest, a major objective on France's north coast, and the Twenty-ninth Division was poised to grab the prize. But after two days of strenuous effort, the German lines still held; it was a time for individual initiative. Staff Sergeant Sherwood H. Hallman realized that the crucial position facing his battalion's line had to be reduced, and assigned himself that task. He jumped a hedgerow into a sunken road and launched a solo attack against thirty German infantrymen. Incredibly, he not only won, but survived. With his carbine and grenades, he killed or wounded four Germans and forced a dozen to surrender. As the rest of his company advanced, some seventy more enemy soldiers capitulated. Hallman's battalion commander was thrilled: the Americans advanced two thousand yards nearer Brest, leading to the capture of an outlying fort later that day. The Pennsylvanian demonstrated that there was still a place for the individual rifleman in a global war.

Tragically, Hallman did not have long to savor his achievement. He was killed by a single rifle shot in Brest the next day.

Another determined GI demonstrated comparable resolve at the cost of horrible wounds. At Reichicourt, First Lieutenant James H. Fields of the Fourth Armored Division led his infantry platoon in a counterattack that sustained heavy casualties. The twenty-three-year-old officer left cover to aid a wounded man, when an exploding shell smashed his face. The Texan lost teeth, gums, and his nasal passage but refused evacuation. Concerned that his depleted eleven-man platoon would be left leaderless, he retained command by hand signals. Later, he picked up a light machine gun and provided suppressing fire for his men to advance, finally taking the position. Before being evacuated, Fields drew a tactical map for his battalion commander showing locations of friendly and enemy forces. Fields survived his horrific injuries and entered the oil business after the war but died shortly before his fiftieth birthday.

Another Texan made history on October 7, as Second Lieutenant James L. Harris of the 756th Tank Battalion earned the unit's second medal. Only three weeks had passed since Lieutenant Raymond Zussman had led an action in southern France that resulted in eighteen enemy killed and ninety captured. Now, under cover of night, German armored infantry threatened the battalion command post. Harris Sherman arrived in time to intervene, and he dismounted to scout the situation on foot.

Capt. James M. Burt, 2nd Armored Division

Gunfire erupted in the darkness and Harris fell, shot through the stomach. He managed to crawl back to his M4 but lacked strength to climb aboard. Nevertheless, he passed orders to the crew until his "track" was destroyed by panzers; the high school dropout lost a leg at the hip in the exchange. But despite their advantage, the Germans withdrew, leaving the 756th's command post intact. Even then, Harris refused treatment until one of his tankers was cared for; in the process, the heroic twenty-eight-year-old bled to death.

Near Wurselen, Germany, on October 13, a tanker from Massachusetts logged a notable action. Twenty-seven-year-old Captain James M. Burt of the Second Armored Division had more life experience than most soldiers. During the Depression he received both academic and football scholarships, earning a degree in chemistry and an ROTC commission in the cavalry. Burt was already a veteran of Tunisia and Sicily, but he met his greatest test outside Aachen, Germany. When his supporting infantry was stopped by heavy gunfire, Burt dismounted and personally scouted ahead, showing his Shermans the best firing positions. He climbed atop his command tank to direct the company's movement, accepting better visibility in exchange for exposure to gunfire. Though wounded, over the next two days he repeatedly scouted on foot and survived two tanks being knocked out. At one point, he drove three hundred yards into enemy territory, calling targets for American gunners. Additionally, he rescued wounded men before his own injuries were treated.

Private Wellborn K. Ross of the Third Division survived a five-hour ordeal near St. Jaucques on October 30. That morning, his company had lost fifty-five of its eighty-eight men attacking a dug-in company of *Alpenjaeger*, German mountain troops, who attacked in turn. Ross took his light machine gun ahead of his squad, firing controlled, accurate bursts amid small arms fire and grenade explosions. The Germans were extremely persistent; so was Ross. The twenty-two-year-old gunner remained through seven attacks, and by the eighth his supporting riflemen were out of ammo. Some crawled forward to obtain a few rounds from his own dwindling supply.

At one point, the Germans were within twelve feet of Ross, trying to kill him with grenades. Ross fired his last belt of ammo, and the surviving GIs fixed bayonets for a final stand. At that moment, more ammunition arrived and Ross quickly reloaded. He opened fire again, using his Browning to stop the last German charge at point-blank range. Their strength depleted, the *Alpenjaeger* withdrew, leaving forty or more dead and ten wounded. The Kentuckian stayed at his post through the night into the next morning; he had been on duty for thirty-six hours when relieved.

Two Ninetieth Division men received the medal for actions on November 12. Before daylight, the 359th Infantry was engaged near Kerling, facing determined efforts to prevent a crossing of the Moselle. German armor punched through on the left with heavy infantry support, poised to overrun a platoon led by Technical Sergeant Forrest E. Everhart. He ran nearly a quarter mile, literally dashing to the sound of the guns, to assess the situation. There, he aided the remaining machine gunner in stopping the *panzertruppen* who still persisted. Everhart had two advantages: courage and grenades. For fifteen minutes, he hurled "pineapples" at the Germans, who finally withdrew. Everhart then ran back to his right flank, directing the light machine gun there. In the eerie predawn light, illuminated by bursting mortar rounds, he scooped up handfulls of more grenades that lasted him a half hour. In all, the Germans lost fifty soldiers, most attributed to Everhart's furious grenade barrage.

Later that day, PFC Foster J. Sayers was yet another Pennsylvanian who came to the fore. During an uphill attack near Thionville, he sprinted ahead of Love Company, 357th Infantry, drawing most of the defenders' fire toward himself while the rest of the outfit maneuvered for position. Already within twenty yards of the German line, he picked up his air-cooled Browning and survived the dash through gunfire, somehow avoiding injury. At the lip of the enemy trench, he killed a dozen Germans, then flopped behind a log and fired from the enemy flank. In the process, he was killed while covering Love Company's advance.

The next day, the Thirty-fifth Division's Staff Sergeant Junior J. Spurrier fought a remarkable action at Achain. That afternoon, his company attacked from the east, but Spurrier circled the town alone, approaching from the west. The Kentuckian spent the next few hours using almost every weapon in both armies' inventories. He killed three Germans with his M1, then used a BAR, bazooka, *panzerfaust* rockets, a German submachine gun, and U.S. and enemy grenades. By nightfall, he had eliminated the equivalent of an enemy platoon, capturing two German officers and two soldiers. Yet his citation is one of the shortest of the war: merely eleven lines of text. His citation does not mention that the twenty-two-year-old "one-man army" captured other Germans that night by setting fire to their barn. Small wonder that the erstwhile farmer also was known as "Task Force Spurrier."

On November 20, a battalion commander in the Fourth "Ivy" Division led by example: from the front. Lieutenant Colonel George L. Mabry was no stranger to emergencies. As a boy, he entered the family's burning home to rescue a younger brother; later he ran four hundred yards to provide first aid for a girl who fell from a seesaw. Now, in the tree-splintered Hurtgen Forest, his Second Battalion of the Eighth Infantry was halted by heavy gunfire inside a minefield. Taking the initiative, he found a way out of the field and assisted in disarming visible mines. Later that day, with fixed bayonet, he took a sergeant's job to assault three bunkers ahead of his scouts. Not surprisingly, Mabry's family was fond of noting that he insisted on doing the same work as anyone else—including taking out the trash.

THE BULGE

On December 16, the German Army did something it had seldom done since the eighteenth century: it launched a winter offensive. General George S. Patton, an admirer of Frederick the Great, was aware of that fact and anticipated the possibility. But Eisenhower disagreed and accepted the risk. Consequently, Hitler's generals achieved strategic surprise in the Ardennes, aiming their armored drive toward Antwerp, the Allies' main logistics port. Timed with poor weather, the Wehrmacht assault relied on overwhelming local superiority, unimpeded by Allied airpower.

Three panzer armies struck a sixty-mile front held by just two American corps: original odds were nearly 200,000 Germans versus 83,000 GIs. Hitler committed his first team to the operation. At some points, it was an elite forces Olympics: Waffen SS and Luftwaffe paratroopers against American airborne units.

Seventeen soldiers from eleven divisions received the medal for the Bulge, including three armored units and both airborne divisions. Casualties were heavy: four recipients were killed and one captured.

Sergeant Ralph G. Neppel of the Eighty-third Division heralded the Bulge action. On the night of December 14, his machine gun squad watched the approaches to Birgel, Germany, having slogged its way eastward since D-Plus 13. Now, when a German tank and twenty soldiers attacked, the Iowan held his fire until the enemy was a hundred yards out. Though several Germans went down, the panzer continued unimpeded, firing its 75mm gun from pistol range. The explosion killed

Sgt. Ralph G. Neppel, 83rd Division

Neppel's crew and amputated one of his feet. Nevertheless, he dragged himself to the Browning, picked it up from the snow, and opened fire again. More Germans fell; the panzer stopped and the commander dismounted, Luger in hand. The German strode within a few paces of the crippled American and shot him in the head before the tank backed away, shorn of infantry support.

Ralph Neppel's guardian angel stood duty that night: the 9mm bullet scarred his head, but he survived. Later, both legs were amputated, but Neppel had turned back an enemy armored assault.

On the first day of Hitler's last gamble, Technical Sergeant Vernon McGarity was a Ninety-ninth Division GI near Krinkelt, Belgium. Just turned twenty-three, he was wounded in one of the opening German barrages but hastened back to his company and rescued one of his men. That was just the start.

The next day, the Volunteer State GI was confronted by an armored attack with supporting infantry. McGarity picked up a bazooka, selected a favorable position, and stopped the lead panzer with one rocket. Three other tanks and their grenadiers withdrew under covering fire, and McGarity rescued another soldier.

Subsequently, McGarity went for extra ammunition, encountering a German machine gun crew that had infiltrated American lines. He fired his M1, killing and deterring enemy gunners until his last clip pinged in the air and his Garand locked open. Though completely out of ammunition, the GIs remained in place until the Germans rolled through, capturing the surviving Americans. McGarity's medal was approved twelve months later.

That same day, First Lieutenant Charles P. Murray observed two hundred Germans assaulting his battalion of the Third Division near Kayserberg, France. The enemy poured in mortar, machine gun, and antitank rounds, saturating the area. Nevertheless, Murray crawled ahead of his company's lines to register friendly artillery until his radio failed. At that point he could have withdrawn, but he was a confident marksman. His grandfather had taught him to shoot a .22 rifle, a skill that paid off in combat. "Shooting was almost second nature to me," he said, "and I qualified expert with most weapons available in infantry units."

He proved the point repeatedly, using a Garand, rifle grenades, BAR, and hand grenades to disrupt the German onslaught. He drove off three mortar crews by destroying their truck, then led a patrol to seize a bridge, capturing ten Germans en route. Another enemy threw a grenade that burst close enough to knock Murray down. Though struck by eight fragments, he remained with his company to complete the deployment.

Four recipients served in the Second Division; three of the latter actions occurred on December 17, the second day of the offensive.

Near Krinkelter, the division's Twenty-third Infantry put up a determined resistance. Sergeant Jose M. Lopez carried his Browning heavy machine gun back and forth across the company's front, serving as a one-man fire brigade. The gun and tripod weighed about a hundred pounds, but the determined Texan continually lugged the weapon on his back, going where the need was greatest. Along the way, he was twice stunned by nearby shell explosions, but each time he shrugged off the concussion. Using move-and-shoot tactics, he cut down a hundred or more Germans before firing his last belt. By then, his fellow soldiers had been able to disengage and pull back into town. Lopez had given them time to withdraw, preventing them from being surrounded.

Another machine gunner was PFC Richard E. Cowan, whose company repulsed six frontal attacks, but the seventh effort brought panzers. With perhaps twenty soldiers still effective, Cowan bolstered the thinning U.S. line as Lopez had done, moving as needed. He shot down dozens of enemy infantry but drew retribution in the form of direct fire from a Tiger tank. The 88mm round shook him, but he remained behind his Browning, ignoring German automatic weapons and *panzerfauste* rockets aimed at him. Finally, enemy pressure was too great and the GIs pulled back; Cowan was the last to leave, providing covering fire while ammunition lasted.

That same day, Lieutenant Colonel William McKinley (a grand-nephew of the former president) distributed antitank teams from his battalion of the Ninth Infantry astride the Laudel crossroads. They were attacked by elements of the Twelfth SS Panzer Division, the *Hitler Jugend* that earned an awesome reputation fighting to destruction in Normandy. PFC William A. Soderman was defending a road junction when, in gathering dark, he heard enemy armor approaching. A bazooka man, Soderman's loader had been wounded that day; he was on his own.

Shortly, he could discern five tanks (probably tank destroyers) of *Kampfgruppe Zeiner*. Waiting until the last possible moment, the Connecticut soldier rose and fired at point-blank range. The vehicle lurched to a stop, spewing flames as the crew bailed out.

Being unassisted, Soderman needed extra time to reload and was unable to engage the other four panzers. They clanked past him, leaving King Company alone in the damp, misty darkness.

Just after daybreak, five more tanks approached, supported by panzer grenadiers. Carrying his bazooka, Soderman sprinted along a ditch that offered partial cover. There, he stepped into the road, fully exposed to the German gunners. He leveled his rocket launcher, tripped the firing handle, and sent a 2.5-inch projectile into the lead panzer. It lurched to a halt, blocking the road and preventing the other vehicles from passing. Lacking a way around the crippled vehicle, they gnashed gears and reversed out of danger.

Soderman dashed back toward his position, under fire most of the way. En route, he encountered a German platoon and dropped his bazooka to use his rifle. He killed three and wounded others before rejoining his company.

However, by then, German numbers forced a withdrawal. At the assembly area, Soderman again heard the chilling familiarity of tank treads and realized that

PFC William A. Soderman, 2nd Division

King Company had been caught in the open with enemy armor approaching. With one rocket remaining, he met another tank head-on, disabling the nearest panzer. But tank gunners spotted the lone American and opened fire. Soderman took 8mm bullets in his right shoulder. Wounded, alone, and unarmed, he crawled to a ditch and was evacuated.

Hitler's Ardennes offensive faltered on the courage and determination of soldiers like Bill Soderman, one of only twelve bazooka men to receive the Medal of Honor.

Not everyone was as fortunate as Soderman and his colleagues. On December 19, Tech/4 Truman Kimbro of the Second Division was directing his squad in planting mines at a crossroads near Rocherath, Belgium. German forces arrived, however, preventing completion of the task; the engineers were beaten back. Nevertheless, the Texan returned alone and, nearing the crossroads, was struck by gunfire. Somehow he found the strength to crawl forward and placed his mines at the intersection. When finished, he turned to drag himself to cover but was shot to death by rifles and machine guns. His determination helped slow the dash into Belgium.

On December 21, Corporal Horace M. Thorne led a Ninth Armored patrol to clear Germans from a wooded area near Gruffingen. Supported by Stuart light tanks, Thorne's men disabled a Mark III panzer with its own infantry escort. Thorne used his light machine gun to shoot two Germans abandoning their machine, then he dashed forward to finish off the crippled tank. Meanwhile, his German counterparts opened fire with their own guns. The New Jersey noncom was undeterred; he reached the Mark III and shot two more crewmen, then took a position on the rear deck. From there, he fired at visible enemy nests, knocking down eight more Germans. When his M919 jammed, Thorne stayed in place, trying to clear the malfunction. At that point, he was killed by concentrated gunfire directed at his exposed position.

That same day, Sergeant Francis Currey fought with everything available in the Thirtieth Division's area around Malmedy. Powerful German armor swept past the 120th Infantry's tank destroyers and antitank guns, forcing a retreat. Currey traded his BAR for a bazooka but had to search for rockets and a loader. He and his new partner destroyed one tank at close range, then he scurried back for his Browning to repel German infantry. Throughout the action, he used the bazooka again, rifle grenades, and two machine guns. With the latter, he covered the withdrawal of some wounded GIs, remaining in the fight long enough to see the Germans pull back.

About noon on Christmas Day, Private Paul J. Wiedorfer found himself far from the holiday celebrations he knew in Baltimore. His platoon in the Eightieth Division was pinned down by two German machine guns protected by rifle squads on either flank. Nevertheless, Wiedorfer rose to his feet and ran forward, slipping on the snow-covered ice. Somehow he avoided being hit, and grenaded the nearest machine gun nest, following up with his M1. He immediately turned right, taking the second position from the side. He shot one gunner, compelling six more to raise their hands.

As if that were not enough, that afternoon Wiedorfer's lieutenant and platoon sergeant were wounded. He assumed command, soon being promoted to staff sergeant. Many years later, Wiedorfer mused, "The older I get, the more I think how wonderful it would be if there were no longer a single living holder of the Medal of Honor. That would mean that we finally learned how to live in peace."

The next night, Private James R. Hendrix earned his medal for slaying the enemy and saving lives. The Fourth Armored Division was deployed around Assenois, driving to relieve the 101st Airborne at Bastogne when stopped by heavy artillery fire. The Arkansas trooper left his halftrack, approached the 88mm battery, and used his rifle to capture the crews. Later, he again dismounted to silence two machine gun nests, holding off German reinforcements while wounded GIs were evacuated. Finally, he climbed into a burning halftrack to help a GI trapped there. Despite exploding mines and ammunition, Hendrix pulled the soldier away, then smothered the man's burning clothes.

Near Flamierge on the fourth day of 1945, Staff Sergeant Isadore Jachman tangled with tanks built in his native land. Jachman had been born in Berlin and emigrated with his family to escape persecution as Jews. Like most of his fellow troopers in the Seventeenth Airborne Division, he was new to combat. He had turned twenty-two on December 14.

Baker Company, 513th PIR, was stymied by German artillery, mortar, and small arms fire, when two panzers attacked. The paratroopers took increasing casualties, unable to engage the tanks on equal terms, so Jachman sprinted across open ground to a fallen bazooka man. Both tank crews recognized the danger and concentrated their fire on the lone American, who stood his ground. He stopped one panzer and forced the other to withdraw, but suffered mortal wounds in the process.

Though widespread, the battle focused on the Bastogne crossroads, and there the Sixth Armored Division counterattacked on January 11. Staff Sergeant Archer T. Gammon's platoon was heavily committed that day, fighting through hip-deep snow that favored any defender. When his mechanized unit was shot up by German machine guns, the twenty-six-year-old Virginian slogged through thirty yards of snow to destroy the MG.42 and crew. Hardly had the advance continued through nearby woods, when greater resistance emerged: a Tiger tank supported by infantry and automatic weapons. Again Gammon attacked alone, grenaded the machine gun and shot two enemy riflemen. The panzer backed away, the crew aware that one GI had deprived it of essential infantry support. Whether in fear or in spite, the German gunner expended an 88mm round on Archer Gammon—fatal tribute to the value of one soldier.

The Battle of the Bulge was over by the end of the month, leaving both sides bloodied and the Wehrmacht depleted. The Americans sustained more than 80,000 casualties, including 15,000 captured: the largest number since the surrender of the Philippines. But Germany took as many as 100,000 casualties and some 800 tanks. Neither the men nor matériel could be replaced.

The European war entered its final phase.

INTO GERMANY

During the Battle of the Bulge, the war continued apace in southern France. Six more medals were presented for December actions and another nine through January. Six of the fifteen were posthumous; two examples illustrate the tenacious nature of the fighting.

On January 8, the Third Division's 30th Infantry assaulted Hill 616 near Kayserberg, France. Technical Sergeant Russell E. Dunham wore a mattress cover as camouflage in the snow, but he was laden with twelve carbine magazines (180 rounds) and a dozen grenades. Well ahead of his platoon, he took on three German machine guns—and won. In attacking the first position, he was shot across the back; his friends could track him by the fresh blood seeping through his smock. Knocked down by the blow, Dunham kicked away a German grenade that detonated as he shot two gunners and dragged the third away. The Illinois NCO then grenaded the next position and assaulted the third, shooting flanking riflemen along the way. He got within fifteen yards of the last gunner, who somehow missed, and Dunham destroyed the nest with more grenades. He had emptied eleven of his dozen magazines,

Tech. Sgt. Russell E. Dunham, 3rd Division

retaining about five rounds, and used all but one grenade. He had killed nine Germans and captured others in reducing the three positions alone, fighting an uphill battle.

Dunham characterized his wartime service as "a great adventure" but found greater satisfaction in peacetime. He worked with the Veterans Administration for thirty years, continuing to support his fellow soldiers in quieter battles, but no less desperate.

On January 26, twenty-one-year-old Audie Murphy fought the best known of the Third Division's medal actions. Having received a battlefield commission, Murphy led his company against German forces near Holtzwihr, France, and stayed alone to call artillery fire. As enemy infantry approached from three sides, he climbed atop a burning M10 tank destroyer to man the .50 caliber Browning. Fighting a lopsided battle for nearly an hour, the young Texan shot down as many as fifty enemy, despite incurring a leg wound. He then re-formed his company for a counterattack before accepting treatment. Subsequently, he played himself in the film biography *To Hell and Back*.

At the other end of the age scale, the Eightieth Division's PFC George B. Turner disproved the conventional view that combat is a young man's endeavor. The forty-five-year-old artilleryman was cut off from his battery at Philippsbourg on January 3, but he came across an infantry company pulling back from a German attack. Turner spotted two panzers with some seventy-five troops coming down the main street and grabbed a bazooka. Advancing through small arms and cannon fire, he stood in the street, leveled his rocket launcher, and hit two Mark IVs. One was destroyed, the second disabled. Then he obtained a light machine gun from a halftrack and turned it on the German infantry, which withdrew.

During the American counterattack, Turner used his Browning to cover the crews of two U.S. tanks that had been hit. Turner dropped his gun, sprinted through enemy fire, and tried to rescue the driver from the burning vehicle, but the main gun ammo cooked off. Turner was knocked down, injured, but stayed with the infantry through the following day. Despite his wounds, he drove a truck through more gunfire to evacuate four critical casualties to an aid station.

George Turner, veteran of two world wars, died in 1963, two days past his sixty-fifth birthday.

Two Thirty-sixth Division soldiers were among the last to receive medals for European action. The events occurred within two days of one another in mid-March.

Technical Sergeant Morris E. Crain was a Kentucky-born NCO leading his platoon of the 141st Infantry at the Haguenau bridgehead across the Moder. On March 13, he led his GIs in securing a position near a crossroads, occupying nearby buildings amid heavy German shelling. After dark, enemy armor with supporting panzer grenadiers advanced to dislodge the Americans, shelling the houses repeatedly. Though a noncom, Crain found himself directing two platoons as increasing German pressure drove the dogfaces back. Despite intense, close-range gunfire, Crain sprinted to the building farthest forward to assist five men isolated there. He ordered them out while he covered their retreat with his Thompson. He was seen to drop three Germans in room-to-room fighting before another shell collapsed the roof, destroying the building. Crain saved his men at the cost of his own life.

On March 15, PFC Silvestre Herrera of Phoenix was patrolling with his platoon near Mertzwiller, France, when automatic weapons opened fire. As other men dived for cover, Herrera ran head-on into machine gun fire, somehow reaching the position unharmed. He took eight prisoners and held his ground until the advance resumed. Shortly after, another machine gun raked the area, presenting a greater danger since it was dug in behind a minefield. Again, the slightly built Arizonan went straight for the threat, accepting the danger of hidden mines. As he closed the distance he tripped an antipersonnel mine that destroyed one foot. Nevertheless, he limped forward, returning fire, and stepped on another mine. He sagged to his knees, ignored the terrible pain, and fired into the enemy position. While ducking Herrera's suppressing fire, the Germans failed to note a squad flanking them on the edge of the field.

Silvestre Herrera didn't have to be in Europe. With three young children, he had an easy deferment, but he had accepted induction anyway. Years later, speaking of his Hispanic culture, he said, "We have a tradition. We're supposed to be men, not sissies."

MARCH 1945

Thirteen awards eventually were presented for action during March 1945. On March 19, Staff Sergeant Herbert H. Burr of the Eleventh Armored Division demonstrated his belief in an "offensive defense." Near Dorrmoschel, Germany, his tank was struck by an antitank rocket, wounding the commander while the rest of the crew bailed out. "Doc"

PFC Silvestre Herrera, 36th Division

Burr, normally the bow gunner, already was nominated for the Distinguished Service Cross. Now, he moved into the driver's seat and led two other M4s seeking a way out of town. Rounding a bend, he found himself looking down the muzzle of an 88, the deadliest tank killer in the war. The Missourian didn't hesitate. Accelerating the Sherman for all it was worth, he double-clutched through the gears, racing toward the lethal cannon. The gunners fled just in time, as Burr drove over the mount, grinding it apart. Then he sideswiped a halftrack, reversed course, and headed back the way he had come. Subsequently, he dismounted to lead medics through gunfire to fetch the wounded platoon sergeant.

Though latecomers to combat, the Seventeenth Division garnered four Medals of Honor: more than any other airborne division in the war. The last three occurred between March 24–28; all posthumously presented for Operation Varsity, the drop north of the Ruhr.

Private George J. Peters jumped near Fluren with the 507th PIR but met immediate opposition. With his unit pinned down by machine gun fire in the drop zone, Peters charged an machine gun nest and was twice knocked down by automatic weapons fire. Despite mortal wounds, he crawled close enough to destroy one nest with grenades and drive enemy riflemen from their positions.

That same day, PFC Stuart S. Stryker of the 513th took charge of a desperate situation nearby at Wesel. His company came under extremely heavy artillery and small arms fire some two hundred yards from a large building with four cannon plus machine guns. Stryker recognized that the troopers would likely be killed if they remained in the open, so he got to his feet and, with only his carbine, called for the GIs to follow him. His group's dash into the teeth of the defense occupied the defenders and permitted other paratroopers to flank the position. The twenty-year-old Oregonian was killed within yards of his objective but was instrumental in the capture of some two hundred Germans and rescue of three fliers held there.

Technical Sergeant Clinton M. Hedrick was a twenty-six-year-old noncom fighting near Lembeck on March 27–28. Hedrick's company was assigned to assault Lembeck town and castle, and the West Virginian used his BAR to advance his men through automatic weapons fire. The next day, he and four troopers crossed the drawbridge into the castle, where they encountered a self-propelled gun, which opened fire. Hedrick was fatally wounded but continued firing long enough for his friends to escape.

The last three medals awarded in Europe went to Third Division soldiers on April 17–18, all from the much-decorated 15th Infantry.

Private Joseph F. Merrell was a New Yorker confronted with the last roadblock before Nuremberg, with his company pinned down by heavy gunfire. Merrell ran a hundred yards across open terrain, taking the fight to four Germans blazing away with machine pistols. The 9mm rounds ripped his clothes, but he killed all four with his Garand. Almost immediately, his M1 was struck by a rifle bullet, but he made a broken-field run of two hundred yards to drop two grenades into the machine gun nest. Instantly, he was on his feet after they exploded, seizing a Luger to finish the surviving gunners. He then destroyed another nest despite two critical wounds. He had killed twenty-three opponents before an MP40 submachine gun ended his spectacular feat and his life.

First Lieutenant Frank Burke was a twenty-six-year-old Easterner who survived the vicious street fighting in Nuremberg. As a prewar site of spectacular Nazi Party pageants, the city was bitterly defended.

■ Quotations

"Having the Medal of Honor has meant a lot to me, although it's hard to live up to it. I don't want anything to tarnish or hurt the medal's reputation, so I must always watch what I do or say, requiring me to live at a higher level than most."

—Oscar G. Johnson (Italy 1944)

"I volunteered for the paratroopers because a girlfriend asked if I would write her a letter on the way down. That was the lady I married!"

—Melvin E. Biddle (Belgium, 1944)

"In life, as in war, no one knows what he or she is capable of doing at a given moment. You rise to the occasion."

—Nicholas Oresko (Germany 1945)

Though assigned as battalion transport officer, Burke demonstrated exceptional skill with a variety of infantry weapons in a four-hour shooting spree. He used a light machine gun to break up an attack on the U.S. lines and killed an enemy gun crew. Then he used a Garand to slay a German sharpshooter in a cellar shootout. Next, he won a grenade duel, retrieved his M1 to kill four more opponents, and rejoined the GIs behind him. He helped a platoon repel a half-hour attack, then joined a group of GIs in destroying a 20mm cannon. In addition to group combat, he was credited with killing eleven enemy soldiers and capturing three single-handedly.

Lieutenant Michael J. Daly and other Third Division men reached Nuremberg the next day. There, Daly picked his way through the rubble, reducing one position after another. He killed a three-man machine gun crew, then shot down all six members of an antitank team. He picked off a machine gunner, directed his troops in finishing the nest, and finally closed on another position to kill the crew from only ten yards away. Daly's medal was approved in September 1945.

There was a postwar reckoning as new Medal of Honor men received their awards in the months after victory. Among other occasions, President Truman presented twenty-seven medals in two ceremonies during October 1945. At both events, he said, "I told these young men that I would rather have that medal around my neck than to be president of the United States. It is the greatest honor that can come to a man. It is an honor that all of us strive for, but very few of us ever achieve."

CHAPTER SEVEN

KOREA

■

A MERICA was caught off guard by the North Korean invasion of the South on June 25, 1950. Following its two-ocean victory only five years before, the United States had allowed its military to wither with astonishing speed. Beset by penurious budgets and inter-service feuds, the new Department of Defense was run by service politicians and political appointees generally unconcerned with war fighting. Furthermore, the Truman administration had virtually assured Communist aggression by stating that South Korea lay outside America's sphere of interest.

Rather than meeting force with force, the initial U.S. response was necessarily limited: lead elements of the Twenty-fourth Division arrived from Japan on July 1; Major General William F. Dean followed two days later. The "Tropic Lightnings" were in combat almost immediately, and the first Medal of Honor actions occurred later that month.

On July 20, a company of the Third Engineer Combat Battalion attempted to break through Communist lines at Taejon. When fired upon, Sergeant George D. Libby was the only man in his truck not killed or

Sgt. George D. Libby, 3rd Engineer Battalion

Maj. Gen William F. Dean, 24th Division

wounded. He flopped into a ditch, alternately returning fire and sprinting across the road to help casualties to cover. When an artillery tractor approached, Libby flagged it down and informed the driver that wounded men needed rescuing. Libby sat on the engaged side, shielding the driver from persistent enemy gunfire, taking repeated hits. Nevertheless, he refused treatment and provided covering fire whenever the tractor stopped to load casualties. By the time the vehicle reached safety, the thirty-year-old Maine soldier was beyond help. His self-sacrifice was undeniable; his medal was approved in three weeks.

Meanwhile, Libby's division commander made his own mark. Major General William F. Dean had assumed command of the Twenty-fourth in October 1949. He had been commissioned in the California National Guard in 1921 and commanded the Forty-fourth Division in Europe during 1944–45. Now he entered his second war not quite fifty-one years old. However, only 15 percent of his soldiers had seen combat in World War II.

At Taejon on July 20–21, Dean demoted himself from division commander to squad leader. Keenly aware of his troops' inexperience, facing massive opposition, he scurried from one crisis to another, leading, demonstrating, encouraging. With his aide and interpreter, he went tank hunting in city streets. He personally destroyed a T-34 tank with a grenade, then took up a bazooka. The division had 3.5-inch rockets that were more effective than the original 2.36-inch projectiles, and Dean set his tank-killer teams to work. He also directed tank fire from exposed positions, sustaining a broken shoulder in the process.

On July 20, Dean became isolated from his troops, who reported he was last seen carrying a wounded man. As it developed, in the dark he slipped down an embankment, hit his head, and passed out. He spent the next five weeks wandering alone, trying to rejoin his far-flung command. On August 25, he collided with a North Korean detachment and was captured on the short end of fifteen-to-one odds. In captivity, he attempted suicide to prevent extortion.

Dean was repatriated in September 1953, astonished to learn he had received the Medal of Honor in February 1951. Though pleased, he was uneasy with the acclaim he received. A deeply introspective man, Dean carried no illusions about his selection for the medal. In part, he said, "There were heroes in Korea, but I was not one of them. There were brilliant commanders, but I was a general captured because he took a wrong road. I am an infantry officer and presumably was fitted for my fighting job."

Three other Army POWs also received the medal, including Corporal Hiroshi Miyamura of the Third Division. Near Taejon-ni, the New Mexico machine gunner used his Browning and bayonet to kill as many as fifty enemy while covering his company's withdrawal. Myamura was unconscious when taken in April 1951 and, like General Dean, was repatriated in 1953. Almost forty years later, Miyamura said, "I believe if we have faith in God and live by His rules, He will not let us down. That same faith is what made this country the greatest country in all the world."

Near Sokkogae in November 1951, Lieutenant James L. Stone and a half dozen First Cavalry troopers fought a rearguard action. He repaired a flamethrower while under fire, used a light machine gun and finally a carbine before his position was abandoned. Stone was too badly wounded to be evacuated and was captured. Stone and Miyamura received their decorations from President Eisenhower in October 1953.

Sergeant First Class Ray Duke of the Tropic Lightnings was captured in circumstances similar to Stone. Holding back Chinese attackers so other soldiers could escape, Duke was critically injured in April 1951. He received typical Communist treatment: no medical care, little food, and repeated torture. Nevertheless, he refused to part with worthwhile information and died after seven months in captivity. His well-deserved medal was awarded in March 1954.

Meanwhile, reinforcements were en route. The advance section of the Twenty-fifth Division arrived in Korea on July 10, and the First Cavalry landed a week later. The new units were almost immediately committed to combat.

On the night of August 6, the Twenty-fourth Infantry Regiment, Twenty-fifth Division, was attacked by swarms of North Koreans near Haman. PFC William Thompson responded to the surprise attack by setting his machine gun astride the enemy's advance and opened fire. The Communist troops halted long enough for the New Yorker's platoon to pull back. He refused to withdraw, sustaining multiple grenade and gunshot wounds until killed by another grenade blast.

Thirty-one-year-old Master Sergeant Melvin O. Handrich of the Twenty-fourth Division brought "untold glory upon himself" August 25–26. That night as many as a hundred enemy soldiers infiltrated the lines of Charlie Company, Fifth Infantry, and Handrich left his position to direct mortar and artillery fire. He remained there for eight hours,

■ *The Korean War*

At the end of World War II, the Allied powers divided the Korean peninsula at the 38th parallel. The former Japanese colony was separated into the Communist-dominated north and the approximately democratic South, to no one's satisfaction. While Pyongyang's despotic dictator Kim Il Sung planned a coercive reunification, President Harry S Truman's secretary of state committed an egregious error. Dean Acheson stated publicly that Korea lay beyond America's area of interest: a clear invitation to aggression. The invitation was soon accepted.

On the morning of June 25, 1950, the North Korean army displaced southward. In less than five years, the "Democratic Republic" had turned itself into a paragon of Marxist virtue, while Seoul's government contented itself with minimal preparation. Nor was the U.S. position much better. The American army of occupation in Japan had, with few exceptions, gone soft. The ennui common to garrison duty had combined with the Truman administration's miserly defense budgets to reduce combat readiness in the Far East. Washington's attention, such as it was, faced toward Europe, not Asia.

The Communist steamroller swept south, all but driving the last allied forces off the peninsula. But the Soviet Union committed its own error by boycotting a United Nations meeting, allowing a vote to support Seoul. Subsequently, fifteen other nations sent troops to Korea and five more provided medical detachments.

Tactically, the Korean War pitted allied firepower and technology against Communist manpower and logistics. Strategically, the United Nations lashed one fist behind its back, refusing to attack enemy bases north of the Yalu River for "fear" of inviting a Chinese response. Incredibly, the policy remained in effect after the Peoples' Republic committed nearly a quarter million troops.

Following stunning losses, the U.S. command under General of the Armies Douglas MacArthur reversed the Korean debacle at one stroke. In September, his semi-impossible amphibious landing at Inchon turned the tide almost overnight. By November, U.S. Army and Marine divisions neared the Yalu, but then the vainglorious Medal of Honor recipient committed his own sin. Arrogantly confident that China would not come to North Korea's aid, MacArthur ignored both overt and tactic warnings and found himself facing 200,000 Communist Chinese "volunteers."

It was a grim, brutal holiday season as, in appalling weather, the Americans retreated southward for the second time in six months. Fortunately, however, Communist supply lines played out along the 38th parallel, and there the war bogged down. MacArthur was relieved of command in April 1951, replaced by General Matthew Ridgway, who fought the Chinese and North Koreans to a standstill. After prolonged, erratic negotiations, an armistice was effected on July 27, 1953.

For decades, the Pentagon bean counters misrepresented the human cost of the Korean "conflict." (Being undeclared by the Senate, it was not a war.) The numbers change frequently, but in the 1990s, the previous figure of some 55,000 American dead was revised to 36,500, though hundreds of POWs have never been accounted for, as the Eisenhower administration was unwilling to pursue the matter. Army casualties included at least 24,957 dead and missing, plus 77,600 wounded among the 2,834,000 soldiers who served in Korea.

More than half a century later, Korea remains a source of tension in the world. Yet consecutive U.S. administrations continue sending fuel, food, and nuclear technology to the most radical Marxist regime left on the planet—evidence of successful extortion from the puppet masters in Pyongyang.

dropping mortar shells within fifty feet of himself to hold back the enemy. After dawn, the Communists tried again, bringing heavy pressure on Charlie's line. Handrich scrambled across the fire-swept terrain, reorganized the GIs, and again called indirect fire. Though severely wounded, he insisted on remaining to coordinate the defense and was killed when the Communists finally overran his position. The New Yorker's medal was authorized twelve months later.

Three men of the Second Infantry Division received medals for the period August 31–September 3, in an action called the Second Battle of the Nakong Bulge.

Near Tongsan, Master Sergeant Travis E. Watkins and PFC Joseph R. Oullette fought with Hotel Company, Ninth Infantry. Fighting in his second war, Watkins led a cut-off platoon in establishing a perimeter amid the encircling Communists, directing the defense until ammo ran low. At that point, he shot two enemy soldiers within fifty yards of the line and scrambled to retrieve their weapons. Before he could return, he was beset by three others who wounded him, but the Southerner killed all three and returned with five guns. During a later assault, Watkins exposed himself to kill some grenadiers and was shot, but kept firing, killing six of the enemy. Then he collapsed, unable to move. He declined food in deference to his soldiers, ordered them to leave while they could, and wished them good luck. He was buried in Gladewater, Texas.

Oullette, a Yankee from Massachusetts, emulated Watkins in risking death or capture to retrieve enemy weapons. In the process, he killed a Communist in hand-to-hand combat, adding more ordnance to the supply. He also made a vain attempt to obtain water from air drop zones, crossing enemy terrain in the process. On September 3, the Communists made a headlong rush behind a grenade barrage; Oullette scrambled from six foxholes to escape the explosions and accepted the danger of gunfire. Badly wounded, he continued fighting until he collapsed. Twenty-two GIs survived to tell the tale; Watkins' and Oulette's posthumous awards were approved in 1951.

Near Agok, some five hundred enemy troops launched yet another midnight attack, forcing an American withdrawal. The Communists destroyed one tank, swarmed over two others, and repelled another one. Sergeant First Class Ernest Kouma of the Seventy-second Tank Battalion found that his M4A3 Sherman was the only vehicle in the enemy's path, and he stood fast. He directed the fire of his crew throughout the night, surviving an incredible nine hours of close-quarter combat. When he expended the ammunition of the turret-mounted .50-caliber machine gun, he drew his Colt and

SFC Ernest Kouma, 72nd Tank Battalion

threw grenades at the enemy. Finally, wounded and with no other option, he directed the tank through eight miles of hostile territory, destroying three machine gun nests en route. At the end of the action, he was credited with killing as many as 250 Communist troops. The Wisconsin NCO was the only Medal of Honor recipient in the first four months of the war who was not killed or captured.

During September, nine Medals of Honor were awarded to soldiers; a record for the Korean War. All were posthumous. Five went to the Second Division, including four on the first day of the month. In separate actions at Am-Dong and Agok, Lieutenant Frederick F. Henry and PFC Luther Story were badly wounded but stood off more attackers, enabling other "Indian Head" soldiers to escape.

Sergeant First Class Charles W. Turner of the division's recon company directed tank fire that destroyed seven enemy automatic weapons,

1st Lt. Frederick F. Henry, 2nd Division

remaining on the rear deck of a tank for better visibility and firing the .50 Browning until killed. Meanwhile, Kentucky PFC David M. Smith absorbed a grenade blast to protect his comrades. He was the first of eight GIs who received the medal for such selfless acts in Korea.

From the infantryman's perspective, Korea was World War I with hills. Trenches snaked along the peninsula's mountain ranges, where short, sharp fights contested control of ridgelines and hilltops. Though artillery and aircraft were important allied assets, much infantry combat was at muzzle-contact range, in brutal nocturnal clashes. Most shooting was done at ranges under 150 yards; bayonets were used more often in Korea than in the Great War.

On September 4, the first cavalry medal went to PFC Melvin Brown of the engineers. Brown's platoon advanced to the walled city near Kasan, where he scaled a fifty-foot wall to fire into the defenses. When his Garand was emptied, he used his grenades, then other GIs tossed theirs up to him. The Pennsylvanian remained in position, drew his entrenching tool, and successively clubbed ten or more North Koreans as they raised their heads over the wall. Brown was reported MIA the next day.

That night, Sergeant First Class Loren R. Kaufman's Ninth Infantry platoon provided flank protection, when Company G was hit by a Communist battalion. In a series of firefights for control of a ridgeline the twenty-seven-year-old Oregonian used his rifle, bayonet, and grenades

■ *Korean War MoHs*

Seventy-eight soldiers have received the Medal of Honor for Korean War action; two-thirds were posthumous. Of the eight Army divisions committed to the conflict, the Second "Indian Head" Division led with eighteen awards, followed by the Twenty-fifth "Tropic Lightning" with thirteen, the "Bayonets" of the Seventh garnered twelve, while the old-timers, the Third "Rock of the Marne" Division, received eleven.

Casualties were massive: in the first six months of hostilities, twenty-one of the twenty-four medals were posthumous, and General Dean was captured. Even after the front stabilized, nearly half the medal recipients were killed during 1951; the rate was maintained throughout 1952 and even increased in the seven months of 1953.

Overall, two-thirds of the Army's Medal of Honors in Korea were awarded to dead soldiers.

The "fightingest" regiments were the Seventh Infantry (Third Division) with eight medals, the Ninth (Second Division) with seven, and the Seventeenth (Seventh Division) and Twenty-seventh (Twenty-fifth Division) with six. Five each went to the Twenty-third (Second Division) and Twenty-seventh (Twenty-fifth Division).

Medal of Honor recipients filled almost every grade from private to major general. Twelve of the nineteen officers were lieutenants, while thirty-nine NCOs received the Medal of Honor. Thirteen of the noncoms were senior NCOs: three master sergeants and ten sergeants first class. Twenty enlisted men completed the tally, though only two were "slick sleeve" privates.

---

to kill enemy scouts and seize machine gun positions. At one point, he turned a Communist weapon on its former owners, and later led an attack that destroyed a mortar position. When the enemy retreated into a village, Kaufman led a patrol to town, routed the defenders and burned the buildings. Kaufman survived that night but did not live to receive his medal; he was killed five months later.

A Tropic Lightning hero was Sergeant William R. Jecelen, leading his platoon to secure a ridge on September 19. Taking heavy fire at the base of the hill, the Marylander realized the only way to gain the crest was straight ahead. The GIs fixed bayonets, gathered their nerve, and dashed uphill, running through antitank fire to reach the Communist lines. There, the soldiers stabbed, shot, and bludgeoned their way toward the crest. When a grenade rolled into their midst, Jecelen leapt on it to save his men. The survivors killed or drove off the reds.

On the same day, in the Twenty-seventh Infantry's sector, Corporal John W. Collier raced ahead of his squad to destroy a machine gun position. Upon rejoining his friends, a grenade rolled into the group. The

PFC Robert H. Young, 1st Cavalry Division

young Kentuckian flopped onto the ground, smothering the blast with his body and sacrificing himself in the process.

PFC Robert H. Young was a twenty-one-year-old cavalryman from California. North of Kaesong on October 9, Company E of the Eighth was leading the squadron advance under extremely heavy mortar and machine gun fire. Though hit in the face and shoulder, Young returned fire until hit again. Awaiting treatment at the aid station, he spotted Communist infiltrators and shot down five despite being shot himself. Still untreated, he left the medics to direct tank fire, took hits from a mortar shell, and assisted other casualties before being evacuated. He died three weeks later.

On October 12, Lieutenant Samuel S. Coursen of the Fifth Cavalry leapt into an enemy trench to save one of his wounded men from several Koreans. In the close confines of the dugout, the New Jersey officer used his rifle butt in a vicious brawl, killing seven Communist soldiers before he was overwhelmed.

That month, the 187th Airborne Regimental Combat Team arrived in Korea. On October 21, PFC Richard G. Wilson's company walked into a narrow valley where the enemy lay in wait. Mortars, machine guns, and small arms opened fire, knocking down troopers on all sides. Wilson, an aid man in Item Company, immediately began tending the wounded, but the Communist pressure was too heavy. As the company began to withdraw to prevent being encircled, Wilson realized that a wounded GI had been left behind and headed back for him. His friends called for him to return, but Wilson disappeared. Two days later, a patrol found his body with the man he had shielded. He was the first of three medics awarded the medal in Korea; two were posthumous.

While soldiers were fighting, freezing, and dying, the geopoliticians were playing their own game. As Allied forces pressed closer to the Yalu River, dividing North Korea from Manchuria, Peking's threats went largely unheeded. The first indication of Chinese activity occurred north of Unsan on October 25, when South Korean forces captured Chinese soldiers. A week later, GIs clashed with Communist Chinese forces (CCF). More was to come.

On November 5, Corporal Mitchell Red Cloud was a Victory Division BAR man on the crest of a ridge, guarding his company command post. He spotted several Chinese approaching through heavy brush perhaps thirty yards away and opened fire. His first bursts chopped down several Communists, alerting the company of its peril. While a response was formed, the Winnebago soldier continued firing from his exposed position but was shot in return. Nevertheless, he refused help and pulled himself erect. Holding to a tree for support, firing one-handed, he continued shooting until mortally wounded.

Sergeant John A. Pittman of the Second Division beat the odds on November 26. The Mississippian volunteered to lead a counterattack to regain lost ground and was advancing against mortar and small arms fire, but the greatest threat came from a grenade. He smothered the enemy ordnance with his body and, though grievously wounded, he asked whether anyone else were hurt. He recovered to receive the medal in 1951, only the third surviving recipient among two dozen citations in the first six months of hostilities.

The next day, Captain Reginald B. Desiderio of the Twenty-fifth Division placed his company as security for a task force command post near Ipsok. Scouting forward in the dark, he ignored enemy gunfire to disperse his men but was wounded shortly thereafter. As with so many other Medal of Honor men, he declined treatment to concentrate on the tactical situation. Even though wounded again, he wielded a rifle, carbine, and grenades to blunt the next Communist attack until fatally shot.

On November 27, the roof fell in. Massive Communist attacks were launched against X Corps units near Chosin Reservoir, leading to the enduring legend of the "Frozen Chosin."

Among the units trying to stem the Communist tide was Task Force MacLean under Colonel Allan D. MacLean. He had three battalions of the Thirty-first and Thirty-second Regiments plus a tank company, a field artillery battalion, and eight antiaircraft vehicles: in all, some 3,200 men, including 700 South Koreans. On November 26, 1/32 relieved the Fifth Marines east of the Chosin Reservoir, but the next night the Communist Eightieth Division swarmed out of the dark, blowing bugles and screaming war cries. In the confusion, MacLean rushed forward, trying to stop what he thought was friendly fire; he was shot and dragged away, dying of his wounds in captivity.

Lieutenant Colonel Don C. Faith Jr., took over immediately. Unlike MacLean, he had combat experience: he had jumped into Normandy with the Eighty-second and was well regarded by General Matthew Ridgway. However, there was no stopping the Chinese avalanche rolling out of Manchuria; it buried everything in its path.

Faith directed a fighting withdrawal toward the frozen reservoir, leading local counterattacks when necessary. He personally scouted the best route, directing movement of his remaining vehicles over the Chosin's eighteen-inch-thick ice. Once his command was across, he joined his men on the far side and resumed his place at the head of the column. On the fifth day, December 1, his command element was stopped by a Communist roadblock on a narrow, winding path. He dismounted, organized a reaction force, and led from the front, throwing grenades and firing his pistol until mortally wounded. The roadblock was overcome, and Task Force Faith reached safety. However, barely

1,000 Americans and South Koreans survived the frozen horror, and of those, just 385 were rated combat effective.

Don Faith's body was never recovered, but Brigadier General Donald C. Faith, who died in 1961, arranged for a tribute to be inscribed on his own Arlington headstone in memory of his son.

In the same time period as Faith's action, an artillery officer died while doing more than expected of him. Lieutenant Colonel John U. D. Page of X Corps was a Philippine-born veteran, forty-six years old, but new to war. He had spent World War II training troops

Lt. Col. Don C. Faith, Jr., 32nd Infantry

in the United States. Having effected liaison with the First Marine Division near the Chosin Reservoir, he remained to help where possible, receiving a Navy Cross in the process. He rescued his driver from an ambush, then reached the Marine outpost near Koto-ri. There, the bespectacled Princeton graduate prepared a reserve force of soldiers trapped with the leathernecks, and repeatedly sought combat. He ignored Communist gunfire to call artillery on enemy troops, manned a machine gun atop a tank, and even flew a "strafing" mission in a liaison aircraft, dropping grenades and firing his M2 carbine from low level.

As the casualty-laden column made its way southward, Page was alternately at the tail, providing cover, or at the head, engaging blocking forces. On the night of December 10, another Chinese unit had worked its way into the American rear, firing from three sides. Page again pushed his way to the fight and led the counterattack, disrupting enemy

■ Korean War Weapons

Because the Korean War erupted less than five years after VJ-Day, the infantry weapons were nearly identical to those of World War II. The M1 Garand was the standard rifle, though some M1903 Springfields remained as sniper weapons. Carbines proliferated in Korea, still valued for their light weight and portability, but the anemic .30-caliber round led to development of the M2 model with full automatic capability.

Browning-designed machine guns were holdovers from World War II: the water-cooled M1917 heavy .30 caliber type plus the lighter M1919 air-cooled model. The heavy M2 .50 caliber was, if anything, more valued in Korea than World War II because of its exceptional range in mountain combat.

Sidearms remained the legendary M1911 .45 pistol and assorted revolvers.

Mortars and artillery were nearly all of the type used in Europe and the Pacific, though some new tanks appeared. However, armored combat was almost nonexistent in Korea, and tanks served largely in infantry support roles.

Fighting in Korea often was at night and therefore at close range. The statistics prove the point: grenades were by far the most used weapon, being employed in 60 percent of Medal of Honor actions. The bayonet was used proportionately more in Korea than previously: 19 percent versus 10 and 4 percent, respectively, in World War I, and II.

---

cohesion. His last words to a subordinate were, "Get back, that's an order. I'll cover you." Shortly thereafter, his body was found amid sixteen dead Chinese. His medal was authorized in 1957.

1951

The first medal of the new year went to Sergeant First Class Junior D. Edwards for action on January 2. His Second Division platoon was pushed out of its defensive position near Changbong-ni, exposing the GIs to fire from a machine gun on higher ground. The Iowan rushed the nest alone, throwing grenades that forced the gunners to retreat. However, they returned and opened fire again, requiring Edwards to grab more "pineapples" and attack once more. This time, he killed the enemy crew. Nevertheless, another Chinese gun opened fire, but the Buckeye noncom was just as persistent. He made a third solo charge across exposed terrain, killing the crew but sustaining mortal wounds in the process. His medal was approved a year later.

First Lieutenant Robert M. McGovern led his cavalry troopers against enemy bunkers on January 30. Though wounded early in the action, he insisted he could continue to fight and crawled up a rocky slope to reach the Chinese lines. The defenders rolled a deluge of grenades downhill, halting the U.S. advance. But McGovern pressed ahead until his carbine was shot from his hands a dozen paces from the bunker. He drew his Colt, threw grenades inside, and ended all resistance by killing seven Communists. When his men reached the position, he was dead, lying before the gun he had captured.

2nd Lt. Carl H. Dodd, 24th Division

A twenty-five-year-old platoon leader did much the same on the last two days of January. Second Lieutenant Carl H. Dodd led his soldiers against Hill 256 near Subuk, when the advance was halted by small arms and mortar fire. After deploying his squads, the Kentuckian attacked a machine gun nest alone, killing or capturing the gunners. His soldiers fixed bayonets and charged behind him, seizing every Chinese position while Dodd personally killed a mortar crew with his last grenade. The platoon dug in for the night, and next morning, Dodd continued his attack with bayonet and grenades to secure the crest of the hill. He lived to receive his medal six months later.

Master Sergeant Hubert Lee provided the Second Division a lesson in determination near Ip-ori on February 1. With his platoon leader wounded and the unit forced to withdraw, Lee assumed command and led repeated counterattacks. The GIs were repulsed four times, and though Lee was wounded, each time he regrouped his soldiers. On the fifth attack, a grenade exploded close by, knocking him down. Unable to walk, he crawled forward, occasionally rising to his knees to shoot, and directing the others. He was hit a third time by gunfire, but the Southerner would not be stopped. When the position was secured, I/23 counted eighty-three Communist corpses. The next morning, Lee celebrated his thirty-sixth birthday.

Two days later, another senior noncom survived similar circumstances. Sergeant First Class Stanley T. Adams occupied a Twenty-fourth Division outpost shortly after midnight on February 4, when as many as 250 Communists attacked from three sides. Adams believed that a good offense was truly the best defense, and ordered his platoon to fix bayonets. Within fifty yards of the Chinese, he was shot in the leg but immediately got up, only to be knocked down four times by grenade explosions. In an incredible display of stamina, Adams and his GIs fought with bayonets and rifle butts for almost an hour, killing more than fifty of the enemy. Working on raw adrenaline, the soldiers then made an orderly withdrawal while Adams provided covering fire.

Another bayonet action occurred on February 7, when Captain Lewis Millett led E Company, Twenty-seventh Infantry, on patrol near Soam-ni. He was a career soldier from a family of soldiers; he had received a battlefield commission in World War II and filled the large boots of Reuben Desiderio, killed during a medal action in November. Millett had already earned a Distinguished Service Cross on February 5; now he faced a greater challenge. One of his scouts noted an enemy machine gun position and called a warning. As the "Wolfhounds" deployed, the Communists opened fire and threw grenades. Millett caught a fragment in his right shin that, "made me madder than hell."

Thus began the last major bayonet charge in American history.

Millett realized that the only way out of the kill zone was an uphill attack. Advancing behind phosphorous grenades, his men closed with

Capt. Reginald B. Desiderio, 25th Division   *Capt. Lewis Millett, 25th Division*

the enemy and engaged with bayonets and rifle butts. Without time to reload, Millett successively bayoneted three Communists to death.

At the end of the fight for "Bayonet Ridge," an arcane ritual was performed. Having killed at least forty-seven Chinese compared to the nine Wolfhound dead, Millett's men indulged in a celebratory dance, chanting "We're good! We're good! We're good!" Eighteen of the enemy corpses had bayonet wounds.

Millett's youngest son died in a plane crash following peacekeeping service in the Middle East in 1985. The old warrior penned this heartfelt tribute, which he called An Old Soldier's Prayer.

"I have fought when many feared to serve. I have gone where others failed to go. I have lost friends in war and strife who valued duty more than love of life. Now I understand the meaning of our lives, the loss of comrades not so very long ago. So to you who answered duty's siren call, may God bless you, my son. May God bless you all."

Four more medals were awarded for actions later that month; three posthumously. It was the second-highest medal count for the war.

Two Second Division men received the medal for actions the following week. About 3:00 A.M. on February 12, Sergeant Charles R. Long's company was subjected to heavy attack. The weight of the enemy numbers overwhelmed the perimeter, and the Kansas City forward observer volunteered to cover the withdrawal. He controlled mortar fire to slow the Communist attack, then lost radio contact. He was seen firing his carbine and throwing grenades until fatally wounded and overrun. At the price of his life, he gave M Company, 38th Infantry, time to regroup and counterattack to retake the hill.

Two days later, the 23rd Regiment's Sergeant First Class William S. Sitman jumped on a grenade to spare death or injury to his machine gun crew. His loss enabled the other five men to continue firing on "the ruthless foe" and repel the attack.

Corporal Einar H. Ingman Jr., received the Seventh Division's first medal of the war for his courageous leadership on February 26. Automatic weapons forced both squads of the platoon's maneuver element to seek cover, and the squad leaders were wounded. The Wisconsin soldier took charge, assigned fields of fire, then leapt to his feet and sprinted toward a machine gun nest. He grenaded the position and finished off the survivors with his rifle. Just then, another gun opened fire only fifteen yards away; Ingman was struck by bullets and grenade fragments, knocking him to the ground. But he raised his M1 and killed the enemy gunners before collapsing from shock and loss of blood. The rest of his men captured the position, chasing as many as a hundred Chinese from their holes. Ingman received his medal in less than six months.

Two men received Medals of Honor for actions in March 1951. On March 7, Sergeant First Class Nelson V. Brittin went on a one-man rampage, using a variety of weapons. Leaving his squad to provide a base of fire, he used grenades to destroy the first Communist position, but in turn was wounded by a grenade. Nevertheless, he grabbed more "pineapples," flushing out enemy soldiers from one position after another and shooting them as they ran. When his rifle jammed, the New Jersey noncom didn't hesitate; he jumped into an enemy fighting hole and bayoneted the occupants. Resuming the advance, Brittin's men again encountered automatic weapons fire, but he charged the position and was killed in the process. He had destroyed or captured four machine guns and killed twenty Communist troops.

Captain Raymond Harvey commanded C Company, Seventeenth Infantry, but largely acted singly on March 9. Primarily alone, he ran through gunfire and bursting grenades to destroy four Communist machine gun nests or bunkers in succession. All the while, he maneuvered his first platoon, ignoring severe wounds, and finally consolidated Charlie Company's position before he was removed for treatment. Harvey had turned thirty-one eight days before; he was the Seventh Division's seventh Medal of Honor recipient in the war.

The Third Division had reached Korea in November 1950; its first medal in the new war went to Lieutenant Darwin Kyle, killed leading a bayonet charge on February 16. "The Rock of the Marne" had garnered two Medals of Honor in World War I and led the entire Army with nearly forty in World War II. Only the Second Division matched the Third, earning Medals of Honor in three consecutive wars.

Four Marne Men added to the division's historic tally during April, including Corporal Miyamura, already mentioned as one of the few Medal of Honor prisoners. The Seventh Infantry's three other awards were all posthumous. Corporal John Essebagger Jr. volunteered to delay the swarming Chinese threatening to encircle Able Company. He was last seen advancing into the Communist tide, firing his Garand and throwing grenades.

Corporal Clair Goodblood performed similar heroics in Dog Company, shielding a fellow machine gunner from a grenade, then manning his

Cpl. Hiroyoshi Miyamura, 3rd Division

Browning while other GIs scrambled to safety. Following a counterattack, the Americans found the Maine soldier's body with nearly a hundred Chinese dead within his range.

Similarly, in Item Company, PFC Charles Gilliland used John M. Browning's automatic rifle and pistol to defend the company's withdrawal. Wounded, with his assistant killed, the Arkansan refused the medics' offer of help and volunteered to remain behind. He died protecting his friends as they pulled back.

Sergeant First Class Donald R. Moyer was a twenty-one-year-old noncom in the Thirty-fifth Infantry. On May 20, his platoon leader was wounded during an uphill attack, so the Michigander took over. He led the GIs through increasingly heavy gunfire and a storm of grenades but, near the top, one well-placed grenade threatened several men. Moyer threw himself on it, protecting his soldiers with his own body.

The Seventh Division's PFC Joseph C. Rodriguez survived exceptional odds at Munye-ri the next day. The assistant squad leader recognized that his men were pinned down by automatic weapons fire from five positions. Gathering his strength, he leapt to his feet and sprinted about sixty yards through heavy gunfire. In sequence, he destroyed all five positions with grenades, killing fifteen Communist troops in the process. The twenty-two-year-old Californian was promoted to sergeant and, though subsequently wounded, insisted on returning to his unit. He was commissioned in 1952 and retired as a colonel of engineers in 1980.

A lone GI fought a desperate battle to save his friends near Pachidong on June 7, 1951. A company of the Thirty-first Infantry was almost overwhelmed in a nocturnal attack and was forced to withdraw to an adjoining hill. PFC Jack G. Hanson volunteered to remain in position, covering the retreat. In the darkness and confusion, after about two hours, the platoon realized that four soldiers supporting Hanson had been wounded and moved to cover. The remaining GIs counterattacked, regaining their lost ground, and found a heartrending sight. The Southerner's body lay ahead of his empty Browning, his Colt's slide locked back in his right hand, and a bloody machete in his left. Protecting his squad mates, he had killed as many as twenty-two enemies before dying.

On June 24, PFC Emory Bennett, a Third Division BAR man, earned the forty-eighth Army Medal of Honor of the war, which had begun 364 days before. The twenty-one-year-old Floridian was killed holding off an enemy night attack, permitting his outnumbered company to withdraw. His was the thirty-third posthumous award of the war to date.

Usually, holidays had little meaning in Korea. But on July 4, Sergeant Leroy Mendonca earned a posthumous medal in all too familiar fashion. When his Third Division platoon was threatened with encirclement on Hill 586, he offered to man an exposed position to protect his friends' withdrawal. The Hawaiian NCO fired all his rifle ammunition, expended his grenades, and fought with his bayonet until overrun. Subsequently, he was credited with killing or wounding thirty-seven Communist troops. His incredible one-man stand had enabled Bravo Company of the Seventh to regroup and retake the hilltop.

That same month, armistice talks began between North Korea and the United Nations command. The deliberations waxed and waned over the next two years.

Sometimes a soldier's most effective weapon is a radio. Certainly that applied to Lieutenant Lee R. Hartell, a forward observer of the Fif-

Lt. Lee R. Hartell,
15th Field Artillery Battalion

teenth Field Artillery Battalion on August 27. Early that morning, the Chinese attacked Second Division positions on a ridgeline near Kobangsan-ni. Hartell, working with the Ninth Infantry, called for illumination rounds, then called "Fire for effect" to drop howitzer fire onto the onrushing enemy. Nevertheless, the Communists swarmed uphill, threatening to overrun the defense. The New Englander was shot in one hand but shifted his radio to the other and expertly called for a box barrage sealing off the company's front and left flank. During a short lull, the Chinese quickly regrouped and came on again, oblivious to casualties. Hartell was seriously wounded but called for simultaneous fire from both batteries he was controlling, then collapsed and died.

Most Medal of Honor actions occur in the course of one day or even one minute. Others extend over far longer periods, such as Lieutenant Colonel Don Faith's ordeal at the Chosin. A Second Division officer made his mark in four frantic days of fighting around Tondul in 1951. Captain Edward C. Krzyowski commanded B Company, Ninth Infantry, in an attack against Hill 700 on August 31, but the advance was halted by crossfire from bunkers. The Illinois officer took it upon himself to solve the problem, destroying one position with grenades and killing gunners of the second with his carbine. The next morning the advance continued but was repelled by the seemingly inexhaustible Communist numbers. Though wounded, Krzyowski helped cover the withdrawal and remained in the line. On September 3, he moved forward to call in mortar fire on enemy positions and was killed by a rifle shot.

Other leaders appeared where needed, often without officer's bars.

On the day that Krzyowski began his campaign, Corporal William F. Lyell found himself the ranking noncom in his Seventh Division platoon. He used a 57mm recoilless rifle to destroy one bunker then resumed command of his GIs. They had barely begun moving again, when two more bunkers opened fire. The Tennessee soldier ignored wounds to destroy both positions, then took a third one single-handedly as well. Lyell was deploying his men in support of another unit when his platoon was beset by mortar fire. Like so many others who led from the front, William Lyell was killed in action.

Capt. Edward C. Krzyowski,
2nd Division

Of four medals awarded for September, ironically a "grenade jumper" was the only survivor. On the night of September 6–7, Corporal Jerry K. Crump of the Third Division distinguished himself by standing his ground against superior numbers, meeting the attack with rifle and bayonet. He rejoined his squad, guarding several casualties, and dived on a grenade to protect the GIs. The Tarheel teenager recovered from his injuries to receive his medal in 1952.

The next day, during Twenty-fifth Division action near Pyongyang, Private Billie G. Kanell established an almost unattainable level of courage and self-sacrifice. Dozens of soldiers and Marines have received the Medal of Honor for smothering enemy grenades to protect comrades, but the Missouri man absorbed two. Barely had he suppressed the first, when another dropped into his buddies' position; somehow he rolled onto it before it detonated, inflicting fatal injuries.

Time and again, Medal of Honor recipients stress, "Never give up." That attitude was fully shared by Lieutenant Jerome A. Sudut, a platoon leader in the Tropic Lightning's Twenty-seventh Infantry attacking dug-in Communist forces near Kumhwa on September 12. The U.S. advance was halted by a large bunker, so the Wisconsin officer used his submachine gun, pistol, and grenades to take the position. He killed three reds and chased off the survivors but sustained painful wounds. Nevertheless, he organized his men and continued the attack. Meanwhile, the persistent enemy had reoccupied the bunker, again firing from various apertures. Sudut took a BAR man, who was then wounded, so the officer picked up the Browning, killed three of the four enemy, and was fatally shot. With waning strength, Sudut rushed the survivor and killed him with a knife.

The Second Division's Twenty-third Infantry entered legend at Heartbreak Ridge near Pia-ri on September 17. Attacked by hordes of Chinese, Company C fired most of its ammunition and had to pull back to prepared positions. PFC Herbert K. Pililaau volunteered to cover the retrograde movement, firing his BAR and expending his grenades. Rather than retreat, the twenty-two-year-old Hawaiian fought hand-to-hand, using his trench knife and bare hands until shot down. Later Charlie Company counted more than forty North Korean corpses around his position.

On October 8, the Second Division continued the fight around Heartbreak Ridge. Company L of the Thirty-eighth Infantry was attacking an enemy trench line, when Sergeant First Class Tony K. Burris made a solo dash for the objective. With a stash of grenades, he smothered the defenders beneath an explosive barrage, killing as many as fifteen. The next day, the Oklahoman was at the head of an attack on the next ridgeline and was twice hit by machine gun fire. Nevertheless, he called up a recoilless rifle team, standing erect to draw fire for the gunners to spot targets. After accepting temporary treatment, Burris resumed the advance and personally destroyed two more Communist positions, then collapsed with fatal wounds. His efforts were credited in large part with securing Hill 605, part of the Heartbreak complex.

Lieutenant Lloyd L. Burke set an example that any cavalryman might envy, mounted or otherwise. With lead elements of his troop stopped by a bunker complex, the twenty-seven-year-old officer took the assignment upon himself. Using hand grenades, rifle grenades, and pistol, he reduced three bunkers in succession. At the last, he caught enemy grenades in midair and tossed them back before they exploded.

Burke then obtained an M1919 with three boxes of ammo and established himself on the enemy flank. Firing downhill, he used the Browning expertly, dropping about seventy-five Communists. Incredibly, though wounded, the Razorback was not finished. He lifted the gun off its tripod and led his platoon in taking two mortars and a machine gun nest, killing a couple dozen more of the enemy in the process.

PFC Herbert K. Pililaau, 2nd Division

Many Korean War recipients were decorated for sacrificing themselves in rearguard actions, as did PFC Mack A. Jordan of the Twenty-fourth Division on November 15. Not quite twenty-one, Jordan single-handedly destroyed a Communist machine gun position and forced a temporary withdrawal of the force threatening his platoon. While crawling toward another machine gun nest, he lost both legs in a grenade attack but continued firing until his friends were out of danger. His medal is displayed in the Mississippi War Memorial in Jackson.

The last of thirty-seven Army medals in 1951 was awarded to a twenty-one-year-old GI for self-sacrifice the night of November 23–24. PFC Noah Knight manned a bunker in the Third Division line near Kowang-San, when two shells struck his position. The South Carolinian was wounded but made his way from the structure to start shooting at the attackers. However, he was unable to see from defilade and moved to an exposed position. Eventually, he used up his rifle ammo in repelling two assaults almost single-handedly. When he saw three infiltrators scurrying along a communication trench, he intercepted them, clubbed down two with his Garand, and went for the third. The last enemy soldier detonated his satchel charge, killing himself and mortally wounding Knight.

1952

Corporal Ronald E. Rosser found himself a long way from Ohio when his Second Division company assaulted a fortified hill near Ponggilli on January 12, 1952. As a mortar observer, he was well forward, seeing the effect of enemy automatic weapons and artillery. The twenty-two-year-old soldier gave his radio to his assistant and charged the nearest enemy bunker with his M2 carbine and grenades. He not only took the position alone, but twice returned to his lines for more ammunition and grenades, methodically taking one bunker after another. In all, he killed thirteen Chinese in successive actions, leading GIs who fell in beside him, while personally sustaining wounds in the process. Yet he helped move other casualties to the rear and somehow survived to receive his medal that summer.

Looking back on his Korean War experience, Rosser said, "I picked up one orphan and made him the platoon houseboy. I felt I needed to save at least one." Then he reflected, "Wouldn't it be nice if the people who start wars had to raise the orphans of that war?"

Medics were constantly in demand, and their devotion was amply demonstrated by the Twenty-fifth Division's PFC Bryant E. Womack. On the night of March 12, he accompanied a patrol that resulted in a "meeting engagement" with Communist forces. The enemy outnum-

PFC Bryant E. Womack, 25th Division   *Sgt. David D. Bleak, 40th Division*

bered the Tropic Lightnings, and casualties quickly accumulated. The medic ignored the enemy fire, rushing to reach wounded men but taking hits himself. While treating one GI, Womack's right arm was amputated by a shell fragment. Rather than move to the rear, he stayed put, telling other soldiers how to treat the critical cases. He was the last man to withdraw, walking unaided until he collapsed. His friends carried him away, but the devoted Tarheel died from excessive blood loss.

The year's third and fourth medals resulted three months later, both from the Fortieth Division's 223rd Infantry. On June 14, Sergeant David B. Bleak demonstrated the ferocity with which medics defended their men. When the patrol was ambushed, Bleak treated some wounded and moved toward other casualties, when fired upon from a nearby trench. The Idaho NCO entered the trench, killed two Communists with his bare hands and stabbed a third with a knife, his only weapon. Upon returning to his casualties, he shielded one soldier from grenade fragments and then was shot. Nevertheless, he carried a casualty downhill, when attacked by two Communists brandishing fixed bayonets. The twenty-year-old Bleak went straight at them, dodged their thrusts, and knocked both unconscious. He then carried his man to safety.

Meanwhile, Corporal Clifton T. Speicher was part of a squad attacking a hill not far away. He was wounded early in the action but, seeing his friends pinned down, he left cover and ran at the bunker. He was hit again within thirty feet of the position but reached the entrance, shot two gunners with his rifle and bayoneted the third to death. While other GIs secured the objective, the young Pennsylvanian walked to the base of the hill, collapsed, and shortly died. The Grizzly Division had two Medals of Honor in one day.

Other actions that summer included Corporal Lester Hammond Jr., whose 187th Airborne Company sent a six-man patrol almost two miles behind enemy lines. With the troopers ambushed and nearly encircled, Hammond shrugged off gunshot wounds to call down artillery fire, remaining in the open for best visibility. He died while preventing the GIs from being overrun. Help arrived too late to save his twenty-one-year-old life.

In the predawn blackness of September 6, Corporal Benito Martinez manned a listening post ahead of the Twenty-seventh Infantry's main line of resistance. Though the young Texan realized he was being surrounded by infiltrators, he opted to stay, in hope of spoiling the attack. He opened up with his BAR, shooting down several Communists. During the six-hour ordeal, he refused repeated offers to send a patrol to fetch him, believing the danger was too great. When the Chinese returned the last time, he took his Browning out of the foxhole and fired it until forced to use his pistol. Martinez's posthumous medal was authorized at the end of 1953.

The next day, a similar action involved another Tropic Lightning soldier. Sergeant Donn F. Porter's four-man outpost came under heavy mortar fire, killing two GIs and destroying the radio. But Porter opened fire, repelling the first attack. On the second effort, he fixed bayonet, leapt from his foxhole, and killed six Communists hand-to-hand. An artillery shell killed him shortly thereafter, but he single-handedly averted a surprise attack on his company.

On October 12, PFC Ernest E. West joined a patrol to find a Communist observation post near Sataeri. The Twenty-fifth Division soldiers were ambushed en route, sustaining multiple casualties. West spotted the patrol leader lying in the open and directed the others to pull out of the kill zone. He then sprinted through gunfire to reach the lieutenant, where he was attacked by three opponents, shooting and throwing grenades. West shot down all three but received serious injuries, including the loss of an eye. Then, he hefted the immobile officer over one shoulder and staggered for safety. While helping move two more casualties, he killed three more Chinese. At twenty-one, Ernest West was among the youngest Medal of Honor recipients of the war.

On October 14, First Lieutenant Edward R. Schowalter Jr. led his platoon of the Thirty-first Infantry in an attack near Kumhwa. Though wounded early in the assault, the Louisianan remained at the head of his men. Next, he shrugged off a severe grenade wound, reached the trench line, and threw grenades into enemy bunkers. When shot by flanking fire, he refused to turn over command and continued directing his GIs in securing the objective. Only then did he consent to being moved to the rear. It was the eighth medal awarded a Seventh Division man in Korea.

The next day, the regiment was engaged in an area called Jane Russell Hill ("named for obvious reasons"), where PFC Ralph E. Pomeroy was a machine gunner on the flank of his platoon's position. When Chinese attacked head-on, he killed several, temporarily stopping the attack. The Communist response was predictable: heavy mortar and artillery fire. But the West Virginian stood his ground, continuing to hold his position. When a mortar shell burst nearby, his tripod was damaged and he was wounded. Nevertheless, he hoisted the fifty-pound M1917 off the mount and carried it forward, sweeping the oncoming horde with .30 caliber rounds. Pomeroy continued ahead despite another wound, firing the last of his 248 rounds within ten feet of the enemy. There, he swung the unwieldy Browning as a massive club, fighting until fatally shot. His incredible devotion to duty enabled his platoon to maintain its perimeter.

The last Army Medal of Honor for 1952 went to PFC Charles George, a Cherokee from North Carolina. With two other Forty-fifth Division soldiers, George provided withdrawal support for a trench raid the night of November 30. As the GIs were leaving, a Communist soldier threw a grenade into their midst. George saw the danger, shouted a warning to one man, shoved the other aside, and smothered the grenade as it exploded. Though severely wounded, he suppressed any sign of pain as he was carried off. However, his injuries were fatal; he died at age twenty.

1953

Six medals were awarded for combat in the last seven months of the war. Private Charles H. Barker of the Seventh Division was a member of a patrol screening his company's approach to Pork Chop Hill on June 4. The patrol surprised a group of Chinese preparing positions on the slope but the Communists quickly reacted to the situation. They called for mortar fire, which halted the American flanking effort, and a prolonged firefight depleted most of the GIs' ammunition. Barker offered to fight a one-man delaying action so the soldiers could withdraw to a perimeter; his friends last saw him in close combat. The South Carolinian was listed MIA and received a promotion to private first class before his death was confirmed. His medal was approved two years later.

Sergeant Ola L. Mize of the Third Division was a defender of Outpost Harry near Surang-ni on June 10. When the Chinese attacked, the Alabaman ran forward to rescue a wounded man from a listening post. Back in his own lines, he joined the close-range gunfight but was knocked off his feet three times by artillery or mortar explosions. More Communists infiltrated the position, and Mize shot one before the enemy soldier could kill his intended victim. Subsequently, Mize ran from post to post, firing to maintain the illusion of full strength, distributing ammo, and coordinating the defense. When a machine gun crew was overwhelmed, Mize shot and clubbed his way to the gun, killing ten enemy soldiers in the process. During a rare lull, he took a radio to call down friendly artillery fire and prepared the GIs for a successful counterattack.

Another defensive action was fought on June 16–17, 1953, in the Third Division operating area. Corporal Charles F. Pendleton fired his machine gun into the massed attackers, killing fifteen or more. He then pulled the Browning from its tripod to fire at enemy troops flanking his position, forcing them to retreat. But the Communists were determined; they launched a second attack, advancing behind a wave of grenades. The Southerner scooped up one and tossed it back; he was shortly wounded by another grenade but continued shooting. Yet another grenade destroyed his gun, but he raised a carbine and fired it until he was killed by a mortar shell.

Though the bulk of Communist forces were Chinese, the North Korean Army remained a factor. As hostilities approached an end, Pyongyang's III Corps opposed the U.S. Fortieth Division sector.

Lieutenant Richard T. Shea Jr. fought near Sokkogae, July 6–8. He was supervising a reinforcement of the Seventeenth Infantry's lines the first night, when Communist troops attacked in force. Shea quickly formed a reaction force and counterattacked. In the dark, Americans and Chinese grappled at fist-fighting distance; the Virginian killed two men with his knife then rejoined his impromptu command. Fighting continued through the night. At daybreak, the Communists came on again; once more he repelled them. With Able and George Companies badly depleted, Shea reorganized them and again charged head-on into the surging enemy forces, sustaining wounds in the process. Later, he single-handedly destroyed a machine gun crew pinning down some of his men. On July 8, the Chinese came once more, and Shea again met them head on. He fell fighting hand-to-hand, but the line held.

Corporal Dan Schoonover was a Seventh Division engineer near Sokkogae on July 8. Owing to heavy Communist resistance, he offered his demolition team as an impromptu rifle squad and helped assault enemy positions. He jumped into a partly destroyed bunker, killed one enemy and captured another, then took a second position with grenades and pistol. Upon reaching the crest of the hill, the Americans were subjected to a powerful counterattack. Over the next two days, Schoonover remained in place, alternately firing a machine gun, attacking another emplacement, and shooting a BAR, until he was killed by artillery.

Corporal Gilbert G. Collier was assistant leader of a contact patrol on the night of July 19–20. In the darkness, the twenty-two-year-old noncom and his platoon leader slipped off a steep slope, falling some sixty feet. Both were injured: Collier's back and Lieutenant Richard Agnew's ankle prevented them from moving with the other men, who were ordered back to their lines. The crippled pair managed to climb over the treacherous slope, hiding in the brush until the next night.

Under cover of darkness, they painfully made their way toward safety. However, they were ambushed and a close-range fight ensued. The Arkansas soldier killed two and was wounded in turn, losing contact with his lieutenant. Out of ammo, he defeated four more enemy soldiers with his bayonet but received severe wounds. Even so, he managed to reach Agnew, who was found by rescuers the next morning, clinging to two grenades. Collier was taken to a MASH unit but died on July 21.

The armistice took effect one week later.

The "final" Korean War recipient (as of 2005) is Tibor Rubin, an immigrant who felt he owed a debt to the United States Army.

"Ted" Rubin was a Hungarian Jew who survived fourteen months in a German concentration camp liberated by U.S. forces in 1945. Determined to become an American citizen, he made his way to the United States and enlisted in time for the Korean War. Assigned to the First Cavalry Division, his citation spanned almost three years of combat, imprisonment, and unfailing fortitude.

Cpl. Gilbert G. Collier, 40th Division

In the 8th Cavalry Regiment's retreat to the Pusan perimeter, Corporal Rubin fought a spectacular solo delaying action, holding a vital road for twenty-four hours and inflicting "a staggering number of casualties on the attacking force." During the subsequent advance to retake lost ground, Rubin helped capture several hundred North Korean troops. Then, following the massive Chinese attack in October, he manned a machine gun after three previous gunners had been killed or wounded. He remained in place that night and through the next day until out of ammunition. Badly wounded, he was captured by the Chinese.

In prison camp, the Communists offered to release Rubin to his native Hungary, but he refused. Instead, he scrounged food and stole supplies for his sick and starving POW comrades, including his Turkish allies. Knowing he would be executed or tortured if caught, Rubin continued his clandestine mercy errands.

Rubin's commanding officer had intended to recommend him for the Medal of Honor, but the CO was killed in action, and the senior noncom, reportedly an anti-Semite, lost the papers. Only in the 1980s did Rubin come to the Army's attention via his fellow prisoners. After an investigation, the award was approved, with President Bush making the presentation in September 2005.

Fifty years on, the effects of the Korean "police action" still are felt around the world as Pyongyang continues its nuclear weapons program. Nevertheless, when Kim Il Sung died in 1994, President Bill Clinton and former President Jimmy Carter expressed condolences upon the demise of the Stalinist despot responsible for the deaths of 36,000 Americans.

U.S. Army veterans of "the forgotten war" felt betrayed.

CHAPTER EIGHT

VIETNAM

■

APTAIN Roger H. C. Donlon was a thirty-year-old Green Beret commanding a Special Forces "A" camp near Nam Dong in South Vietnam's central highlands. Before dawn on July 6, 1964, a large Viet Cong force estimated at battalion strength assaulted Detachment A-726. For the next five hours, Donlon moved amidst mortar shells, bursting grenades, and unrelenting gunfire to direct the defense of his beleaguered outpost. He braved flames to help empty the ammunition locker, then spotted three VC breaching the main gate. He killed all three with six rounds, then sprinted to help man the camp's 60mm mortar. Before he got there, he was shot in the stomach and, though most of the crew was wounded, he directed moving the tube thirty-three yards to avoid being overrun. Donlon ignored his injury to cover the withdrawal. He returned to the position to drag a wounded sergeant to cover, then retrieved the mortar unaided. Despite receiving another wound, he fetched a 57mm recoilless rifle and secured more ammo and grenades for his troopers.

The Arkansas officer then crawled 175 yards, under fire, to direct an

Capt. Roger H. C. Donlon, Special Forces

81mm mortar to fend off an attack from the eastern perimeter. As if that weren't enough, Donlon survived a trek to the eastern mortar position, largely ending the pressure from that flank. But other VC came ahead, and Donlon moved from one position to another, firing his rifle, throwing grenades, and keeping his men organized. At that point, he was wounded a third time by an exploding mortar shell, but he shrugged off the pain to reorganize his men and treat more casualties. The VC abandoned the attack after sunup, leaving fifty-four corpses behind.

Roger Donlon received the first Medal of Honor for the Vietnam War. It was authorized before end of the year and subsequently awarded by Lyndon Johnson.

At the time of Donlon's action, another elite forces officer was facing even greater trials. Captain Humbert R. Versace had been captured with two other Rangers on October 29, 1963, but Versace continued the fight in captivity. "Rocky" Versace was a second-generation West Pointer who intended to become a Catholic priest upon completion of his obligated service. Within weeks of leaving the army, he was an intelligence advisor in the Mekong Delta. Versace, Lieutenant James "Nick" Rowe, and Sergeant First Class Dan Pitzer led their provincial forces against the Viet Cong in An Xuyen Province but were overwhelmed by enemy numbers. The three Americans were wounded and taken into captivity.

Over the next two years, Versace was the living embodiment of the Code of Conduct. He not only refused to provide any information beyond name, rank, and serial number, but consistently engaged the Communists in philosophical arguments. Said one friend, "Rocky could tell the VC to go to hell in English, French, and Vietnamese." He made four unsuccessful escape attempts, each resulting in additional torture. Rowe and Pitzer felt that Versace intentionally focused the enemy's cruelest efforts upon himself in order to spare his wounded friends as much as possible.

On September 26, 1965, Versace was murdered in retaliation for the deaths of reputed Communist sympathizers in South Vietnam. Nick Rowe escaped in 1968, after five years in enemy hands and told Versace's story. An interim Silver Star was granted, and President Nixon approved Rowe's recommendation for Versace's Medal of Honor. However, the paperwork languished until 1971, when the Medal of Honor was denied. Rowe felt the reason was political:

Capt. Humbert R. Versace,
Military Assistance Advisory Group

he had been vocal in his criticism of antiwar senators. Nevertheless, Rowe continued his counterinsurgency work until assassinated by Philippine Communists in 1989.

The case languished for a decade, then in 1999, Versace's admirers petitioned the Army to reconsider. By then, the 1970s Democrats were mostly gone and Rocky Versace's brother accepted the medal on behalf of the family in 2002.

1965

During 1965, U.S. troop strength in Vietnam rose from 23,000 to 184,000, with 1,000 killed in action.

■ Vietnam 101

Following France's defeat in 1954, Vietnam was partitioned north and south, much as Korea had been nine years previously. Under Communist control, the north established itself as the Democratic Republic of Vietnam (DRV); the south (nominally democratic) was the Republic of Vietnam (RVN). As in Korea, the Communist north intended to return the south to "unified" status by force. With backing from Russia and China, Hanoi began a patient campaign throughout Indochina, employing overt and covert means to undermine established governments in the region.

America got into Vietnam via the back door of Laos. In the early 1960s, Washington's focus lay in that direction more than South Vietnam, but the geography drove the politics. Because South Vietnam was bordered by Laos and Cambodia, clandestine operations were conducted in both nations. Meanwhile, the indigenous "progressive" movement in the RVN grew into the Viet Cong, allied with Hanoi.

In the summer of 1964, several events brought large-scale American military involvement to the region. Communist guerrillas blew up U.S. and RVN facilities, and DRV torpedo boats attacked American warships in the Tonkin Gulf. The first event, on August 2, was genuine: a response to U.S. support of Saigon commando operations. A purported second incident two nights later did not occur; it was the result of nervous American sailors reporting "enemy" radar contacts, a fact known to some Washington officials.

Nevertheless, the administration of Lyndon B. Johnson seized upon the second "attack" to demonstrate its anticommunist resolve. With a presidential election only three months away, Johnson and Defense Secretary Robert Strange McNamara used the Tonkin Gulf attacks to launch retaliatory raids against North Vietnam. American troop strength eventually reached half a million men, and the bombing campaign—never fully prosecuted—waxed and waned according to the domestic and geopolitical situations.

In early 1968, the Communists violated the Tet holiday cease-fire to launch massive attacks throughout the south. Allied forces inflicted serious losses on the Viet Cong, but much of the U.S. press represented Tet as a Communist victory. Consequently, Johnson announced he would not seek re-election. Republican Richard Nixon won, pledging to end the war, but four years later, the process was no closer. When Hanoi launched its 1972 "Easter offensive," Nixon finally ran out of patience and loosed the bombers. Air power won a limited victory, forcing Hanoi back to the Paris bargaining table. Meanwhile, "Vietnamization" had taken effect with RVN forces increasingly replacing U.S. and Allied troops. The formal armistice took effect in January 1973, at which time most (not all) American POWs were returned. The U.S. Senate then withdrew most financial aid to Saigon, and barely two years later the Communists triumphed. Some Americans cheered: the bitter Vietnam experience had produced cultural and political tremors that sent aftershocks echoing for years.

Some 58,000 Americans died in Vietnam, Laos, and Cambodia between 1961 and 1975. The latter two countries were subjected to socialist genocide in the wake of Saigon, but the total human loss of the Second Indochina War can never be known. However, the specter of Vietnam cast a long-lived shadow over American foreign policy that did not begin to dissipate until the first Iraq war in 1991. While politicians continued to meddle and fumble, the junior officers of the 1960s learned the appropriate lessons and applied them at the turn of the millennium.

Prominent among the reinforcements was the First Cavalry Division (Airmobile), based at An Khe beginning in September. In October, the First Infantry Division entered its third war, assigned to III Corps. "Back in the world," the first draft card burnings occurred that same month.

As of 2003, six Medals of Honor had been awarded for 1965 actions. The first went to South Carolinian Charles Q. Williams, a Special Forces officer, at Dong Xoai on June 9–10. Like Roger Donlan, Williams defended a Special Forces camp against prolonged, determined attack. As a second lieutenant, Williams was executive officer of the Green Beret detachment when it was attacked by a VC force of regimental size. Over the next fourteen hours, Williams was wounded repeatedly but kept moving, rallying the defenders, and coordinating efforts of two compounds. After firing a rocket launcher to destroy an enemy machine gun, he pulled his wounded loader to cover. He then supervised the withdrawal, calling in air strikes and ensuring that no wounded were left behind when helicopters arrived. His medal was authorized thirteen months later.

Williams' loader was a Navy Seabee, Petty Officer Third Class Marvin Shields. Already wounded, Shields was killed while returning from the volunteer sortie to destroy the VC machine gun nest. The Dong Xoai battle was the first in Vietnam resulting in Medals of Honor for members of different services.

Meanwhile, three members of the independent 173rd Airborne Brigade received medals for actions that fall. The 173rd was the Far East "fire department." Based on Okinawa, the "Sky Soldiers" were rushed to South Vietnam in May 1965, the first major Army unit involved in the expanding war. The brigade's major component, the 503rd Airborne Infantry, was committed to combat in War Zone D.

On September 20, Sergeant Larry S. Pierce was engaged with the regiment's First Battalion near Ben Cat. While his squad was pursuing a Communist force, he noticed a mine in the road. With no time to call a halt, Pierce flung himself on the mine as it exploded, saving the nearby Sky Soldiers.

Another trooper sacrificed himself on October 22. The Second Battalion was assaulting an enemy defensive line at Phu Cuong, when a grenade rolled among five troopers. PFC Milton L. Olive III grabbed the grenade and fell on it as it exploded. He was two weeks short of his nineteenth birthday.

Almost twice as old was Spec. 5 Lawrence Joel, at thirty-seven, operating with the First Battalion's headquarters company. On November 8, the lead squad was ambushed and every man was killed or wounded. While treating casualties, Joel was struck in his right leg by a 7.62mm round. He stopped long enough to bandage his own wound and inject enough morphine to deaden the pain so he could continue treating his soldiers. Knowing that more troopers lay ahead, he moved toward the initial contact despite constant enemy gunfire and the shouted warnings of his friends.

Reaching more wounded soldiers, Joel administered plasma, which required him to rise to a kneeling position. The gunfire continued unabated while he held the bag upright, rifle fire kicking up dirt on both sides. He was hit again by a bullet in the thigh, but once more he ignored his own wounds to continue searching for and treating the injured. Incredibly, he survived in the kill zone to treat thirteen more men before emptying his medic's kit. Joel's resourcefulness saved one man with a chest wound, by pressing a plastic bag over the entry hole and congealing the blood.

While a platoon engaged the nearest VC, another Vietnamese force announced itself with a volley of gunfire. More Americans went down; many were wounded. Joel had resupplied himself and continued crawling through the gunfire, treating men in turn.

The firefight lasted almost twenty-four hours. Joel received a promotion and the Medal of Honor eighteen months later. He was the first of at least fifteen Army medics to receive the medal for service in Vietnam. It was a startling contrast to two medics decorated in World War I, ten in World War II, and three in the Korean War.

The last medal of the year went to Lieutenant Walter J. Marm Jr. of the First Cavalry, for action on November 14. In relieving another unit, Marm's platoon clashed with a larger enemy force and went to ground. The young Pennsylvanian killed four Communist troops infiltrating his line, then drew fire upon himself to gauge the position of a camouflaged machine gun. He maneuvered to the flank and fired an antitank rocket that hit the position but failed to

Spec. 5 Lawrence Joel, 173rd Airborne Brigade

destroy the gun. Consequently, Marm sprinted across open ground, closing the distance to grenade range. He was wounded in the attack but pressed ahead and finished off the eight-man gun crew with his rifle.

Marm's medal was the first awarded to the cavalry in Vietnam. More than twenty others would follow for the Airmobile division.

1966

In January 1966, U.S. troops conducted their first operations in the Mekong Delta. It was an area that would become familiar to GIs over the next six years. But war activity was expanding at home, too. That March, an estimated 200,000 antiwar marchers appeared in New York City.

▪ Vietnam Weapons

One of the greatest weapon scandals in U.S. history occurred literally during the middle of the Vietnam War. In 1966–67 the Army and Marine Corps decided to replace the proven .30 caliber M14 rifle with the smaller, lighter .223 caliber M16, leading to widespread dissatisfaction and an unknown number of avoidable casualties. Designed by Eugene Stoner, and originally adapted by the Air Force, the AR-15 used space-age composites for uncommon strength and lightness. However, Army Ordnance made fundamental changes in the M16 version, including the type of powder employed. More incredibly, the new rifles were issued without cleaning kits, and the Department of Defense balked at chrome lining the chambers for budgetary reasons. The result was a morale-sinking series of failures in combat. Some infantry companies broke regulations to reissue M14s.

Eventually, "the black rifle" was turned into a reliable weapon, though the theory behind a small, high-speed bullet remained controversial. Said one rifleman, "With my M14, nobody I shot ever did anything but lay right down and assume ambient temperature. You could carry more ammo with the sixteen, but you needed more ammo, too."

Other widely used infantry tools included the M60 machine gun, firing the same .30 caliber cartridge as the M14. Partly based on Germany's superb MG.42, the '60 was a rugged, reasonably portable squad automatic firing about six hundred rounds per minute.

The M79 grenade launcher was popularly called the "bloop tube" for its distinctive sound when fired. It was a single-shot weapon, firing a 40mm projectile to three hundred meters or more.

Various figures have been cited for the number of rounds-per-confirmed-enemy-kill in Vietnam. Even the base figures are controversial, owing to the exaggerated "body count" mentality evoked by the McNamara passion for quantification. However, most infantry shooting in Vietnam was suppressive or "reconnaissance by fire" without identifiable targets. In any case, more than 50,000 rounds were fired for each Communist soldier known killed: twice the World War II figure.

Vastly more efficient were sniper rifles, owing to the marksman's creed of "one shot, one kill." Scoped M14s were used, as were militarized versions of civilian hunting arms such as the Winchester 70 and Remington 700. Night sights became increasingly popular as thermal technology evolved.

GIs took the same pistol to Southeast Asia that their grandfathers used in the Great War. The M1911 proved just as rugged in jungles and swamps as it had in the trenches fifty years previously.

As of 2003, eighteen awards had been presented for actions in 1966. The first of those also was the first awarded the 101st Airborne, which had garnered two Medals of Honor in the Second World War, shortly after Lieutenant James A. Gardner was born. The young Tennessean received his medal for a series of actions on February 7.

Attacking near My Canh, Gardner's platoon encountered a well-designed enemy defensive line with overlapping fields of fire, preventing further movement. Not even U.S. aircraft or artillery had been able to breach the line, so the airborne troopers maneuvered on the flank. More

Communist gunfire erupted, but Gardner splashed across a rice paddy and tossed grenades into two bunkers. The Tennessean immediately went after a third, meeting an enemy soldier at near muzzle-contact distance. Gardner shot the man down, then regrouped his platoon and continued advancing.

The GIs found another layer of the Communist defense, but Gardner was undeterred. With more grenades, he charged two more bunkers, firing his rifle to suppress defensive fire. At the last bunker, he was mortally wounded but still managed to fling a grenade inside,

1st Lt. James A. Gardner, 101st Airborne Division

clearing the position. Gardner's soldiers found his body on the rim of the bunker. He died on his twenty-third birthday.

Nine days later, the Twenty-fifth Division logged its first medal in Vietnam. It was typical timing, as throughout the war the heaviest combat occurred in February and March, reflecting the weather as much as offensive operations. Spec. 4 Daniel Fernandez was a quiet, well-regarded soldier on his second Vietnam tour. On February 18, his patrol was ambushed by a Viet Cong company in Hau Nghia Province. The squad's machine gunner was critically wounded and unable to withdraw with his comrades, so Fernandez, Sergeant Ray Sue, and two others volunteered to attempt a rescue. They fought their way through gunfire and grenades, reached the downed soldier, and found him dead. Nevertheless, they prepared to retrieve his body. But Sue took a gunshot to one knee, forcing a temporary halt. While the NCO was receiving treatment, Fernandez held

Spec. 4 Alfred Rascon, 173rd Airborne Brigade

the left flank amid increasing opposition. The VC fired a rifle grenade that landed next to Fernandez; in his haste to get out of the blast pattern, he accidentally kicked the grenade toward Sue and the medic. Realizing time was nearly up, he instantly dived on it. The explosion mortally wounded the twenty-two-year-old New Mexican, but he saved his friends.

In February 2000, Spec. 4 Alfred Rascon of the 173rd Airborne Brigade accepted his medal from Bill Clinton. Army paperwork had been lost for thirty-four years, but his buddies insisted that Rascon deserved "the big one." Their patience and persistence were rewarded.

On March 16, 1966, the Mexican-born Rascon accompanied his reconnaissance platoon in an effort to link up with an isolated unit. His platoon was pinned down by heavy automatic weapons fire, with casualties beyond immediate aid. The twenty-one-year-old medic ignored warnings to stay under cover, dashed forward to tend a wounded machine gunner, and covered the man's body from exploding grenades. Rascon sustained a bullet wound in the process. With one gunner still in action but running low on ammunition, Rascon again braved enemy fire to deliver linked rounds. A grenadier then was hit, and Rascon ignored his own injuries to reach the soldier, repeatedly protecting him by absorbing more grenade blasts.

When the firefight ended, Rascon insisted on treating other casualties before he boarded a med-evac helicopter.

Alfred Rascon became an American citizen the next year and returned to Vietnam for a second tour in 1970.

In March, the First Infantry Division logged its first Medal of Honor for its third war. Having missed Korea, the "Big Red One" nonetheless had received five medals in the First World War and sixteen in the Second.

Lieutenant Robert J. Hibbs of the Twenty-eighth Infantry was operating around Don Dien Lo Ke on March 5. By then, he was nearly halfway through his tour, and he was experienced in "the bush." Leading a fifteen-man ambush patrol, he initiated the fight by detonating claymore mines as the VC closed within seven yards of his position. Nearly half the Communist troops went down in the initial flurry of mines, grenades, and gunfire, but about fifty remained. Hibbs conducted an orderly withdrawal, though his rear element tangled with an undetected VC company. The fight turned badly; in the confusion, one GI was trapped between the enemy units.

Hibbs shrugged off a leg wound and took a sergeant to find the missing soldier, PFC Johnnie Holloway. The noncom's identity is uncertain, but he may have been Staff Sergeant David Payne. In any case, the pair found Holloway and shoved him toward safety, dodging a crossfire from two enemy machine guns. Hibbs shouted that he would cover the NCO and wounded man while they escaped. Then Hibbs charged both machine guns. The twenty-two-year-old Midwesterner was shot down but found the strength to destroy the starlight scope on his M16 before he died.

The division's third brigade named its chapel at Lai Khe after Robert John Hibbs.

Another Big Red One recipient was Sergeant James W. Robinson Jr., a husky, athletic, former Marine. His extraordinary heroism was demonstrated when his company tackled a VC battalion east of Saigon on April 11.

Delta Company of the Sixteenth Infantry took increasing casualties from enemy riflemen in a tree line, but Robinson located the most threatening sniper and silenced him with a grenade launcher. Shortly thereafter, the Illinois NCO noticed wounded men and medics taking fire. He sprinted across open ground and dragged two casualties to cover, applied first aid, and was credited with saving both men.

Then the twenty-five-year-old sergeant realized that some of his GIs were low on ammunition. He again exposed himself to enemy gunfire, retrieving weapons and ammo before spotting another downed American. Robinson returned to the open ground, took gunshots to a shoulder and leg, yet moved the man to safety and again administered life-saving treatment.

Robinson stopped his one-man campaign long enough to patch his own wounds, then sighted an enemy machine gun position. Though out of rifle ammo, he grabbed two grenades and attacked. He was shot in the leg by a tracer round that ignited his clothes, but he ripped off the burning portions, and continued his attack. The machine gun fire hit him twice, but Robinson put his grenades on target before he collapsed and died, face to the enemy.

Delta Company had taken 80 percent casualties, but others certainly would have died except for the treatment provided by an Air Force Pararescue man, Airman William H. Pitsenbarger, who received a posthumous Air Force Cross.

A long-delayed postscript occurred to Robinson's action. In December 2000, Pitsenbarger's Air Force Cross was upgraded to the Medal of Honor.

Subsequently, Robinson's father, James, established a website in honor of his courageous son. The site notes that two schools, an Army training center, and an annual award bear Sergeant Robinson's name.

The Americal Division was formed at New Caledonia in 1942, hence the name rather than a number. It fought through the Pacific War and was designated the Twenty-third Infantry Division in 1954 but retained the name through most of its subsequent history. The division's first Vietnam Medal of Honor went to Staff Sergeant Nick D. Bacon of the Twenty-first Infantry. The Arizona noncom found himself leading two rifle platoons west of Tam Ky on August 26. With his own platoon leader a casualty, Bacon led his soldiers against an enemy bunker complex. He reached the nearest position alone and killed the Communist machine gunners by himself. However, when the adjoining platoon moved forward, its leader also was shot. Bacon immediately assumed command and directed the remainder of the action. Again leading from the front, he killed four more Communist soldiers and destroyed an antitank weapon that threatened U.S. armor.

However, enemy gunfire remained heavy and Bacon scrambled atop a tank for a better view of the situation. Ignoring automatic weapon rounds snapping around him and pinging off the turret, he directed covering fire into other bunkers. The suppressing fire allowed removal of casualties.

Bacon retired after twenty-one years in the Army, including a second Vietnam tour. Becoming vice president of the Congressional Medal of Honor Society, the devoted veteran wrote, "I'll fight for this great land and even die for her—for this is my land, secured by God and man . . . be proud that you are an American, and thank God that you are."

Five medals were awarded for November, a new record for the Vietnam War. Four went to men of the Twenty-fifth Division; two members of Able Company, Twenty-seventh Infantry were decorated for the same action on November 5. The company commander was Captain Robert F. Foley, three years out of West Point. His unit was moving to help extract another company from danger near Quan Dau Tieng, when the advance element was halted by heavy Viet Cong gunfire from well-camouflaged positions. Foley ran forward, assessed the situation, and directed one platoon to flank the enemy while he led the other two in the attack.

When both of Foley's radio operators were shot, he moved them to cover and resumed his advance. When a machine gun crew went down, he took the M60 and pressed ahead, alternately firing on the move, shouting directions, and covering removal of more casualties.

Shortly, the Massachusetts officer learned that his flanking platoon had been stopped, so he moved to investigate. While taking command of the maneuver element, he was knocked down by a grenade blast, sustaining multiple injuries. Nevertheless, he continued leading from the front, taking three enemy positions by himself.

One of Foley's soldiers was PFC John F. Baker Jr., less than a week past his twenty-first birthday. When the point man was killed, Baker ran to the head of the column and, with another GI, destroyed two Communist bunkers. The other soldier was shot, but Baker stood fast, killing four VC snipers and taking the mortally wounded man to safety. With a machine gunner, the Midwesterner then attacked two other positions, destroying one before his partner was hit. Like Foley, Baker seized the M60 and finished the attack on the next bunker. Then he helped the gunner to cover, retrieved more ammo, and returned to the fight. With enemy resistance increasing, Baker alternately fired his "hog," killed other VC, and retrieved more casualties.

Almost miraculously, Foley and Baker survived to receive their medals in person.

Staff Sergeant Delbert O. Jennings of the Air Cav also used an M60 in the last medal action of the year. In the Kim Song Valley on December 27, his company was defending Landing Zone Bird, which came under attack by North Vietnamese regulars. Having moved into position during the Christmas truce, the Communists arrived in regimental strength, supported by heavy weapons.

Jennings, a thirty-year-old veteran, used his weapon to stop the initial enemy advance, cutting down a dozen North Vietnamese soldiers. He covered his squad's retreat to better positions, then gunned two en-

■ *The Medal in "The Nam"*

The Vietnam conflict was America's longest war. Hostilities lasted from 1961 to 1975, though the greatest activity occurred from 1965 through 1972. As of 2003, about 150 Army medals had been awarded for ground actions throughout Southeast Asia, plus six for Army aviation personnel. Ninety-six were posthumous—over 60 percent. That was comparable to the Army figure for Korea and more than the ratio for World War II.

By far the greatest number of awards for Army ground actions in one year was forty-one in 1968, about one-quarter of the total. The next most active years were 1967 and 1969.

Army units receiving the most medals were the First Cavalry Division, with twenty-five (plus two aviation awards); the Tropic Lightnings of the Twenty-fifth Division, twenty-one; 101st Airborne Division, seventeen; the 173rd Airborne Brigade garnered thirteen; an even dozen to the Fourth Division; the First and Americal Divisions, eleven each; and the Ninth Division, ten. Special Forces soldiers received eighteen medals; eight for the Fifth Special Forces Group.

Occasionally, the Medal of Honor was exploited for political purposes. At least one military aide to Lyndon Johnson recalls the president saying, "I need to make a speech. Trot me out a hero, son."

Nevertheless, Vietnam recipients represented the gamut of soldiers in the 1960s and early '70s. There were lifers and teenagers. Some were on their second or even third war. Some were draftees. At least one admitted to being stoned on marijuana at the time of his action. Whatever their background, the recipients are unanimous: all gave some; some gave all.

---

emy sapper teams. During the next withdrawal, he fought hand-to-hand, clubbing one Vietnamese to death.

Badly in need of reinforcement, the firebase received heli-borne troopers whom Jennings directed to a safe landing amid heavy gunfire. When the NVA pulled back, Jennings then volunteered to lead a sweep beyond the perimeter searching for eight missing GIs. The wounded men were recovered despite booby traps and sporadic rifle fire.

Apart from the Medal of Honor, Jennings later became command sergeant major of the First Cavalry Division. He passed away in March 2003.

1967

Thirty-one medals have thus far been awarded for 1967 actions by soldiers in ground combat. That year, Lyndon Johnson announced that more American troops were needed in South Vietnam. Meanwhile, the antiwar movement gained momentum. In October, 50,000 protestors marched at the Pentagon; many soldiers "in country" saw them as traitors.

In February, some eight hundred Sky Soldiers of the 173rd Airborne Brigade jumped in Operation Junction City near Kontum. It was the only significant combat drop of the Vietnam War. However, combat increased throughout the country that month, as a new record was set. Six GIs eventually received the Medal of Honor for actions during February 1967.

Three members of the Fourth Division earned posthumous awards in a three-week period. On January 27, Spec. 4 Donald W. Evans Jr. met the high standard of combat medics. Despite being wounded himself, he repeatedly ran through gunfire and explosions to reach downed GIs and was killed while tending yet another soldier.

On February 15, PFC Louis E. Willett's company tangled with a larger Communist force. In the prolonged firefight, the New Yorker covered the withdrawal of his pinned-down squad. He shrugged off painful wounds to exchange close-range rifle fire with the VC, permitting his friends to regroup at cost of his own life.

The next day, Staff Sergeant Elmelindo R. Smith displayed incredible stamina in a prolonged firefight. Though repeatedly wounded—he was knocked unconscious when struck by a rocket-propelled grenade—the thirty-two-year-old Hawaiian refused to quit. When finally immobilized by blood loss, he positioned himself in the open, knowing he would draw fire but also providing warning of approaching Communist troops. He died in place, still vigilant on behalf of his friends.

Sergeant First Class Charles E. Hosking Jr. was a career infantryman who had been wounded in the Battle of the Bulge but was still a combat soldier twenty-three years later. In March 1967, with Company A, Fifth Special Forces Group, he was an advisor to a South Vietnamese civilian defense group in Phuoc Long Province. While preparing to move a captured Viet Cong sniper to the team's base, Hosking was startled when the Vietnamese snatched a grenade off his belt. The VC pulled the pin and ran toward four U.S. and Vietnamese officers nearby. The forty-two-year-old Hosking overtook the enemy and wrestled him to the ground, forcing the grenade against the man's chest. Hosking then rolled atop the Vietnamese, pinning him until the grenade exploded. Both men died in the blast. Hosking was posthumously promoted to master sergeant.

In May of that year, a battalion of the Ninth Division's Sixtieth Infantry was operating in the Ap Bac area. A platoon was taken under fire from bunkers and trees, so Sergeant Leonard B. Keller moved for a better position and shot one VC who fled a bunker. Joined by twenty-two-year-old Spec. 4 Raymond R. Wright, Keller seized an M60 and began taking on each bunker in turn. With Keller providing suppressing fire, Wright dashed ahead to toss a grenade in the next position, killing the enemy soldier there. The duo repeated the process on the next position, then leapfrogged ahead once more. The third bunker contained a VC with an automatic rifle who pinned down much of the platoon. Keller and Wright dealt with him as well. With their teamwork well established, they assaulted four more bunkers, killing the VC inside each time.

Once beyond the enemy defensive line, Keller and Wright spotted enemy snipers fleeing the trees. The two GIs kept up the pressure, forcing the remaining Vietnamese out of position to threaten the platoon. Between them, Keller and Wright had killed or dispersed the equivalent of an enemy platoon. Theirs were the division's first medals of the Vietnam War.

A double award went to the Fourth Division on May 20, both posthumous, for saving friends from grenades. The First Battalion, Eighth Infantry was engaged in Kontum Province that day. PFC Leslie A. Bellrichard of Charlie Company, occupying a fighting hole with four other GIs, was knocked down by a mortar explosion. Bellrichard dropped the grenade he was ready to throw and, with no time to retrieve it, rolled on top of it before it detonated. Meanwhile, Staff Sergeant

Frankie Z. Molnar of Bravo Company helped repel repeated assaults and crawled through heavy fire to fetch extra ammunition. While helping others move a badly wounded GI, Molnar used his body to stifle a grenade explosion.

PFC Sammy L. Davis served with the Fourth Artillery, Ninth Infantry Division. Defending a fire-support base west of Cai Lay, Davis had just observed his twenty-first birthday. At 2:00 on the morning of November 18, 1967, the base came under mortar fire while a VC unit of battalion strength swarmed the perimeter. As his howitzer crew pointed the gun to bore-sight the enemy, Davis used an M60 to hold off the Communists. A recoilless rifle round struck the howitzer, blowing the crew off the mount and flinging Davis into a hole. He rebounded, dashed to the burning "tube," rammed home a shell, and fired. The recoil knocked him down but he bounced back to his feet and, though wounded, repeated the process four more times with the same result.

As if that weren't enough, the Midwesterner swam a stream bordering the facility to rescue three GIs, fought off more VC in the process, and returned to the gun line. There, he ignored his injuries to help man another howitzer until the attackers fled. He was not the first "cannon cocker" to receive the medal in Vietnam, nor was he the last.

The 173rd Airborne garnered three medals in November. PFC John A. Barnes III was far from Boston on November 12. When he saw his platoon's machine gun crew killed, he dropped his M79 grenade launcher and sprinted through NVA fire to reach the M60. He got there in time to kill nine Communist soldiers assaulting the position. When Barnes turned to grab an ammo box, an enemy grenade rolled beside some wounded men nearby. John Barnes sacrificed his twenty-two-year-old life to save his buddies.

Over Thanksgiving, the Second and Fourth Battalions of the 503rd fought their way to the summit of Hill 875. Medals went to Chaplain Charles J. Watters and PFC Carlos J. Lozada.

Watters was a forty-year-old major, practically ancient by infantry

---

■ *Other Redlegs in Vietnam*

A half dozen Army artillerymen received the medal in Vietnam; two in October 1967 alone. SFC Webster Anderson of the 101st Airborne fought from the parapet of his battery's position near Tam Ky on October 15. Two days later, Lieutenant Harold B. Durham Jr., of the Big Red One, died as a forward observer directing "arty" for his regiment. Critically wounded, he called fire on his position to repel enemy forces.

Commanding the First Battalion, Fifth Artillery, Lieutenant Colonel Charles C. Rogers fought as an infantryman on November 1, 1968. Though wounded three times, he led his cannoneers in repelling assaults against his position.

In March 1970, Sergeant Mitchell Stout of the 44th Artillery waited for an enemy mortar attack to abate. When it did, Communist troops tossed a grenade into his crew's bunker. The twenty-year-old noncom scooped up the grenade and just made the exit when he was killed in the explosion.

Another forward observer who made the ultimate sacrifice was Lieutenant Brian M. Thacker of the 92nd Artillery. When his hilltop firebase was overrun in March 1971, he directed fire "on my pos" (position) and survived the shelling. Though wounded, he survived eight days in the bush, returning to safety.

---

standards. He had earned jump wings at thirty-eight, twice the age of the youngest paratroopers. But when a support company ran into heavy opposition near Dak To, he did not hesitate. The chaplain ran forward, moved wounded men from the line of fire, provided treatment as well as consolation, and administered last rites to the dying. At one point, he dashed between the two opposing forces to carry a shell-shocked trooper to safety. Once a perimeter was established, the New Jersey priest went alone beyond the lines to bring in critically wounded soldiers. He made at least three such treks through gunfire and mortar shells, then distributed food and water. He was killed while treating casualties.

Meanwhile, Carlos Lozada manned a machine gun in the 503rd's Second Battalion. With three other troopers, he was positioned in a listening post ahead of the company lines, when a company strength NVA attack developed. The Puerto Rican M60 gunner shot twenty or more, some within ten yards of his position, but the Vietnamese were persistent. They threatened to envelop the company, which was ordered to pull back. Lozada shouted for his three-man crew to join the withdrawal while he covered them. With NVA closing from three sides, he kept firing until severely wounded. He was carried rearward but died shortly thereafter. The Second Battalion lost 117 killed and missing in the vicious, close-range combat.

Medal of Honor history was made in December when a second Vietnam War chaplain earned the award. Captain Angelo J. Liteky was a Roman Catholic priest dedicated to fighting Communism. At age thirty-six, he remained in the forward area of the 199th Infantry Brigade, an independent unit operating in Bien Hoa Province.

Able Company of the Fourth Battalion, Twelfth Infantry, contacted a far larger force that gained fire superiority. With most GIs hugging the ground, Liteky was constantly on the move throughout the night. By the time reinforcements arrived the next morning, the chaplain had retrieved more than twenty casualties under fire while administering the last rites to mortally wounded GIs.

That was only the beginning of the story.

Liteky left the army in 1971; four years later, he left the priesthood and changed his name to Charles. After two tours in Vietnam, he turned to social activism and became a tax protester.

In 1986, Liteky renounced his Medal of Honor, leaving it at the Vietnam Memorial in protest of the Reagan administration's anticommunist policy in Central America. Eventually, he served two federal prison terms, the first (six months) for vandalism at Fort Benning in 1990, the next in 2000 (one year) for trespassing to protest training of foreign special forces there.

Only one other recipient had renounced the medal, former Marine Corps Captain (then Staff Sergeant) John J. McGinty. He received his award for 1966 combat and later declined it on religious grounds.

1968

In the Chinese zodiac, 1968 was the Year of the Monkey. In the history of the war, it was the year of Tet. During April, U.S. and North Vietnamese representatives began discussing prospects for peace negotiations in Paris. Meanwhile, U.S. troop strength peaked at some 550,000; a record 15,000 were killed. In November, Richard Nixon won the presidency, partly on the strength of a "secret plan" to end the war.

It was the banner year for Vietnam Medals of Honor: forty-four for the army, including three aviators. Six actions in January tied the record again; each award to a different organization.

The first award for the pivotal year went to Corporal Jerry W. Wickam of the Eleventh Armored Cavalry Regiment. On January 6, he dismounted from his "track" to clear a bunker complex of VC troops, largely unaided. He was killed after returning to the area to assess damage following an air strike.

February was the season of the Tet holiday. It was also the signal for the largest Communist operation of the war to date. Late on January 30, at least 70,000 NVA and VC troops launched a well coordinated series of attacks against a hundred South Vietnamese cities, towns, and facilities. Six GIs received Medals of Honor for actions in the next four weeks.

One of the province capitals targeted by the Communists was Chau Phu, hard on the Cambodian border, one hundred miles west of Saigon. There, on the first two days of Tet, Staff Sergeant Drew D. Dix helped fight off two VC battalions, despite the near collapse of the South Vietnamese command structure. As an advisor, Dix led ARVN soldiers in rescuing a nurse isolated in the city center, then returned to lead eight more civilians through mortar and gunfire. Subsequently, he retrieved two Filipino citizens by killing six VC.

The twenty-three-year-old NCO continued his rescue efforts the next day. He led twenty Vietnamese soldiers in clearing the major buildings downtown, taking twenty prisoners in the process. When he learned that VC held the deputy province chief's wife and children, he entered the house and freed them. Most likely, Dix saved their lives, as Communist forces routinely executed the civilian leadership. In two days, Drew Dix had saved fourteen U.S. and other civilians, killed at least fourteen enemy, and took twenty prisoners.

Sergeant First Class Eugene Ashley Jr. was a senior advisor leading an ad hoc Laotian force to relieve Green Berets at Lang Vei on February 6. It was a desperate situation: eleven light tanks supported an eighteen-hour Communist attack on the outpost near the Laotian border. Ashley's flanking movement relieved pressure on the Special Forces compound, and he seemed everywhere at once, doing everything possible. He fired mortar rounds, directed artillery and air strikes, and led five attacks against the North Vietnamese. During the last assault, he called friendly fire within lethal distance of his own men to repulse the Communists. He took his team to the crest of a hill overlooking the area and, though badly wounded, he continued fighting until he fainted from blood loss. Friends carried him toward the command bunker, but he was killed by artillery. Nevertheless, most of the survivors were evacuated by air.

On the same day as Ashley's action, PFC Thomas J. Kinsman participated in a Ninth Division reconnaissance mission near Vinh Long. His company's armored personnel carriers were ambushed by VC with rocket-propelled grenades and automatic weapons, and the GIs dismounted to attack the enemy positions. In dense foliage, a VC got close enough to throw a grenade into a group of eight Americans. Kinsman dropped onto the grenade, taking most of the blast and saving his friends. Miraculously, he survived severe head and chest wounds.

Staff Sergeant Fred W. Zabitosky's Medal of Honor citation says he was leading a long-range reconnaissance patrol (LRRP) in South Vietnam on February 19. Like many documents of the era, it misrepresents the facts. Zabitosky's nine-man team was inserted to gather intelligence across the Laotian border, where officially no Americans operated.

But the North Vietnamese did. In ten-foot-high elephant grass the Special Forces men walked into a large NVA camp. Both sides realized the other's presence at the same time. It became a running gunfight.

As the Green Berets withdrew toward their landing zone, Zabitosky

■ Across the Line

Staff Sergeant Fred Zabitosky was not the only Medal of Honor recipient whose action posed a political embarrassment to Washington. His February 1968 citation stated that he fought in South Vietnam, when in fact he was leading a long-range patrol into Laos. Though badly burned, he rescued two crewmen and survived to receive his medal.

A year previously, Lieutenant George K. Sisler also was operating in Laos; his citation said he was "deep within enemy dominated territory."

Spec. 5 John J. Kedenburg sacrificed himself in a June 1968 patrol, giving up his position in a helo extraction to permit a South Vietnamese soldier to reach safety. Kedenburg died fighting as the helo lifted off.

In December of that year, Sergeant Robert L. Howard was seriously wounded and, unable to walk, crawled among his outnumbered platoon members to provide first aid. For more than three hours, the GIs and Vietnamese held off two enemy companies until evacuated by air.

Staff Sergeant Franklin D. Miller led a U.S.-ARVN LRRP unit in January 1970, single-handedly covering the team's withdrawal to an extraction point. He made repeated solo counterattacks, permitting his wounded soldiers to reach safety.

Some wartime citations have been corrected, but it is unknown if others reflect the geographic reality.

Semantic disingenuousness also attended Staff Sergeant Roy P. Benavidez's 1968 citation. The Pentagon allowed that he was operating "west of Loc Ninh." In truth, he was across the border from Loc Ninh. The courageous Green Beret received his Medal from President Reagan in 1981.

---

planted claymore mines, fired his rifle, and had the radio operator call for air support. Shortly, A-1 "Sandys" were overhead, raining 750-pound bombs and napalm on the area. The air strike bought some time, but precious little.

Forming a small perimeter at the LZ (landing zone), Zabitosky directed the defense while calling helicopter gun runs. The rescue would be a helo pilot's nightmare: "dustoff on a hot LZ."

When two Hueys landed, the troopers scrambled aboard, but Zabitosky's helicopter took repeated hits and spun out of control. The team leader was ejected from the doorway and landed mere yards from the crash. He regained consciousness with his clothes on fire. He didn't know it, but his back was fractured and he had broken several ribs. Yet he suppressed the pain, forced his way through the burning wreckage to retrieve the pilot, and dragged him away. Then the NCO returned through the searing flames, hefted the critically burned copilot, and hauled him to the second Huey as well. The copilot died of his wounds; Zabitosky and the pilot recovered.

On February 21, the Second Battalion, 501st Infantry was assaulting Communist positions along a river near Hue and encountered heavy fire from rifles, machine guns, and rocket-propelled grenades. Staff Sergeant Joe R. Hooper pulled together several D Company troopers and crossed the river, under fire, overrunning bunkers on the opposite bank. As the rest of Delta resumed the attack, Hooper dragged some wounded to safety but was hit in the torso. Ignoring the wound, he continued leading attacks on successive bunkers, destroying them with rifle fire and grenades. He then slew two enemy soldiers who had shot the battalion chaplain.

Hooper then regrouped his men and began a sweep of the area, reducing three structures defended by Vietnamese riflemen. He was attacked by an enemy officer, whom he killed by bayonet, then dashed ahead to assault another stronghold that was holding up his unit. Again he used his rifle and grenades to destroy the objective.

Hooper's strength had begun to fade from the bullet wound and successive grenade blasts. However, he remained in charge and pressed ahead to another line of bunkers. His men were pinned down by fire from four positions on the left, but Hooper gathered more grenades and sprinted along a shallow trench, tossing grenades into each one. Only two Vietnamese survived his attack.

By then, Hooper's men reached the last line of Communist defenses. He personally destroyed one with an incendiary grenade and took two more with rifle fire. Then, aware of a wounded GI huddled in a trench, Hooper dashed through heavy gunfire to retrieve the man, but was confronted by a North Vietnamese officer. Hooper shot him with a pistol and pulled the casualty to safety. He was still not finished, however, and shot three more enemy soldiers in the final defensive position.

Hooper then reorganized his men, established a perimeter, and declined evacuation until the next day. He had used the full arsenal of personal weapons: rifle, bayonet, pistol, and grenades, overcoming a dozen or more enemy positions almost single-handedly.

Another Delta Company NCO received the medal for the same action. Staff Sergeant Clifford C. Sims, a twenty-five year-old Floridian, was advancing toward a bunker in thick foliage, when he heard a loud, distinct click just ahead. Recognizing it as a command-detonated mine, Sims shouted a warning and threw himself on the likely position. His body absorbed most of the blast, killing him instantly. It was the only time in 101st Division history that two men received the medal for the same event.

The Tet offensive was declared ended on February 22, by which time four more medals were earned. Some 10,000 NVA and VC had been killed; their organization badly mauled. But the demonstration of Communist strength and resolve sent tremors through the American political landscape. In March, General William Westmoreland asked for an additional 200,000 troops; a wholly unrealistic prospect. That same month Johnson announced he would not seek re-election.

On March 9, Captain Jack H. Jacobs was temporarily assigned as an advisor to the ARVN Ninth Division in Kien Phong Province. Jacobs, with the first company in contact with VC bunkers, was wounded by mortar fire but assumed command when the South Vietnamese commander was hit. With blood running in his eyes, Jacobs not only directed his impromptu command but also helped move seriously wounded men and provided first aid. Repeatedly, he ran across open terrain, exposed to machine gun fire, retrieving a total of fourteen soldiers. He killed at least three VC in the process, then accepted treatment of his own wounds.

The eight medals awarded for May 1968 set a record for the war, as of 2003. Five were posthumous; two went to the 101st Airborne.

Among the Screaming Eagles, Spec. 4 Peter M. Guenette sacrificed himself on a grenade. Meanwhile, in an action reminiscent of 1918, Sergeant Robert M. Patterson single-handedly took five enemy bunkers, killing eight enemy in the process.

In the Sixth Infantry of the Americal Division, Platoon Sergeant Finnis D. McCleery fought as expected of a Texas-born Irishman. Ignoring grenade wounds, he crossed about sixty yards of fire-swept ground to reach a bunker complex and secure the enemy line.

Lieutenant Douglas B. Fournet of the Seventh Cavalry died trying to disarm a mine, while PFC James W. Fous of the Ninth Division dived on a grenade to protect his friends.

Grenades proved even more troublesome that month. Sergeant Anund C. Roark of the Fourth Division died protecting his soldiers from an enemy grenade. In a similar action, the 199th Brigade's Spec. 4 Kenneth L. Olson dropped a grenade when shot. Rather than try to kick it away, he fell on it to protect other GIs.

The devotion of one soldier to his organization is called "unit cohesion" by military professionals. Frequently, it amounts to a type of love. However defined, it was demonstrated by Staff Sergeant Marvin R. Young near Ben Cui on August 21. Taken under heavy fire by a larger NVA force, Young's company was forced to withdraw to more defensive positions. However, the Texan noted that his point element was unable to disengage. Despite wounds to the head, arm, and leg, he refused to be moved. In staying behind, he provided covering fire for his squad to withdraw.

The last medal of the year went to a Green Beret noncom, Sergeant First Class Robert L. Howard. He had been nominated for the Medal of Honor twice before, but his was a case of "third time lucky." On December 30, operating in Laos, his platoon survived more than three hours of close contact with perhaps two Communist companies. Howard's rifle was destroyed by a grenade blast and he was wounded. Though unable to walk, he risked gunfire to retrieve casualties, provided first aid, and supervised the team's defense before helicopters arrived. Also presented the Distinguished Service Cross, Silver Star, and Bronze Star, he was probably the most decorated GI of the Vietnam War. Howard was commissioned shortly after his Medal of Honor action, served in Desert Storm, and retired as a colonel after thirty-six years of active duty.

1969

American forces began a slow withdrawal in August 1969, with 480,000 men in-country at year end. By that time, another 10,000 Americans had been killed. In November, Nixon's "Vietnamization" program got underway, with ARVN forces accepting a greater combat role.

Nearly thirty medals were awarded for 1969 combat, five each to the Cavalry and the Americal Divisions. But the first went to PFC Don J. Jenkins of the Ninth Division on January 6. While on a reconnaissance patrol, Jenkins' company came under fire from concealed Communist forces. The twenty-year-old machine gunner independently moved to the flank and began suppressive fire, but his M60 jammed. Subsequently, he used lightweight rocket launchers and a grenade launcher to destroy enemy bunkers. Then, although wounded, he risked death to make three trips to retrieve wounded men, alone and in darkness. Jenkins was promoted to staff sergeant at the time of his medal presentation.

A lifesaving machine gunner also figured in one of the six medal actions during March. On the third, Sergeant Lester R. Stone Jr. took over an M60 when his Americal platoon's gunner was wounded. The squad leader ignored AK-47 rounds impacting around him, working feverishly to clear a malfunction, then laid down fire on Communist positions while casualties were pulled back. The North Vietnamese, probably sensing a temporary advantage, rushed Stone's position. Taking hits, he rose to a kneeling position and coolly shot down six before falling dead.

Two weeks later, another Americal soldier died saving comrades in the First Infantry. Twenty-year-old Spec. 4 Thomas J. McMahon was a devoted medic who saw three GIs fall with severe injuries. He ran forward, applied first aid to the nearest man, and carried him to safety. On the second trip into enemy gunfire, McMahon was wounded by a mortar shell but retrieved the second soldier as well. He declined treatment of his own wounds to make a third effort and was killed before he could reach him.

Yet another Americal medic earned a posthumous medal, when PFC

Spec. 4 Thomas J. McMahon, Americal Division

Daniel J. Shea matched McMahon's dedication. The Connecticut soldier left cover four times to bring fallen GIs to safety. On his fifth effort, Shea was critically wounded as he reached the casualty. Nevertheless, Shea treated the man and carried him to the platoon position. Just before reaching cover, Shea was knocked down by a mortar explosion. He died shortly thereafter but had retrieved five men from almost certain death.

Medics such as Tom McMahon and Dan Shea set the standard for heroism and devotion—not so much to duty as to their friends.

Not only medics saved men under fire. Captain Kern W. Dunagan commanded a company in the Americal's Forty-sixth Infantry on May 13, operating in Quang Tin Province. He was seriously wounded in an early-morning mortar attack but remained in command, directing the disengagement from a superior Communist force. He personally retrieved two wounded GIs, sustaining another wound himself. Nevertheless, when he learned that six soldiers were cut off from the company, he went after them. He found the isolated men and carried one who was unable to walk. The thirty-five-year-old officer further demonstrated his concern for his soldiers by ensuring that all casualties had been treated and evacuated before he accepted treatment himself.

All five of the Air Cavalry's 1969 awards were posthumous, including Sergeant Rodney J. Evans, who placed himself between a command-detonated mine and his men on July 18.

■ *Medics*

Fifteen U.S. Army medics received the Medal of Honor for lifesaving actions in Southeast Asia. Eight of the awards were made posthumously.

The medics were both draftees and lifers, from age twenty to thirty-nine. Two were over thirty; six were under twenty-one.

Sp.5 Lawrence Joel	173rd Airborne Brig.	November 1965
Sp.4 Alfred Rascon	173rd Airborne Brig.	March 1966
Sp.4 Donald W. Evans Jr. *	4th Infantry Div.	January 1967
PFC James H. Monroe *	1st Cavalry Div.	February 1967
Sp.4 Charles C. Hagemeister	1st Cavalry Div.	March 1967
Sp.5 Edgard L. McWethy Jr. *	1st Cavalry Div.	June 1967
PFC Clarence E. Sasser	9th Infantry Div.	January 1968
Corp. Thomas W. Bennett *	14th Infantry Reg.	February 1969
Sp.4 Thomas J. McMahon *	Americal Div.	March 1969
PFC Daniel J. Shea *	Americal Div.	May 1969
Sp.4 Joseph G. LaPointe *	101st Airborne Div.	June 1969
Sgt. Gary B. Beikrich	5th Special Forces	April 1970
PFC Kenneth M. Kays	101st Airborne Div.	May 1970
SFC Louis R. Rocco	Military Assis. Cmd.	May 1970
PFC David F. Winder *	Americal Div.	May 1970

*posthumous award

Another medic who should have received the Medal of Honor was Sergeant Billie Hall of Tulsa, Oklahoma. Fighting with a Special Forces A Team at Camp Ashau in March 1996, he lost both legs at the knee in a mortar explosion but refused to quit. A friend applied tourniquets, and Hall crawled through the position, treating other casualties while refusing further attention himself. He died as a result of his wounds and received a Distinguished Service Cross. Hall left a wife and baby son he had never seen. Five other Distinguished Service Crosses were awarded for the defense of the camp but no Medals of Honor. Speculation held that the Army felt too many Medals of Honor were going to Green Berets.

By one reckoning, 1,357 Army medics are listed on the Vietnam Memorial in Washington, D.C.

On March 21, Spec. 4 Donald R. Johnston was a mortar man at a firebase in Tay Ninh Province. He defended his position against enemy sappers and, while firing from a bunker, he saw a Vietnamese hurl three satchel charges inside. Without hesitation, he covered all three with his body, shielding six other GIs from the worst of the blast.

First Lieutenant Robert L. Poxon led his cavalry troop into a "hot" landing zone (LZ) on June 2. Seeing one of his GIs shot down, Poxon ran toward the man but found him dead and was himself hit by gunfire. Though bleeding badly, he shrugged off the pain and directed his platoon against a bunker blocking egress from the LZ. The Michigan officer crawled within grenade range, rose to his feet, and sprinted the last few yards. The gunners swiveled on the new threat and shot Poxon, but he destroyed the bunker. Crossfire from another position then killed the twenty-two-year-old leader.

Sergeant Donald S. Skidgel was killed while exposing himself to automatic weapons fire on September 14. He had already made two trips through bullet-swept terrain, destroying a bunker and returning for extra ammunition. He then directed his vehicle into an exposed area to draw enemy attention away from his troop's command element and received mortal wounds.

Second Lieutenant Robert D. Leisy was an Eighth Cavalry platoon leader engaged in a firefight in Phuoc Long Province on December 2. He sighted an enemy RPG gunner in a nearby tree and, as the rocket-propelled grenade left the tube, Leisy moved to cover his radio operator. The grenade exploded nearby, and Leisy absorbed the full blast. Nevertheless, despite probably knowing his wounds were fatal, he insisted that other casualties be tended first.

The year also featured three Special Forces actions.

Sergeant First Class William M. Bryant was a Green Beret who died fighting on March 24. Commanding a civilian defense company in Long Khanh Province, his Vietnamese battalion was attacked by portions of three Communist regiments. The ensuing battle lasted thirty-four hours, and Bryant was seldom still. He constantly moved among his troops, directing the defense, moving casualties, and retrieving air-dropped ammunition. When the fighting tapered off, he led a patrol beyond the perimeter to assess Communist intentions, repelled an attack, and led his small force back to base. Subsequently, he led another patrol to break the siege, advancing 220 yards into the brush. Though wounded in an ambush, he remained in charge, directed helicopter gunships, and used the interval to destroy a machine gun position single-handedly. He was regrouping his team when killed by an RPG blast. He was thirty-six.

Spec. 4 Robert D. Law was a Ranger attached to the Big Red One, operating in Tinh Phuoc Thanh Province. On February 22, the twenty-four-year-old Texan was one of six men on a long-range reconnaissance patrol (LRRP) that encountered a Communist unit. A prolonged firefight erupted, but

Staff Sgt. Robert J. Pruden, Americal Division

Law moved to a flank to attempt suppressive fire on the enemy. When a grenade was thrown into the Americans' position, Law could have dived to cover in a streambed but instead smothered the explosion himself.

Another medal-winning Ranger was twenty-year-old Staff Sergeant Robert J. Pruden of the American Division. His team was inserted into enemy territory on November 29, seeking information on enemy units. While establishing an ambush position, his five men were fired upon from two Communist units. Pruden scrambled from cover, firing on the move to cover a Ranger caught in the open. Though hit three times, the Minnesotan caught the enemy off balance, permitting his team to disengage and reach an extraction point. He died of his wounds before helicopters could take him to safety.

1970

From the end of April to the end of June, U.S. forces operated in Cambodia, dislodging traditional North Vietnamese enclaves. But despite increased reduction of American troops in South Vietnam, the Cambodian incursion incited widespread protest. In May, the nation's attention was focused on Ohio, where the National Guard responded to antiwar riots around Kent State University. On May 4, the Guardsmen encountered a violent protest on campus and opened fire, killing four students, including an ROTC cadet.

Thus far, seventeen Army Medals of Honor have been presented for ground combat in 1970.

Spec. 4 Danny J. Petersen of the Twenty-fifth Division commanded an M113 armored personnel carrier while operating against North Vietnamese forces in Tay Ning Province on January 9. When the Communists opened fire, another APC of Petersen's company clanked to a halt. Petersen saw that the crew was trapped amid machine gun fire and rocket-propelled grenades but moved to intervene. He directed his driver to a position between the crippled "track" and the NVA, allowing the crew to dismount long enough to conduct repairs. While firing his machine gun at the Communists, Petersen's vehicle was hit by a rocket-propelled grenade that wounded his driver. Within pistol range of the enemy, the twenty-year-old Petersen carried the soldier across nearly fifty yards of open terrain before reaching cover. As if that weren't enough, Petersen returned to his M113, climbed atop the vehicle, and resumed firing. His suppressive fire allowed other troops to disengage, but he was taking rounds from three sides. Finally, he was mortally hit; his sacrifice was honored in July 1974.

Throughout the medal's history many soldiers have been described as one-man armies. That description fit Sergeant Richard A. Penry of the 199th Brigade on the night of January 31. His company incurred heavy fire from enemy mortars, rockets, and small arms that took most of the leadership off its feet. Even worse, the platoon was scattered in a loose perimeter comprised of isolated pockets of GIs with little or no coordination. Radios repeatedly were damaged or failed, placing communications at a premium. Penry first tended his company commander and other casualties, then began a lengthy, frustrating search for a working radio. He risked death fetching three sets before finding a fourth that functioned. After calling for help, he manned a forward position and almost single-handedly blunted a platoon-sized attack.

Spec. 4 Danny J. Petersen, 25th Division

During a relative lull in the firefight, he learned of five wounded GIs beyond the U.S. lines and brought them to safety. When medevac choppers motored into the area, the Californian again left his lines to establish a homing beach for the "dustoffs." He then triaged eighteen casualties and ensured their evacuation before joining another platoon to pursue the Communist force.

Penry received his medal eighteen months later. He died in 1994, only forty-five years old.

Nineteen-year-old Spec. 4 Peter C. Lemon was a Canadian-born trooper in the First Cav. On April 1, he was a machine gunner defending Fire Base Illingworth against a large attack in Tay Ninh Province. He fired his M60 until it quit, then picked up an M16 and shot it until it too jammed. Lemon then resorted to grenades to repel the next assault, killing or driving off all but one enemy, whom he chased down and killed hand to hand.

Sgt. Peter C. Lemon, 1st Cavalry Division

During the attack, Lemon was wounded by a bursting grenade, but he carried a more seriously wounded casualty to the aid station. Upon returning to his position, he was struck again. He could have pulled out but, recognizing that the Communists were about to break through, he stayed put. Again he expended his supply of grenades and went after the survivors with his bare hands. In the process, he was wounded a third time but still persisted. He found another M60 and hauled it atop the parapet, spraying 7.62mm rounds into the surging attackers. Finally, he collapsed and was carried off for medical attention. Fire Base Illingworth survived—and so did Peter Lemon. He became the twenty-sixth First Cavalry man to receive the Medal of Honor since 1944. Subsequently, he studied child psychology, becoming a motivational speaker, author, and sculptor.

Most Medal of Honor actions are cited for events lasting minutes or hours. Sergeant First Class Gary L. Littrell was in almost constant action for five days in April. As an advisor to an ARVN ranger battalion in Kontum Province, he assumed command when enemy shelling killed or wounded the senior Vietnamese officers and noncoms, leaving him the only uninjured American. From April 4–8, he exhibited "near superhuman endurance" in repeatedly calling in air support and artillery fire to repel Communist attacks. The Rangers saw him constantly in motion, marking the position for aircraft, treating casualties, distributing ammo, and placing himself as both a leader and shooter. His fluency in Vietnamese was essential to co-ordinating the defense, and his skill in "aviation English" was equally important. At one point, he directed attack pilots in dropping their ordnance on advancing enemy within fifty meters of his own "posit." He received the medal in October 1973. Littrell succeeded Nick Bacon as president of the Congressional Medal of Honor Society in 2002.

SFC Gary L. Littrell, II Corps Advisory Group

Spec. 4 Kenneth E. Stumpf led his squad of the Thirty-fifth Infantry against an NVA position near Duc Pho on April 25, 1970. When the Vietnamese opened fire, three of Stumpf's men were hit by automatic weapons fire. Though he occupied a secure trench, he left safety three times to retrieve each man despite close-range gunfire. Then he regrouped his soldiers against the enemy bunker complex, attacking with grenades. Nearing the first bunker, he tossed an "egg" through the firing slit, but the NVA returned it. Stumpf ducked for cover, and after the explosion, he modified his tactics. He pulled the pins on two more grenades, counted off two or three seconds, then threw them inside. Both exploded before the occupants could pitch them back. With the first impediment overcome, Stumpf's company pressed ahead to secure the rest of the area.

The Vietnam War record for a long-term Medal of Honor citation went to Lieutenant Colonel Andre C. Lucas, West Point Class of 1954. He was recognized for his tenacity in defending Fire Base Ripcord, July 1–23. Commanding a battalion of the Screaming Eagles, Lucas was con-

Lt. Col. Andre C. Lucas, 101st Airborne Division

stantly engaged for more than three weeks. He was frequently airborne in a command-and-control helicopter, directing his companies from low level, where the Huey drew heavy ground fire. He also dropped badly needed supplies to his men. When another chopper was shot down, Lucas led the rescue attempt but judged enemy fire too heavy. He ordered other troopers to remain behind and personally risked death from Communist weapons, exploding ammunition, and the helicopter's burning fuel. He remained at the blazing crash site until the entire aircraft was consumed, surviving the multiple risks. However, he was killed while directing the battalion's withdrawal.

1971

The Army's last five Medals of Honor in Southeast Asia were awarded for actions in 1971.

Spec. 4 Larry G. Dahl was a twenty-year-old Oregonian serving in a transportation company based in Binh Dinh Province that February. Manning a gun truck that was escorting a road convoy, he responded to an ambush and participated in the ensuing firefight. As the gun trucks disengaged, a Communist soldier threw a grenade into Dahl's vehicle.

Without time to toss it out, Dahl covered the grenade and was killed protecting his fellow soldiers.

The next month, Spec. 4 Michael J. Fitzmaurice survived a hard-fought battle at Khe Sanh. The 101st Airborne was in static positions near the besieged base, as Fitzmaurice and three other Screaming Eagles occupied a bunker. North Vietnamese infiltrators got close enough to fling three satchel charges inside, but the South Dakota trooper returned two before they exploded. He smothered the third with his flak jacket and his own body, sustaining injuries in the explosion but saving his friends.

Though partially blinded, Fitzmaurice got to his feet and charged the Communist sappers outside. He fired his M16 until it was destroyed in a grenade blast, then he fought hand to hand. He declined immediate evacuation in favor of remaining at his post.

An all-night siege resulted in a medal for Staff Sergeant Jon R. Cavaiani, June 4–5. Assigned to a training and advisory group supporting the South Vietnamese, the native Briton led his platoon at a radio relay post in Communist territory. He directed a successful defense of the platoon's perimeter with most of the weapon types available, then requested helicopter extraction. He called in the first three Hueys, which successfully lifted most of his GIs to safety, but he remained with the others throughout the night. In a foggy dawn, the Communists renewed their attack under cover of machine gun and RPG fire. The odds were too heavy; the NVA pressed ahead, clearly able to take the position. Cavaiani ordered his soldiers to save themselves, while he provided suppressive fire. He stood fully exposed to the attackers, thinning their advancing ranks with an M60 machine gun. When the Communists took the position, Cavaiani "played 'possum," which wasn't difficult: he had been shot and burned. He got away with it, spending ten days in the bush before being captured. He was held until Operation Homecoming in 1973, only then learning that survivors of his firebase had recommended him for a "posthumous" medal.

First Lieutenant Brian M. Thacker survived an extremely hard-fought battle to defend a U.S. and South Vietnamese firebase in Kontum Province. An unusually strong NVA force attacked at dawn on March 31, using flamethrowers to breach the perimeter. After four hours of desperate fighting, the defenders were forced to abandon their position. Upon ensuring that small groups were properly organized to escape and evade, Thacker took his M16 to the perimeter and fought alone to hold back the Communists. Finally, he called down artillery fire on his own position, giving the other American and ARVN soldiers more time to get away. Though wounded, the twenty-five-year-old artilleryman made his way to temporary safety and survived eight days in the bush. Only when the firebase was recaptured was he able to find help.

The Army's last Medal of Honor action in Vietnam was conducted by First Lieutenant Loren D. Hagen. Though assigned to the Training Advisory Group, Hagen's Special Forces team conducted reconnaissance patrols inside the demilitarized zone between North and South Vietnam on August 7. Early that morning, the Green Berets were detected by Communist forces, which attacked with automatic weapons, mortars, and RPGs. After the initial skirmish, Hagen deployed his men to repel the next assault, ignoring the risk of heavy gunfire and explosions to direct the defense. Throughout the firefight, the North Dakota officer used his rifle and grenades while scouting the perimeter and distributing ammunition. When an RPG destroyed a Special Forces bunker, Hagen crawled through heavy gunfire to lend assistance, exchanging rounds with the Communists in an effort to reach his men. He was killed in the effort, providing an eerie symmetry to the Army Medal of Honor. The Green Berets had received the first and last medals of the Vietnam War, seven years and one month apart.

Though Americans remained in direct combat in Southeast Asia, no further Army Medals of Honor were awarded. The last U.S. ground forces departed for home in August 1972, and the Paris peace accords took effect on January 27, 1973.

Subsequently, the U.S. Senate curtailed military aid to South Vietnam, and Hanoi's patience was rewarded. In April 1975, North Vietnamese tanks rolled into Saigon, completing the "reunification" of the nation.

CHAPTER NINE

THE PERENNIAL WEAPON

■

T HROUGHOUT the history of the Medal of Honor, recipients
have wielded an extraordinary variety of weapons. A survey of
twentieth-century citations reveals at least fourteen types of infantry
weapons, with grenades by far the most common, followed by rifles,
machine guns, and sidearms. Of the latter, none comes close to match-
ing the record of the M1911 Automatic Colt Pistol (ACP).

Designed by John M. Browning, the big, rugged Colt fires a .45 caliber bullet at a velocity of 800–850 feet per second. Some 3 million
eventually were obtained by the armed forces, which officially retained
the pistol until the arrival of the Beretta M9 in 1985. However, inventories were not depleted until about 1991. In its own way, the 1911 pro-
vides a concise history of the medal.

SEVENTY-FIVE YEARS OF 1911S

In the seventy-five years from 1918 to 1993, at least fifty-five Medals of Honor were presented to troops carrying the .45 ACP. Forty-two of those were Army men, including eleven in World War I. The next conflicts involved fifteen known Army incidents in World War II, nine in Korea, five in Vietnam, and finally two in Somalia. The exact total is unknown, as most citations only refer to "pistol" or "revolver," and some famous events do not mention sidearms at all. Alvin York's is the best-known case, and while undoubtedly other actions featured Browning's masterpiece, citations and accounts often are inconclusive.

The first medal awarded to a .45 ACP man went to First Lieutenant William B. Turner of the Twenty-seventh Division's 105th Regiment. In a night action on September 27, 1918, Turner rushed a German machine gun that opened fire on his group, and he killed the machine gun crew with his pistol. He then pressed forward to another machine gun post twenty-five yards away, and killed one gunner before the rest of his detachment arrived and put the Maxim gun out of action. Turner continued leading his men over three lines of hostile trenches, cleaning up each one as they advanced. Despite being wounded repeatedly, he pressed the attack, and after his .45 ammo was exhausted, he picked up a rifle and bayoneted several of the enemy in hand-to-hand encounters. He then organized a counterattack until he was finally surrounded and killed.

In all, six officers, three noncoms, and two enlisted soldiers were presented the pale blue ribbon with thirteen white stars for actions involving the .45 ACP in September and October 1918. The most famous episode occurred on October 8, when Corporal Alvin York used his rifle and his M1911 to kill twenty-five German machine gunners and infantrymen while capturing an incredible 132 more. Perhaps more remarkably, four more doughboys used Colts in Medal of Honor actions that same day, including three from the Thirtieth Division. A junior officer from the Twenty-ninth, Second Lieutenant Patrick Regan, wielded an empty M1911 to capture thirty Austrians manning four machine guns.

Another action involving a sidearm was First Lieutenant Samuel Woodfill's exploit of October 12, 1918, but he may have used a revolver—likely a 1917 New Service chambered for .45 ACP.

Two South Carolinians used their Colts to good effect in a combined attack on German positions near Montbrehain on October 8. Lieutenant James Dozier and Sergeant Gary Foster attacked a machine gun nest firing on the Thirtieth Division's 118th Infantry, crawling forward "under the guns" to reach grenade range. The doughboys tossed their grenades, and though Dozier was wounded, they pressed the attack, following up with their pistols. Together they then captured eighteen Germans at gunpoint.

It was a busy month for the Thirtieth Division. Three days later, Sergeant Richmond H. Hilton's company was halted by concealed Maxims near Brancourt. Hilton spotted a machine gun among shell holes and fired his rifle until out of ammo. Then he drew his pistol, closed with the enemy, and killed six and captured ten. He lost an arm to a bursting shell but survived.

WORLD WAR II

The World War II actions were equally divided between the Pacific theater of operations and the European. The first event occurred in the Philippines during February 1942, when First Lieutenant W. C. Bianchi died while leading his Filipino Scouts against the Japanese invaders.

Almost a year later, Major C. W. Davis wielded his Colt while leading men of the Twenty-fifth Infantry Division on Guadalcanal in the Solomon Islands. Neither man was known to have killed enemy troops in these actions, but the citations make it clear that both officers carried M1911s while performing "above and beyond the call of duty."

Two of the most remarkable M1911 actions came in the Marianas in June and July 1944. The Army's Twenty-seventh Division, stalled in its advance on Saipan, met determined Japanese defense in depth. Private Thomas A. Baker of the same regiment as Lieutenant Turner in 1918 had been nominated for his courage and initiative in reducing enemy bunkers during June. By July 7, he was a sergeant manning a perimeter attacked by thousands of Japanese from three sides. Though wounded, Baker remained on the line, fired his rifle until empty, then used it as a club. Baker declined the chance to be evacuated in the forced withdrawal, saying he did not want to slow his men's progress. He asked to be left with the last ammunition available—an M1911 fully loaded with eight rounds.

The citation said, "When last seen alive, Sergeant Baker was propped against a tree, pistol in hand, calmly facing the foe. Later Sergeant Baker's body was found in the same position, gun empty, with eight Japanese lying dead before him."

At that same time, Lieutenant Colonel W. J. O'Brien carried two Colts, firing with enthusiasm if not precision in defense of his battalion's perimeter nearby. After emptying his pistols he mounted a jeep with another Browning classic, the M2 .50 caliber machine gun, and was last seen "firing into the Jap[anese] hordes that were then enveloping him."

As the Central Pacific campaign drove westward, the U.S. Army fulfilled its pledge and returned to the Philippines in the fall of 1944. Two PFCs fired their Colts in the process of earning Medals of Honor that December, providing a symmetry to the M1911 cycle begun by Lieutenant Bianchi almost three years before.

Pvt. Thomas A. Baker, 27th Division   *Lt. Col. William J. O'Brien, 27th Division*

Meanwhile, GIs fighting in Europe made their presence known to the Army Awards and Decorations Committee. In October and November 1943, a Third Division captain and PFC both used pistols to good effect during fighting in Italy's Volturno River region.

Captain Arlo L. Olson was killed while using his pistol, and PFC Floyd Lindstrom died fighting on Armistice Day, November 11.

Following the jump into Normandy, Lieutenant Colonel Robert G. Cole of the 101st Airborne Division carried his Colt the week after D-Day, holding a hard-pressed position until relieved by an armored column. At one point, he used his pistol butt to knock on a tank turret to get the driver's attention.

An M1911 action fought against appalling odds occurred near Besancon, France, on September 7, 1944. Manning an observation post of the 3rd Division, Tech. 5 Robert D. Maxwell and two other soldiers were armed only with pistols when a platoon of German infantry assaulted the position. Supported by 20mm and 7.92 automatic weapons, the Wehrmacht troops must have been confident of success as they advanced within ten yards of the observation post. The three GIs used their Colts to prevent the enemy from coming closer, but a German tossed a grenade into the position. Maxwell instantly grasped a heavy blanket and threw himself on the grenade before it exploded, preventing harm to his men. The enemy withdrew, and though crippled, Maxwell miraculously survived.

Not only infantrymen used the service pistol in Medal of Honor actions. Two tankers were decorated for their exploits in France that October, and in December, Corporal Henry F. Warner of the Big Red One used a bazooka and his Colt to stop a German armored thrust. Warner's citation says he won a pistol duel with the commander of a *panzer* threatening to overrun his position; the tank withdrew.

Using a sidearm in Medal of Honor combat proved a high-risk venture in World War II. Of the twenty known recipients, twelve were killed. It's worth noting that two other medals went to GIs who used a Luger and an unidentified German pistol during their particular actions.

KOREAN WAR

The survival odds were even worse in Korea, as five of the eight Army men lost their lives. The war's first M1911 recipient was Sergeant First Class Ernest R. Kouma, another armored trooper, who used his pistol during the desperate fighting in the summer of 1950. As before, the recipients ranged from privates to lieutenant colonels.

An event eerily reminiscent of Sergeant Turner's posthumous action on Saipan occurred in June 1951. PFC Jack G. Hanson, a twenty-year-old Mississippian, volunteered to cover the withdrawal of four wounded men from his squad. When his platoon counterattacked, his body was found with machine gun ammunition expended, his right hand grasping an M1911 with the slide locked back, and a bloody machete in his left hand. More than twenty enemy bodies were found nearby.

The last Korean War pistol award went to Corporal Dan D. Schoonover of the Seventh Infantry Division for a three-day action in July 1953, the month the armistice was signed. After extraordinary heroics in reducing enemy bunkers, Schoonover was killed while defending his position successively with a Browning machine gun, a BAR, and finally his pistol. The pistol's inventor was never better represented.

VIETNAM WAR

During the Vietnam War, pistols were perhaps best associated with the esoteric world of the "tunnel rat," wherein single soldiers squirmed into Viet Cong tunnels too small for anything but a handgun.

The Army's first M1911 Medal of Honor in Southeast Asia was logged by Second Lieutenant Robert J. Hibbs of the Big Red One. In March 1966, following the ambush of a VC patrol, Hibbs and a sergeant returned to the kill zone to retrieve a wounded man. As the NCO led the GI to safety, Hibbs provided cover with his rifle and pistol. He charged two enemy machine guns and was killed in the process, but his action saved the wounded soldier.

Spec. 5 Dwight H. Johnson used a daunting variety of weapons in January 1968. When his M-48 tank threw a tread, he dismounted with only a pistol and killed several Communist troops engaging other tanks of his platoon. Ammo expended, he returned through gunfire and RPGs, grabbed a submachine gun and returned to the fight, saving the wounded driver of an armored personnel carrier. Subsequently, he obtained more pistol ammo and fought off more NVA trying to mount his "track." He finished the fight with the Patton's pedestal-mounted .50 caliber Browning.

Staff Sergeant Joe Hooper of the 101st Airborne used everything at his disposal near Hue in February 1968. In a prolonged action against enemy positions along a riverbank, he killed at least eighteen Communist soldiers with grenades, rifle, bayonet, and pistol, saving a squad member in the process.

Two months later, a First Cavalry Division officer fought an agonizingly long action. Leading a voluntary night patrol, Lieutenant James M. Sprayberry attempted the rescue of an isolated detachment from his company. He used grenades to eliminate one enemy bunker after another, and at one point shot a VC who tried to intervene. After more than seven hours, the persistent Southerner achieved his mission, returning with the wounded GIs. He was credited with killing a dozen Communists in the process.

Another cavalry officer, Captain Harold A. Fritz of the Eleventh Armored Regiment, used his sidearm to defend his troopers in January 1969. The twenty-four-year-old officer rode in a truck convoy ambushed in Binh Long Province, but he quickly organized a response. The VC regrouped and assaulted the position, threatening to overrun the Americans, when Fritz manned a machine gun, helping repel the attack. But the persistent guerrillas returned moments later, closing within a few paces of the trucks. With his .45 and a bayonet, Fritz led a counterattack that stopped the assault long enough for help to arrive.

SOMALIA AND BEYOND?

Twenty-four years passed before the next Medal of Honor event for the ageless Colt—a period equal to the span between 1918 and 1942.

In Mogadishu, Somalia, on October 3, 1993, two Delta Force commandos volunteered for insertion near the wreckage of a Black Hawk helicopter shot down earlier in the day. In saving the H-60 pilot, Master Sergeant Gary I. Gordon and Sergeant First Class Randall D. Shughart used their rifles and M1911s until killed by overwhelming numbers of Somalis.

1st Lt. James M. Sprayberry, 1st Cavalry Division

No other item in the U.S. military inventory has been used for so long as John Browning's rugged pistol. From adoption in 1911 into the twenty-first century, the timeless Colt remains a frontline weapon that may well outlast its Beretta replacement.

The M1911 has become a multigenerational weapon. Through four major wars and numerous expeditions, operations, and "conflicts," the grandsons of doughboys and the sons of GIs have taken the hefty .45 to war, and the end is nowhere in sight. The history of the pistol and the Medal of Honor remain intimately linked.

Whether future conflicts will result in additional medals for M1911 *pistoleros* is impossible to say. The old warhorse shows no sign of retirement, despite its nominal replacement by the M9. But as long as special operations forces continue carrying John Browning's superb sidearm, its value remains undiluted as the M1911 nears its centennial in the twenty-first century.

■ *Tools of the Trade*

The infantry's inventory of weapons is fully reflected in Medal of Honor actions, but there are surprises. Many Medal of Honor recipients—perhaps most—used multiple weapons in the same fight, but some patterns emerge. Most widely used is the hand grenade, which ran a close second to sidearms in World War I and led all weapons by large margins in World War II and Korea.

Pistols and revolvers exceeded use of the rifle in the Great War but rifles led among firearms in the next two conflicts. The carbine, which did not exist in World War I, trailed only the rifle and machine gun in the next two wars.

Automatic rifles (mostly the famous BAR) were used in all three wars, while submachine guns appeared in World War II and continued in Korea.

Other Medal of Honor weapons included mortars, rifle grenades, flame throwers, bazookas, and recoilless rifles.

Edged weapons were still employed in the twentieth century, as bayonets and knives featured in all three wars. In fact, they were proportionately more important in Korea than either world war.

CHAPTER TEN

RECENT EVENTS

■

THE Medal of Honor's erratic path through history continues wending its way, often driven by political winds. However, questions arise: Was a civilian scout leading an Army patrol that fought Indians eligible or not? What about a contract doctor who joined U.S. Army soldiers in enemy captivity?

The questions eventually were answered affirmatively. In 1989, "Buffalo Bill" Cody and four other scouts were reinstated as Medal of Honor recipients, following their revocation in 1916. Dr. Mary Walker's award already had been reapproved during the Carter administration. The awards for Cody and Walker, et al., had been rescinded owing to the statute limiting medals to active duty military personnel engaged in combat.

However, inconsistencies remain. Adolphus Greely's controversial award was not revoked, even though his 1935 citation was published long after his service ended, and no combat action was cited. Similarly, Charles Lindbergh's noncombat award was allowed to stand.

Meanwhile, soldiers kept fighting and dying, earning the medal as intended.

SOMALIA

In December 1992, the lame-duck Bush administration committed 1,800 Marines to war-ravaged Somalia under "Operation Restore Hope." Critics insisted that America's national interest was not at stake in eastern Africa, but George H. W. Bush thought that U.S. troops could help the United Nations gain a foothold against warring factions. The most notorious was that of Mohammad Farah Aidid, who controlled much of the nation's food supply. A temporary settlement was reached, and most American troops withdrew.

However, Bush already had been defeated by the Democrat candidate, Arkansas Governor Bill Clinton, who took office in January 1993. Though openly contemptuous of the military, Clinton sent more American troops to Somalia in a doomed effort to support the United Nations. Blue-helmeted "peacekeepers" sustained frequent casualties against Somalia militiamen, but persistent press coverage spurred the U.S. government to attempt a resolution of violence and famine. UN troop strength grew, but the Somali factions continued fighting the peacekeepers—and each other.

On October 3, 1993, the U.S. command launched an effort to capture several of Aidid's lieutenants. But the mission turned sour: in a fifteen-hour battle in the streets and warrens of Mogadishu, eighteen soldiers died and seventy were wounded.

During the day, two HH-60 Black Hawk helicopters were shot down by Aidid's civilian fighters. An unknown number of survivors were completely isolated and in danger of being overrun by hordes of Somalis, but two Delta Force snipers insisted on trying to cover the rescue attempt. The Army general in Mogadishu finally granted approval to Master Sergeant

Gary I. Gordon from Maine and Sergeant First Class Randall D. Shughart of Pennsylvania. They were highly skilled, experienced soldiers in their mid-thirties. They knew the odds against them; they went anyway.

The "D boys" were landed a hundred meters from the downed Black Hawk. Shughart had an M14 with optical sight; Gordon an M16. Fighting in the close confines of the wreckage in the street, they also used their Colt pistols as necessary. For several minutes, they defended the surviving helicopter pilot, expending most of their ammunition. When Shughart was fatally wounded, Gordon re-

Master Sgt. Gary I. Gordon, Task Force Ranger
SFC Randall D. Shughart, Task Force Ranger

trieved the M16 with five rounds, gave it to the injured pilot, and said "Good luck." He then continued firing his M1911 until killed.

The Black Hawk pilot survived capture and eventually was released. Total Somali losses were never fully known; perhaps 1,500 killed or wounded in the prolonged fight. But in thirty days, the American Rangers and commandos were withdrawn. For their knowing self-sacrifice, Shughart and Gordon were recommended for the Medal of Honor, which was approved seven months later.

When Bill Clinton presented posthumous medals to the snipers' families in 1994, Shughart's father, Herbert, refused to shake the president's hand, reportedly saying, "My son died for nothing, and you are not fit to be commander in chief." Hardly blinking, Clinton continued small talk with others attending the Oval Office ceremony.

As of 2006 the only Medal of Honor for operations in Afghanistan or Iraq was a posthumous award to an Army noncom. In April 2003 Sergeant First Class Paul R. Smith was a thirty-three-year-old veteran of Desert Storm and Kosovo, serving with the Eleventh Engineer Battalion of the Third Infantry Division.

On the morning of April 4, Smith was supervising a construction project at Baghdad International Airport when his unit was suddenly attacked by an estimated one hundred Iraqis. Smith deployed two platoons in defensive positions, making use of a Bradley fighting vehicle and two M113 armored personnel carriers.

Seeing one of the APCs disabled by rockets and mortars, Smith dashed to the rescue, providing covering fire and helped pull three wounded soldiers to safety. With enemy resistance stiffening, he ran through the kill zone to climb aboard an immobile M113 and manned its .50 caliber machine gun. For half an hour he remained exposed to the Iraqis, shooting and reloading with the help of Private Michael Seaman. Smith remained at the gun, fending off renewed assaults, until shot in the head. He was taken to an aid station but could not be saved. Other engineers reckoned that he killed twenty or more enemy soldiers.

The Floridian's family received his Medal of Honor from President Bush in April 2005. At the same ceremony the Smiths received the first thirteen-star flag that will henceforth be presented to recipients or their survivors.

Seaman received an Army Commendation Medal.

RETROACTIVE AWARDS

From 1993 to 2001, thirty-nine more Medals of Honor were presented, mostly retroactive awards to members of racial minorities.

In July 1986, Dr. Leroy Ramsey, Ph.D., of New York and Representative Mickey Leland (Democrat, Texas) wrote the Secretary of Defense that no black soldier received the medal in either world war. Two years later, the Secretary of the Army directed research to determine whether any racial barriers may have prevented awards to blacks. The medal was posthumously presented to Corporal Freddie Stowers of World War I, who had already received a French decoration.

No black units were committed to combat until 1944, and World War II ended the following year without any Medal of Honor awards. Consequently, the statutory limits on medal presentations had long since lapsed. However, in 1989, the acting Secretary of the Army commissioned a study titled "The Medal of Honor and African-Americans in the U.S. Army during World War II." Eventually, a $320,500 government contract was given to Shaw University in North Carolina, resulting in the recommendation of seven black GIs for the medal. Six had previously received the Distinguished Service Cross; one the Silver Star. The upgrades were approved: four recipients had been killed in action, and three died prior to the awards. Vernon J. Baker was present to receive the medal from Bill Clinton in January 1997.

Additionally, in the National Defense Authorization Act of Fiscal Year 1996, Congress directed a review to upgrade Distinguished Service Crosses to Asian Americans and Native American Pacific Islanders, a class of persons generically called AANAPI. Eventually twenty-two AANAPI received the Medal of Honor since FY96 legislation included a waiver of the three-year time limit for awards not previously considered and upgrades of decorations already awarded. It is now codified in Title 10 USC, Section 1130. In essence, there is no longer a statute of limitations on the Medal of Honor.

The AANAPI awards were made in June 2000—the largest batch since Harry Truman awarded fifteen on October 12, 1945. Twenty of the recipients were members of the 442nd Regimental Combat Team. By comparison, the largest number of medals to another regiment in World War II was about thirteen to the Thirtieth Infantry, Third Division.

The other AANAPI medals involved an additional Mediterranean theater award and one from the Pacific. Nine of the retroactive recipients were still living at time of the presentation.

Medic Alfred Rascon belatedly received his medal in February 2000. His Vietnam buddies were surprised to learn that his recommendation had "fallen through the bureaucratic cracks" so they pursued the matter for his lifesaving efforts.

Additional posthumous Army awards were made in 2001 to Sergeant Andrew Jackson Smith, previously recommended for Civil War service; to President Theodore Roosevelt for the Spanish-American War; to Captain Ben L. Salomon, recommended but not approved owing to his medical status in World War II; and upgrade of the Silver Star to Captain Humbert R. Versace in Vietnam.

Smith's case was advanced by Republican lawmakers from Illinois despite the fact that he had served in a Massachusetts regiment. Though racism was alleged in his case, in contrast to the world wars, thirteen black soldiers were awarded the medal in 1865 and four more through 1914.

FRAUDULENT SALES

In April 1995, an FBI agent, acting on covert information, purchased two Medals of Honor at a collectibles show in New Jersey. It was a violation of federal law; in most circumstances, only recipients are authorized to possess the medal, and sales are forbidden. The seller had obtained the genuine medals from one of the managers of HLI Lordship Industries, the government-approved manufacturer of Medals of Honor. Subsequent investigation determined that as many as three hundred medals had been surreptitiously obtained and sold at trade shows.

HLI Lordship was found in violation of Title 18 US Code, Section 704. The firm was fined $80,000 and ordered to pay the government the value of three hundred medals, some $22,500. HLI Lordship was also prohibited from future business in providing the Medal of Honor or other awards or decorations.

Subsequently, members of the Congressional Medal of Honor Society identified more than five hundred imposters: men who falsely wore the medal or claimed to have received it. The penalty for such fraud was raised from a $250 fine to a year in prison and/or a $100,000 fine, but the maximum is seldom if ever imposed. However, word has spread, and Internet sites are devoted to exposing not only Medal of Honor imposters but imitation ex-POWs and elite forces members.

RETROSPECTIVE

It has been said that the Medal of Honor is earned at the intersection of Happenstance and Hell. Very few soldiers set out to "win" the medal, and the mortality rate is high among those who do. George Custer is Exhibit A. Most recipients insist, "Nobody wins the Medal of Honor. It's not a contest."

However, for some, the medal became the springboard to professional or personal success. Alvin York and Audie Murphy are prime examples: the medal propelled them from commonplace circumstances into the public eye as nothing else could have. Army recipients of the medal now include one president (Theodore Roosevelt), three governors, four U.S. senators, eleven congressmen, an ambassador, and two cabinet members.

Other medal holders, less motivated or less fortunate, passed into obscurity. One troubled veteran died committing a felony at age twenty-three. A few others have done jail time.

But the huge majority of medal recipients have done exactly what their lesser-heralded comrades did. They counted their blessings and spent the rest of their lives devoted to their families, their communities, and their nation. Not a few are devoted to their God. Whatever their opinions, faith, or creed, the dwindling number of men entitled to wear the nineteenth-century medal suspended from the pale blue ribbon can testify to its deceptive weight. It's a burden gladly borne, carried with pride in having served as men among men.

BIBLIOGRAPHY

Canfield, Bruce N. *U.S. Infantry Weapons of the First World War*. Lincoln, RI: Andrew Mowbray Inc., 2000.

Hardy, Gordon (ed.) *Above and Beyond: A History of the Medal of Honor from the Civil War to Vietnam*. Boston: Boston Publishing Co., 1985.

Lemon, Peter C. *Beyond the Medal: A Journey from Their Hearts to Yours*. Golden, CO: Fulcrum, 1997.

McChristian, Douglas. *The U.S. Army in the West, 1870–1880*. Norman: University of Oklahoma Press, 1995.

McPherson, James. *Battle Cry of Freedom: The Civil War Era*. New York: Ballantine Books, 1989.

O'Neal, Bill. *Fighting Men of the Indian Wars*. Western Publications, 1992.

Parrish, Thomas (ed.) *The Simon & Schuster Encyclopedia of World War II*. New York: Simon & Schuster, 1978.

Proft, R. J. (ed). *United States of America's Congressional Medal of Honor Recipients*. Columbia Heights, MN: Highland House, 1998.

Stallings, Laurence. *The Doughboys: The Story of the AEF, 1917–1918*. New York: Harper & Row, 1963.

Trask, David F. *The War with Spain in 1898*. Lincoln: University of Nebraska Press, 1996.

Ward, Geoffrey C. *The Civil War*. New York: Alfred A. Knopf, 1990.

INDEX

Page numbers in *italic* indicate photographs.